1998 FORMULA ONE YEARBOOK

Chronicle OF THE GRAND PRIX YEAR

DK PUBLISHING, INC.
www.dk.com

FOREWORD

Welcome to the *1998 Formula One Yearbook*. Despite the dominance of McLaren-Mercedes and Ferrari, the season has been full of action and surprises. Contrary to early predictions, the World Championship has kept our attention at fever pitch all the way through to the last race. Many people from a number of countries have contributed to this book and helped to get it to press within hours of the results at Suzuka. Thanks to them, and we hope you enjoy the book.

A DK PUBLISHING BOOK

www.dk.com

Translated and adapted for Dorling Kindersley by GLS Editorial and Design, Garden Studios, 11-15 Betterton Street, London WC2H 9BP

Project editor Michael Downey
Translator Alex Stewart
Editorial director Reg Grant
Design director Ruth Shane

Text Adrian Gilbert/Jens Ernat/Holger Joel
Editorial/design JOSCH Werbeagentur GmbH

First published in the United States in 1998 by Dorling Kindersley, Inc
95 Madison Avenue, New York, NY 10016

A catalog record is available from the Library of Congress

ISBN 0-7894-3754-6

Printed and bound by westerman druck GmbH, Braunschweig, Germany

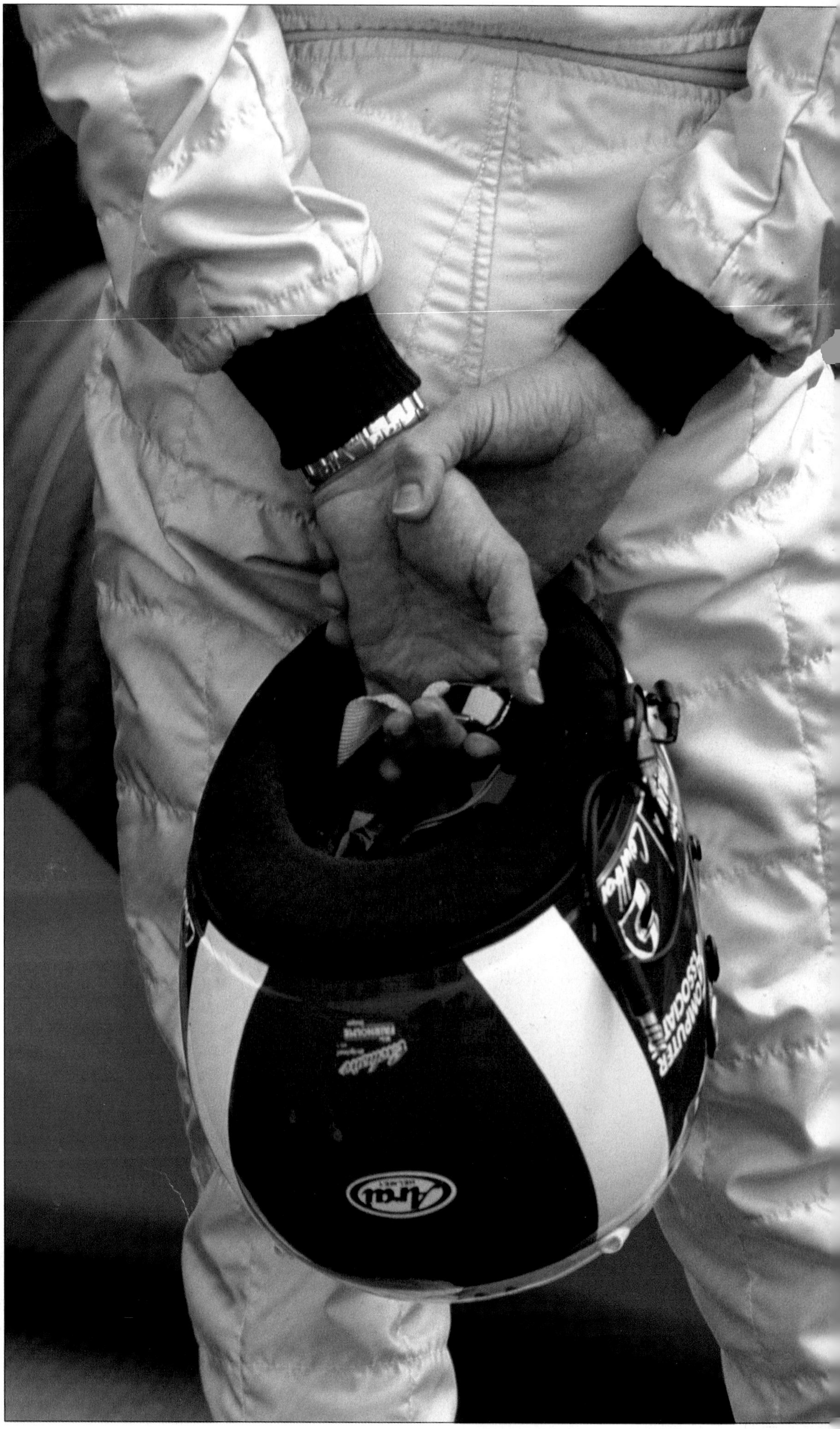

CONTENTS

MILD SEVEN

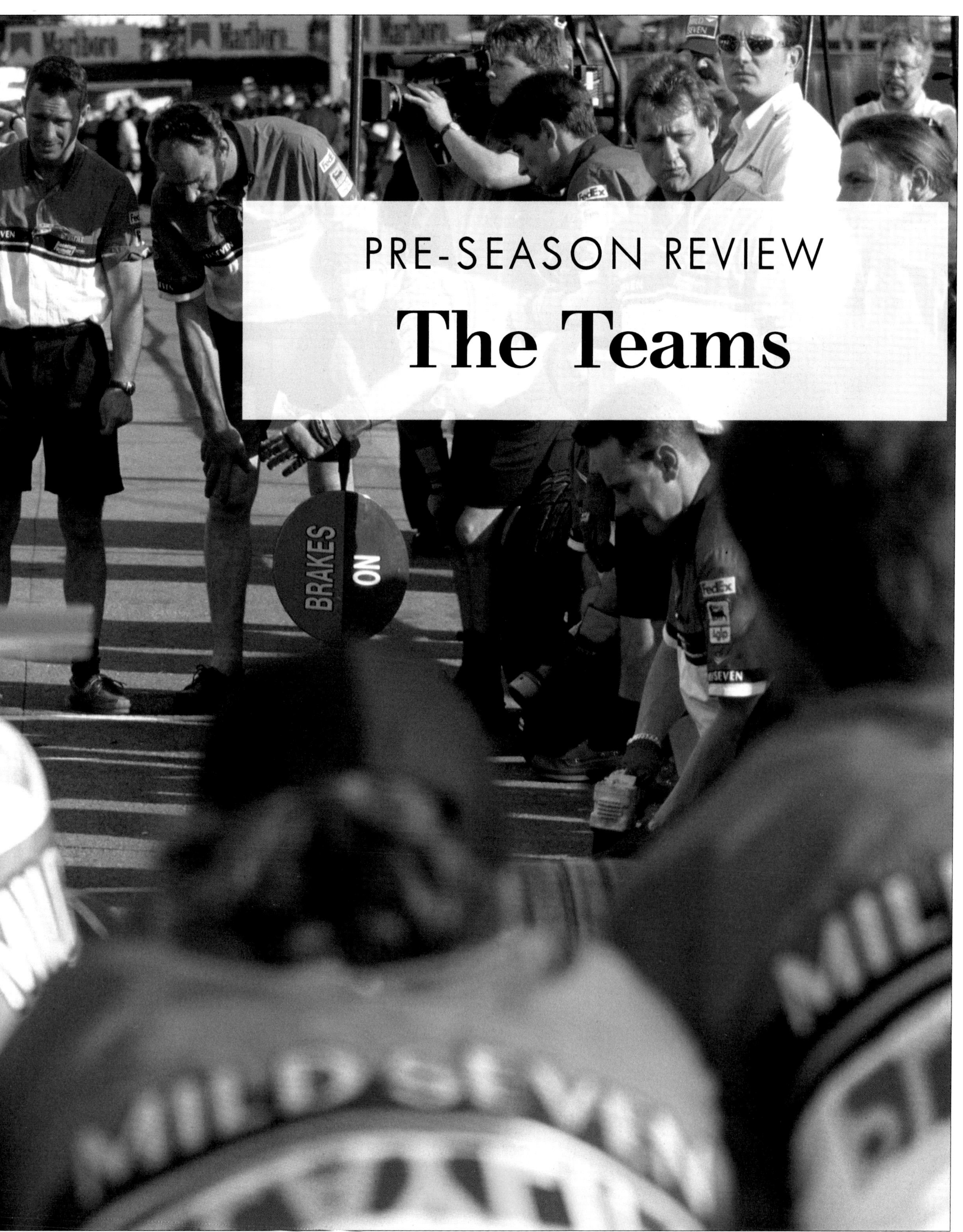

PRE-SEASON REVIEW

The Teams

The 1998 season was as much a battle between the tyre manufacturers as it was between the teams, with newcomer Bridgestone providing real competition for Goodyear. But the decision by Goodyear to withdraw from Formula One at the end of the season would remove this "war of the tyres" – to the detriment of the sport.

WILLIAMS

British powerhouse for world champions

Four individual titles alongside five constructor titles in only six years made the team led by Frank Williams the most successful in Formula One racing during the 1990s.

The 1997 season was one of the finest in Frank Williams' long career in the field of racing. Winning the championship with a total of nine victories gave the Williams team an acclaimed place of honour in the constructors' hall of fame.

Looking forward to the 1998 season, however, it is doubtful whether the team will be able to follow up this success. This is because the new season has forced various changes on Williams. Particularly serious in this respect has been the departure to McLaren-Mercedes of technical guru Adrian Newey, who had made a large contribution to Williams' success in the past.

Williams continue to rely on the engines and technology supplied by Renault, although the French company officially withdrew from Formula One at the end of 1997. The power units are operated under the private label of the engine supplier Mecachrome, which has also obtained the services of a number of Renault technicians. Frank Williams was prepared to accept the changes, convinced that Renault still has the best technology and knowing that engine development will continue for at least the next two years. Williams' co-operation with Mecachrome is contractually secured until the end of 1999, when BMW will take over as Williams' engine supplier.

Men at the wheel

The French-Canadian driver Jacques Villeneuve (the son of the late Gilles Villeneuve, who was killed in a racing accident in 1982) enters his third Grand Prix season as the new Formula One World Champion. Asked what his target for 1998 was, the 27-year-old replied: "Why, a second World Championship of course!" His carefree racing style had already given him a place in racing history when he became the youngest Indycar champion of all time in 1995. Villeneuve's team-mate, Heinz Harald Frentzen, enters the new season in a similarly ambitious state of mind. The 31-year-old Frentzen's mature attitude is firmly based on the career troughs through which he has passed on the way to success.

When Frentzen appeared to be more or less at the end of his career, languishing in Japanese Formula 3000, Peter Sauber took him into his Formula One team in 1994. Sauber, however, was not one of the top teams, so that – apart from a third place in Italy (1995) – all that Frentzen usually saw was the rear lights of the competition.

Williams to the rescue

It was only when Frank Williams took him on for the 1997 season that things began to look up for Frentzen. He appeared to have started well, and during the first race in Australia he led the field for long stretches and looked a likely victor. Then a brake disc failed, and Frentzen was forced to retire. During the next race, he put too much pressure on himself, made mistakes, and was much criticized both in the specialist press and in his own team. Even a first place at Imola in Italy did not seem to help.

Nevertheless, Frentzen's fortunes slowly began to improve – after the Belgian Grand Prix, his performances became more consistent. He ended the season in third place with 42 points. Despite this, the pressure on Frentzen will be intense in 1998.

Technical Details

Chassis	Williams FW20
Tech. Director	Patrick Head
Engine	Mecachrome GC37-01 V10
Weight	121 kg
Engine Manager	Jean-Yves Houe
Tyres	Goodyear
Fuel	Castrol, Petrobras

Results to end of 1997

GP Debut	GP Britain 1972
GP Points	1910.5
GP Victories	103

Address
Williams Grand Prix Engineering Ltd, Grove, Wantage, Oxfordshire, OX12 ODQ, England
Internet
http://www.williamsdb.com

THE TEAM

Team leader Frank Williams (centre) in conversation with Ron Dennis (left) and Bernie Ecclestone (right)

▲ Photographed with the team. Jacques Villeneuve (car no. 1, right), born 9 April 1971 in St Jean sur Richelieu, Canada – F1 debut in 1996 in Australia; 33 races, 11 victories. Heinz Harald Frentzen (car no. 2, left), born 18 May 1967 in Mönchengladbach, Germany – F1 debut in 1994 in Brazil; 65 races, 1 victory.

◀ Patrick Head, the highly influential chief designer and technical director.

FERRARI

"We are poised to take the Championship"

Ferrari are approaching the start of the 1998 season with a renewed determination to regain the World Championship after 19 years. Even the most humble fitter on the home test track in Fiorano knows how important it is to Italian motorsport fanatics to win this title. And, because the team has said that the transition period necessary for restructuring the team is finished, there will be no easy excuse for those responsible if Ferrari do not achieve their objectives.

The new car – the brilliant work of newly acquired designers Ross Brawn and Rory Byrne – is now ready for some racing action. And just in time as Fiat, the Ferrari team's owners, are now expecting a return on their substantial financial investment. Otherwise, Ferrari is threatened with a drastic reduction in budget.

Although all those concerned express great optimism, Ferrari's World Championship title bid has a potential problem in the choice of tyre. The US tyre manufacturer Goodyear gave early notice of its withdrawal from Formula One at the end of the 1998 season and gave its customers the freedom to change to the Japanese competitor Bridgestone. The Japanese, who made their debut in Formula One in 1997, appeared to have had good results during the tests on their tyres in the winter months. Yet Ferrari race boss Jean Todt did not seem very interested in pursuing a deal with Bridgestone, and continued to fit the team's cars with American tyres. For the first time since taking control, a Todt decision brought with it a hail of criticism. If, at the end of the season, there is only a piece of rubber between success and failure, Todt will face some searching and extremely uncomfortable questions.

Making amends

Michael Schumacher – considered by many to be the best driver in the world – has also had to meet some severe criticism after the incident in Jerez when he attempted to force Villeneuve off the track. Following his open confession that he made a mistake, Schumacher – in his third year with Ferrari – is absolutely determined to make amends by winning the title. Ferrari have paid him a fortune to secure the title for them, and there can be few doubts that Schumacher is the man most likely to achieve this result.

Eddie Irvine, born in Northern Ireland and now living in Dublin, is also in his third year with the team but has not yet succeeded in gaining a victory. The Irishman drove a superb race last year in the Grand Prix at Suzuka, when he provided unselfish support to his team-mate during Schumacher's attempt to overhaul Jacques Villeneuve. Irvine, then leading, voluntarily handed over his position to Schumacher and protected him to the end of the race against the hard-pressing Canadian driver. In fact, this unselfish attitude cost Irvine victory in the end – although he did manage to obtain a position on the rostrum in third place. This result did, however, confirm his position as the second driver for Ferrari.

While many of the other teams provide equal facilities and backup to both drivers, Ferrari operate on the basis that Schumacher is the main driver, and anyone else is there only in support. Irvine has loyally accepted this role – but for how much longer?

THE TEAM

▲ *Eddie Irvine (car no. 4), born 10 November 1965 in Newtownards, Northern Ireland – F1 debut in 1993 in Japan; 65 races, no victories.*

◀ *Team manager Jean Todt (left), chief designer Ross Brawn (right) and Michael Schumacher (car no. 3, centre), born 3 January 1969 in Hermüllheim, Germany – F1 debut in 1991 in Belgium; 102 races, 27 victories.*

Technical Details

Chassis	Ferrari F300
Tech. Director	Ross Brawn
Engine	Ferrari 047 V10
Weight	115 kg
Engine Manager	Paolo Martinelli
Tyres	Goodyear
Fuel	Shell

Results to end of 1997

GP Debut	GP Monaco 1950
GP Points	2093.5
GP Victories	113

Address
Ferrari SpA, Via Ascari 55-57, 41053 Maranello, Modena, Italy
Internet
http://www.ferrari.it/comsport/formula1.html

BENETTON

A new outfit for United Colours

The Italian Benetton team is trying to brighten up its colours for the 1998 season with new drivers, new tyres, and a new team manager.

Dave Richards took over as the head of the rather luckless Benetton Formula One team at the end of 1997. A mere two victories in the last two years was considered reason enough for Benetton to hasten the retirement of his predecessor, Flavio Briatore.

Top man at Benetton

In Richards, the job was entrusted to a man who, up to then, had no experience in Formula One. He did, however, know how to build up a successful team, as evidenced by his victories in rally sport in which his team – under the name of Prodrive – won three World Championship titles with Subaru in the years 1990 to 1993. Immediately on his return to the British Touring Car Championship, Prodrive again secured the title – in this case in association with Alfa.

Richards regards the 1998 season more as a period of reorientation than outright victory. He hopes to harvest the fruits of his labours in the 1999 season. The fact that he is not afraid to follow uncharted paths in achieving his objectives is indicated by Richards' choice of tyre company – Benetton was the next top team, after McLaren, to change from Goodyear to their Japanese competitor Bridgestone.

Benetton has a young team with new arrivals Giancarlo Fisichella (Italy) and Alexander Wurz (Austria), who replaced Jean Alesi and Gerhard Berger. Both new drivers made their appearance in the 1997 season and immediately showed remarkable promise. A highly thoughtful driver, Wurz achieved a third place at Silverstone in the British Grand Prix. Fisichella did even better in last year's Grand Prix at Spa in Belgium when he drove his Jordan to second place. And if his engine had not failed at Hockenheim, Fisichella would have almost certainly won the race.

THE TEAM

Team manager Dave Richards (right) in conversation with new arrival Giancarlo Fisichella (car no. 5), born 14 January 1973 in Rome, Italy – F1 debut in 1996 in Australia; 25 races, no victories.

Alexander Wurz (car no. 6), born 15 February 1974 in Waldhofen, Austria – F1 debut in 1997 in Canada; 3 races, no victories.

Technical Details

Chassis	Benetton B198
Tech. Director	Pat Symonds
Engine	Mecachrome GC37-01 V10
Weight	121 kg
Engine Manager	Jean-Yves Houe
Tyres	Bridgestone
Fuel	Agip

Results to end of 1997

GP Debut	GP Brazil 1986
GP Points	772.5
GP Victories	27

Address
Benetton Formula Ltd, Whiteways Technical Centre, Enstone, Chipping Norton, Oxfordshire, OX7 4EE, England

Internet
http://www.jtnet.ad.jp/WWW/MILDSEVEN/F1/

McLAREN

Back on the road to the top

In comparison with their rivals, McLaren-Mercedes were very late in presenting their car for 1998. But the team, led by Ron Dennis, had very obviously succeeded in putting an outstanding vehicle on the road.

When McLaren set about the initial testing phase in Barcelona, Mika Hakkinen climbed into the driving seat and immediately pulverized the track record by almost two seconds. Yet the McLaren crew accepted this result in a relaxed manner as if, even without the tests, they knew their car's potential.

This self-confidence is certainly one of the contributions made by company boss Ron Dennis. He has already succeeded once before – in the 1980s – in gathering the most capable people around him and forging them into a victorious team. Again, it looks as if he is on the verge of a major breakthrough. For one thing, it is clear that the three-year alliance with Mercedes-Benz is finally bearing fruit. Manufactured in Britain, the powerful Mercedes-Illmor engine is now far more reliable than was the case in previous seasons.

New Innovations

The arrival of Adrian Newey has also been crucial to the overall McLaren-Mercedes design. Newey, an aerodynamics specialist, made a substantial contribution to the success of Williams last year and is sure to do so again for the McLaren team.

On the choice of tyres, the British team was the first to accept the offer to leave Goodyear for Bridgestone. Here, again, Dennis left nothing to chance in making the change. Once the deal with the Japanese tyre company had been concluded, the McLaren drivers tested the new racing tyres for a total of 8,000 km (5,000 miles).

Of the two McLaren drivers, the Scot David Coulthard began his third season with the team this year, and the Finn Mika Hakkinen has stood by McLaren since 1993. They are both top drivers with many years of practical racing experience and, fundamentally, they both drive fast.

Now that Hakkinen has won his first Grand Prix – in the final race of the 1997 season in Jerez – many observers think he has the potential to win a World Championship. He has now become an integral part of the McLaren-Mercedes team, but, as ever, race victory will be the acid test.

Technical Details

Chassis	McLaren MP4/13
Tech. Director	Adrian Newey
Engine	Mercedes FO 110G V10
Weight	107 kg
Engine Manager	Mario Illien
Tyres	Bridgestone
Fuel	Mobil

Results to end of 1997

GP Debut	GP Monaco 1966
GP Points	2047.5
GP Victories	107

Address
McLaren International Ltd, Woking Business Park, Albert Drive, Woking, Surrey GU21 5JY, UK
Internet
http://www.mclaren.co.uk

THE TEAM

David Coulthard (car no. 7), born 27 March 1971 in Twynholm, Scotland – F1 debut in 1994 in Spain; 58 races, three victories.

Team chief Ron Dennis (right) in discussion with director Norbert Haug.

Mika Hakkinen (car no. 8) born 28 September 1968 in Helsinki, Finland – F1 debut in 1991 in the USA; 96 races, one victory.

JORDAN

Team under pressure

"We have got to the point where we can win during the coming Grand Prix season." With this statement, team boss Eddie Jordan announced his target for the new season.

The team – built around the ambitious Irishman – is under severe pressure to achieve real results in the 1998 season. If success continues to be elusive, the Jordan team may well lose the rights to the Mugen-Honda engine. When agreeing the contract, the Japanese company left the door open to allow them to cancel co-operation with the Jordan team after the first year if the team had had no real track success.

But the Jordan team does have a good chance of at least one race victory in 1998. In 1997 – with Giancarlo Fisichella driving – the team just failed to gain a place on the rostrum by the narrowest of margins.

According to Jordan's technical director, this year's car is a further development of the previous year's model. The most striking changes apply to detailed modifications, with particular attention being paid to the handling capabilities of the car and to making it more comfortable to drive. Visually, there is not much difference from its predecessor. Apart from the smaller wheelbase as specified by the rules, the paintwork at the front is the only noticeable difference – the snake has been replaced by a hornet.

Technical Details

Chassis	Jordan 198
Tech. Director	Gary Anderson
Engine	Mugen-Honda MF30 1HC V10
Weight	116 kg
Engine Manager	Hiroshi Shirai
Tyres	Goodyear
Fuel	Repsol

Results to end of 1997

GP Debut	GP USA 1991
GP Points	121
GP Victories	0

Address
Jordan Grand Prix Ltd,
Buckingham Road, Silverstone, Towcester,
Northamptonshire, NN12 8JT, England
Internet
http://www.jordangp.com/

Damon Hill, the 1996 World Champion, had a poor season in 1997. After being rejected by Williams, Hill joined the Arrows team. Although well rewarded when with the Arrows, he was unable to challenge the leaders. At the close of the season he had only secured seven World Championship points from 17 races. That was too little for a man of his class and, as the 37-year- old himself said, he felt the need for more success. In 1998, he would like to give his new employer their first Grand Prix victory.

Although a talented driver, some critics wonder whether Hill has the motivation and aggression to fight with the best. This will be a vital year for Damon Hill, one in which the British driver hopes he will have an opportunity to prove his doubters wrong. If not, then it is likely that Hill may retire from Formula One.

Fighting for his place

Ralf Schumacher was with Jordan in his first Formula One season in 1997. For a greenhorn, this is usually an apprenticeship and learning period. For this reason, Eddie Jordan forgave his employee some drives into the gravel. In 1998, however, Jordan will demand greater consistency, and "little Schumi" will have to make great efforts to justify his Formula One claims. In a team-mate like Hill, however, the German driver has a colleague who can provide him with invaluable advice and expertise.

If that is not reflected in one of the leading places by the end of the 1998 season, then the number of Schumachers in Formula One might rapidly drop to just one again – or, if nothing else, then a move to another team will be highly likely.

THE TEAM

▲ *Damon Hill (car no. 9), born 17 September 1960 in London, England – F1 debut in 1992 in England; 84 races, 21 victories.*

◄ *Ralf Schumacher (car no. 10), born 30 June 1975 in Kerpen, Germany – F1 debut in 1997 in Australia; 17 races, no victories.*

Team chief Eddie Jordan.

PROST GRAND PRIX

The "professor" is only interested in the best

Alain Prost is leading his team for only the second season in Formula One, having taken over the old Ligier team he renamed Prost Grand Prix.

Prost was World Champion four times and ambition is one of his main characteristics. As team manager, he has only one objective – success. Even if his intentions seem extremely optimistic, Prost has always achieved whatever he has set out to do. A good example of Prost's approach was revealed last year when he succeeded in freeing Jordan's grip on the exclusive rights to Peugeot's engines by brokering a deal that secured them for his own team for several years. Jordan were thus forced to look elsewhere.

Technical Details

Chassis	Prost AP01
Tech. Director	Loic Bigois
Engine	Peugeot A16 V10
Weight	125 kg
Team Manager	Cesare Fiorio
Tyres	Bridgestone
Fuel	Total

Results to end of 1997

GP Debut	GP Brazil 1976
GP Points	410
GP Victories	9

Address
Prost Grand Prix,
Technopole de la Nievre,
58470 Magny-Cours, France.
Internet
http://www.prostgp.com

Despite his ambitious visions, the Frenchman has both feet on the ground; this is evidenced by the fact that he will not give any precise timetable for realizing his objectives.

THE TEAM

Olivier Panis (car no. 11), born 2 September 1966 in France – F1 debut in 1994 in Brazil; 59 races, one victory.

▲ Four times World Champion, Alain Prost was nicknamed the "professor" because of his careful and knowledgeable driving style.

◀ Jarno Trulli (car no. 12), born 13 July 1974 in Pescara, Italy – F1 debut in 1997 in Australia; 14 races, no victories.

Panis and Trulli

Monaco victor of 1996, Olivier Panis, was involved in a terrible accident at the Canadian Grand Prix last season, in which he broke both his legs. At the time, there were doubts about whether he would ever drive a racing car again. However, only five months later, the 31-year-old Frenchman was again at the steering wheel of a racing car. Given this pugnacious attitude, he should be worth watching in 1998 – if his Prost car proves up to scratch.

This is the first year in the team for the Italian Jarno Trulli, the German Formula Three Champion in 1996. The 24-year-old – who has replaced Japanese driver Shinji Nakano – made a good impression on the team when he deputized for the injured Panis. He fought an exciting duel with Jacques Villeneuve during the 1997 Austrian Grand Prix – a duel that lasted until the 58th lap. Trulli's refusal to be overawed by Villeneuve demonstrated a promise that the Prost team was keen to capitalize upon.

SAUBER

Old engine dogs Swiss hopes

Ɔuring pre-season testing on Ferrari's ɪome track in Fiorano, the team run ɔy Peter Sauber probably broke into he odd grin. Whereas their own car ·an faultlessly during initial tests, heir Ferrari hosts were struggling vith a large number of difficulties on he same track. Although their self-·onfidence has increased, no-one at ·auber would claim to believe that hey will come anywhere near Ferrari ɪuring this season.

The main reason why Sauber annot be competitive in 1998 lies vith the engine. As was the case in .997, Sauber are using a 1996-vintage 'errari engine which is simply not ɪowerful enough. A succession of hanges have been made – such as owering the crankshaft by 10 mm to educe the centre of gravity of the unit · but they are unlikely to make ɪgnificant overall improvements.

In addition to the weakness in the ngine department, the Sauber also uffered from handling problems with ·hich the drivers had to fight all eason. The chassis caused the car to ndersteer on a near permanent basis, making set-up very difficult. Will this be put right for the new season?

The major innovations which Peter Sauber has introduced concern team personnel. Max Welti, his team manager for many years, was dismissed by Sauber on the basis that Welti did not have a sufficiently technical orientation.

Searching for a replacement, Sauber looked to the Williams team, where he landed Tim Preston and appointed him as the test team manager. Andy Tilley, bought in from Jordan, was nominated by Sauber to be co-ordinator between the test team and the racing team.

Against the background of these additions to personnel, Sauber hopes for an improvement in the Constructors' Championship, although he continues to exclude the possibility of an outright Grand Prix victory.

Flair and experience

The Frenchman Jean Alesi, who lives in Switzerland and has raced in 135 Grand Prix, changed from Benetton to Sauber for this season. Alesi is well-known in Formula One racing circles for his extremely fast starts and his mercurial temperament. He has long been one of the top stars of the series, although up to now he has not managed a real breakthrough, scoring only one Grand Prix victory. Johnny Herbert moved to Sauber when Heinz Harald Frentzen went to Williams. Since then, the British driver – now 34 years old – has provided the team with a third place in last year's Hungarian Grand Prix. Herbert finished the 1997 championship in 11th place overall.

Technical Details

Chassis	Sauber C17
Tech. Director	Leo Ress
Engine	Petronas SPE 01D V10
Weight	120 kg
Engine Manager	Osamu Goto
Tyres	Goodyear
Fuel	Shell

Results to end of 1997

GP Debut	South African GP 1993
GP Points	69
GP Victories	0

Address
Red Bull Sauber Petronas,
Wildbachstrasse. 9, 8340 Hinwil, Switzerland
Internet
http://www.redbull-sauber.ch

THE TEAM

Jean Alesi (car no. 14), born 11 June 1964 in Avignon, France – F1 debut in 1989 in France; 135 races, one victory.

Team chief Peter Sauber.

Johnny Herbert (car no. 15), born 2 June 1964 in Romford, England – F1 debut in 1989 in Brazil; 113 races, two victories.

THE TEAM

ARROWS

Team chief Tom Walkinshaw.

Pedro Diniz (car no. 16), born 22 May 1970 in São Paulo, Brazil – F1 debut in 1995 in Brazil; 50 races, no victories.

Mika Salo (car no. 17), born 30 November 1966 in Helsinki, Finland – F1 debut in 1994 in Japan; 52 races, no victories.

The courage to take risks

TWR chief Tom Walkinshaw intends to make every effort during the next few years to enter the inner circles of Formula One with his team. For this purpose, the British manager is prepared to take risks to get there.

The new Arrows A19 from the TWR company has been completely redesigned – from the engine to the paint scheme. The respected chief designer, John Barnard, has radically lowered the tail of the car and transformed the rear airflow. In addition, the British designer has created a carbon-fibre gearbox and installed a new oil supply system. These are all innovations which the top teams would probably never dare to incorporate in their cars.

For all the technical risks taken by Barnard, the car has arrived late for the 1998 season. As a result, the team has not had enough time to test the car. Walkinshaw, however, accepts this state of affairs in a reasonably relaxed manner. For him, 1998 is to be a year in which he acquires a large number of test miles, under race conditions, in order to win points towards the end of the season.

Close partners

Walkinshaw is particularly proud of the new unit which, although developed and built by Brian Hart, carries the name of TWR (Tom Walkinshaw Racing). The TWR boss is also glad to indicate that Arrows is supported by an unnamed motor car manufacturer who could, if necessary, carry the whole project alone.

This statement naturally raises speculation as to whether Nissan will be engaged in Formula One in the near future. A point to note is that the Japanese are already partners of Walkinshaw in the touring car field and that a Nissan delegation was present at the "roll-out" of the A19.

Pedro Diniz will continue to have to live with the image that he is only driving in Formula One because of the money he brings with him. Although the Brazilian millionaire's son has had more than his fair share of spins and racing accidents, he is a far better driver than some give him credit.

The highlight for Diniz in the last season was on the Nurburgring, where he came fifth, giving his employer two valuable championship points. What is more, he reached the finish before his then team-mate, ex-world champion Damon Hill. Although Hill may have often been lacking in motivation during his time at Arrows, the fact that Diniz was able to out-qualify him on a number of occasions provided a good indication of the Brazilian driver's real abilities.

Another "flying" Finn

After three years of "official duties" at Tyrrell, Mika Salo comes as a new recruit to Arrows. The Finnish driver was not able to demonstrate his true capabilities with the uncompetitive Tyrrell team, but he is highly esteemed by many as a very quick driver, in the mould of his better-known compatriot, Mika Hakkinen.

At Arrows, Salo may still be lacking a car which is really good enough to allow him to move a long way forward in Formula One. But he can prove his worth by putting in better times than his team-mate, and when conditions allow, to get into those elusive point-scoring positions which will establish his reputation.

Technical Details

Chassis	Arrows A19
Tech. Director	John Barnard
Engine	Arrows T2 V10
Weight	120 kg
Engine Manager	Pete Dodd
Tyres	Bridgestone
Fuel	Elf

Results to end of 1997

GP Debut	Brazilian GP 1978
GP Points	150
GP Victories	0

Address
TWR Group Ltd, Leafield Technical Centre, Leafield, Witney, Oxon., OX8 5PF, England
Internet
http://www.arrows.com/

STEWART

Ford and Stewart promise to do better

After a fairly unhappy start in Formula One during 1997, the Stewart team is entering a second season in a determined mood. They are also under great pressure from their engine supplier, Ford.

When Ford and three-times World Champion Jackie Stewart presented their first joint Formula One racing car at the end of 1996, they had high hopes for the coming season At the end of the year, however, some 34 combined starts were followed by a total of just six Stewart cars crossing the finishing line, including one second place in Monaco. Like fellow champion Alain Prost, Jackie Stewart was finding life as a team leader harder than that of a racing driver.

A better engine

The weak performance failed to shake the relationship between Ford and Stewart, and both sides promised to increase their efforts substantially in 1998. The major problem with the Stewart cars in 1997 had been their unreliable and underpowered Ford engines. As a result, Ford promised further engine development, and undertook to provide the team with an exclusive engine that was both reliable and powerful.

In return, however, Ford wanted to see success on the track. Otherwise, it was clear that the American motor company would have to reconsider the relationship and look elsewhere.

Against this background, the team chief sought additional financial backers with whose support he could pump another £5 million into the racing car development. The final product is a racing car designed by technical director Alan Jenkins. Given these improvements, more will be expected of Stewart in 1998.

The Stewart team has decided to keep the same drivers it employed in the 1997 season, namely the Brazilian Rubens Barrichello, and the Dane Jan Magnussen. Barrichello is the "old hand" of the team. Although he is only 25 years old, Barrichello is very experienced and has 81 Grand Prix races under his belt. The Brazilian provided the team with a second place in Monaco last year – these were the only points earned by the team in their admittedly short history.

Magnussen, on the other hand, raced his first Formula One season in 1997, and, for much of the time, he found it difficult to cope at such a high level. Although he has doubts about Magnussen, Jackie Stewart decided to keep him on for 1998; it will be up to the young Dane to prove that this was the right decision.

Technical Details

Chassis	Stewart SF2
Tech. Director	Alan Jenkins
Engine	Ford Zetec R V10
Weight	120 kg
Engine Manager	Brian Dickie
Tyres	Bridgestone
Fuel	Texaco

Results to end of 1997

GP Debut	Australian GP 1997
GP Points	6
GP Victories	0

Address
Stewart Grand Prix Ltd, 16 Tanners Drive, Blakelands, Milton Keynes, Bucks, MK14 5BW, England

Internet
http://www.stewartgp.com

THE TEAM

Team chief and three-times world champion, Jackie Stewart.

Rubens Barrichello (car no. 18), born 23 May 1972 in São Paulo, Brazil – F1 debut in 1993 in South Africa; 81 races, no victories.

Jan Magnussen (car no. 19), born 4 July 1973 in Roskilde, Denmark – F1 debut in 1995 in Japan; 18 races, no victories.

TYRRELL

Tyrrell retirement makes way for new team

"Formula One can certainly survive without Tyrrell, but I am not sure how I will manage in future without Formula One." With these words, the 73-year-old Ken Tyrrell made his departure from the Grand Prix circuit. After 31 years in Formula One, the motorsport veteran had sold his team to newly founded British-American Racing (BAR).

The new company combines the cigarette concern BAT, the chassis company Reynard, and Jacques Villeneuve's manager Craig Pollock. The latter will function as the new team chief. With the purchase of the once-great Tyrrell team, BAR have secured no more than an existing base with which to establish a foothold in Formula One. The new team accepts that it must be subjected to a "complete restoration" by the year 1999. A start will be made this summer because BAR intend, by then, to have the first test car of their own on the road, based on the Tyrrell 026.

BAR will probably bring in their own management structure over the coming months, although for the time being the Tyrrell technical director, Harvey Postlethwaite, will remain in office. But when this 53-year-old Englishman also disappears from the Grand Prix scene at the end of the season, the Tyrrell family connection with Formula One racing will pass into motorsport history.

For all their ambitions, BAR have a nagging problem standing in their way – lack of access to a competitive engine. The 1998 car is powered by an overworked Ford V10 customized engine which Pollock and his partners have had to buy at substantial cost from Ford (unlike Stewart who have exclusive rights). It is intended that this will change in 1999. By then, BAR wishes to be the partner of an engine manufacturer, although this bid has so far been unsuccessful.

Drivers required

The Brazilian Ricardo Rosset will be given another chance to prove his driving skills for the first time since his Formula One debut in 1996 with Arrows. Last year, he was a spectator because money problems forced Lola, his then employer, to cease operations after only one race. Expert opinion, however, is far from sure if Rosset has the talent for Formula One.

The 24-year-old Japanese driver Toranosuke Takagi comes from the Nippon Formula and was a test driver with Tyrrell last year. He will drive in his first Grand Prix race when the season starts. Yet it is highly unlikely that such inexperienced drivers will be acceptable to the ambitious BAR team, and Craig Pollock will almost certainly be looking further afield. If Pollock's friend Jacques Villeneuve can be persuaded to leave Williams, his arrival at BAR would be a real coup for the new team.

Technical Details

Chassis	Tyrrell 026
Tech. Director	Harvey Postlethwaite
Engine	Ford ZETEC R V10
Weight	125 kg
Team Manager	Steve Nielsen
Tyres	Goodyear
Fuel	Elf

Results to end of 1997

GP Debut	Canadian GP 1970
GP Points	617
GP Victories	23

Address
Tyrrell Racing Organisation Ltd,
Long Reach, Ockham, Woking,
Surrey GU23 6PE, England

Internet
http://www.tyrrellf1.com

THE TEAM

Craig Pollock: Part-owner and the new team chief of the British-American Racing team.

Ricardo Rosset (car no. 21), born 27 July 1968 in São Paulo, Brazil – F1 debut in 1996 in Australia; 16 races, no victories.

Toranosuke Takagi (car no. 20), born 12 February 1974 in Shizuoka, Japan – F1 debutant.

MINARDI

A team fighting to get on the pace

Minardi was the only team to emerge without any world championship points at the end of the 1997 season. In effect, the cars were not up to the demands of Formula One racing. On most occasions, Minardi would be fighting to avoid last place on the grid, and only half the races were completed by either of its two drivers.

During the winter months, team boss Giancarlo Minardi attempted to improve his key personnel by "poaching" Gustav Brunner from Ferrari. Brunner, an Austrian by birth, has a reputation of being a self-taught polymath in the field of technology – reflected in the current Ferrari F300.

New car construction

As leader of the design department, Brunner has to create a new racing car for Minardi. Such a comprehensive overhaul will obviously take time, and the new car will not come into operation until 1999. It is hoped that this car will make Minardi into a serious motor racing team.

The Japanese Shinji Nakano relieved his private sponsor Mild Seven of a vast sum of money in order to take his place with Minardi. Given support by the engine manufacturer Honda, Nakano had driven for Prost last year but was eventually deemed surplus to requirements by the French team. Nakano had earned his spurs as a driver in cart racing, before going on to compete in the Japanese Formula 3000 championships.

The FIA made an exception in awarding the Formula One "super licence" to Esteban Tuero. This makes the 19-year-old driver the youngest newcomer in the top class since the Formula One series began.

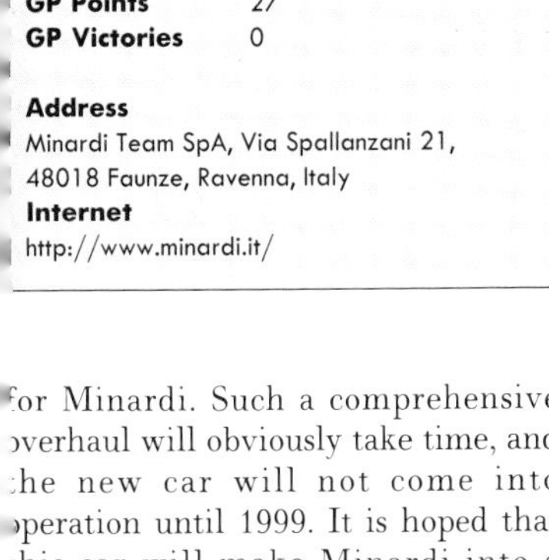

Technical Details

Chassis	Minardi M198
Tech. Director	Gustav Brunner
Engine	Ford ZETEC R V10
Weight	125 kg
Tech. Cood.	Gabbriele Tredozi
Tyres	Bridgestone
Fuel	Minardi

Results to end of 1997

GP Debut	Brazilian GP 1985
GP Points	27
GP Victories	0

Address
Minardi Team SpA, Via Spallanzani 21, 48018 Faunze, Ravenna, Italy
Internet
http://www.minardi.it/

THE TEAM

Shinji Nakano (car no. 22), born 1 April 1971 in Osaka, Japan – F1 debut in 1997 in Australia; 17 races, no victories.

Esteban Tuero (car no. 23), born 22 April 1978 in Buenos Aires, Argentina; F1 debutant.

Team chief Giancarlo Minardi.

BRIDGES

THE 1998 SEASON

The Races

CALENDAR

1–31 January
Now that the Swiss team has severed its connections with team director Max Welti, Peter Sauber himself intends to resume the leadership of the team. The reason for the sacking is the poor showing by the team during the past season (16 points overall and seventh in the World Championship).

The French tyre manufacturer Michelin's return to Formula One sport will not take place in 1999, as formerly planned. "The new regulations don't give us much room for manoeuvre," states Françoise Michelin, the grand-daughter of the company's founder.

The coming season will be the last for the Tyrrell team. The team boss Ken Tyrrell (73) has sold the team to British American Racing (BAR).

Engine supplier Peugeot flies in 400 people to the launch of the new Prost racing car.

1–28 February
The money crisis at Minardi is over. After the dismissal of Tarso Marques, the Japanese driver Shinji Nakamo will, thanks to the financial muscle of his sponsors, occupy the second driving seat beside Esteban Tuero.

Moving from Ferrari to Minardi: technical expert Gustav Brunner.

Minardi has annoyed Ferrari. The reason for the quarrel is that Minardi have enticed the technician Gustav Brunner from Maranello to the Minardi team.

Ferrari is preventing Minardi from using the Ferrari test track in Fiorano and intends to oppose the super-licence for the Minardi driver Tuero.

6 March
The prestigious, and official, Grand Prix ball will give profits raised from the event to an organization for stroke victims and to a foundation for multiple sclerosis sufferers.

7 March
Prost driver Olivier Panis suffers a blow during qualifying for the Australian Grand Prix. Because he left his car standing on the track with a seized gear box, he is censured and made to pay a $2,500 fine.

8 March
The McLaren Silver Arrows complete the opening race of the season in Melbourne, Australia, with a stunning double victory. Controversy is caused, however, when David Coulthard waves second-placed team-mate Mika Hakkinen through to victory.

18 March
The French Grand Prix at Magny-Cours has been confirmed for 28 June 1998 at a meeting of the FIA World Council. The race, which had long been in doubt because tobacco advertisements are forbidden, has been restored to the racing calendar.

28 March
A protest by Ferrari against an allegedly forbidden four-wheel steering arrangement by McLaren is upheld in São Paulo by the race commissioners. McLaren has to remove the so-called "wonder brake".

29 March
São Paulo: The McLaren pair Hakkinen and Coulthard again prove unbeatable during the second race in the Formula One World Championship in Brazil.

1-31 March
New warning lights in the cockpit are being tested for the first time during the South American Grand Prix races. When the yellow or red flag is waved, a corresponding light will now illuminate in the car.

McLaren announces a Formula One two-seater to give selected members of the general public a taste of what it is like to be in a racing car. Each co-driver is charged a hefty sum for the privilege, but any profits go to good causes.

Two years before its proposed entry into Formula One, BMW reports success in acquiring new members for its team. The Bavarians have secured the services of Dieter Gundel, the software expert who has been with McLaren since 1991.

Up to now, nine teams have signed the new Concorde Agreement, which is valid from 1998 to 2008. The agreement regulates the financial relationship between the FIA and the teams.

After a disappointing start to the season, Jordan sends its cars back into the wind tunnel for testing. The intention is to find out why the aerodynamics have got worse compared with the car's performance the previous year.

Prost in a Prost. Team chief Alain Prost gets behind the wheel during testing sessions. He does this "in order to get a feel for the new car and to understand it better".

From next year, Ford will be providing engines to another Formula One team in addition to the Stewart team. The most probable candidate – on the basis of past success – is Benetton.

Tony Blair is again in the headlines with regard to Formula One. An investigating committee has accused the British Prime Minister of having accepted the invitation of the FIA to the Silverstone Grand Prix in 1996 without reporting the visit as he should have done.

Quotes
"The man is a millionaire and always looks like an unmade bed."
Herald Sun, Melbourne, on Jacques Villeneuve's appearance.

"If Hakkinen was the hero of the Grand Prix, then Eddie the Eagle is the greatest Winter Olympics competitor of all time."
Herald Sun after the controversial outcome of the Australian Grand Prix.

"If things get really bad, there will soon be a hearing even before the prize ceremony."
Süddeutsche Zeitung on the wave of protest that takes place before the Brazilian Grand Prix over McLaren's so-called "wonder brake".

BACKGROUND

Objecters ousted

Melbourne was again voted "best Grand Prix" by the FIA.

While the Formula One circus was preparing for its first appearance in the Australian Grand Prix at Albert Park, a fierce battle raged between the motorsport authorities and radical environmentalists.

While the Formula One enthusiasts could hardly wait for the arrival of the containers, drivers, and racing cars that would signal the start of the season, the "Save the Albert Park" association attempted to disrupt the event. The activists claimed that the race would interfere with local wildlife in Albert Park. Some of the more extreme "activists" climbed on to the stands and delayed construction work. But the militancy of these actions annoyed not only neutral observers but many other people sympathetic to the environmental cause. Spokespersons for the Australian Grand Prix also pointed out that before the development of the race track at Albert Park it had been a virtual wasteland.

The general enthusiasm of the local population for Formula One motorsport in the end outweighed the voice of protest, and the FIA considered the Australian Grand Prix to be an unqualified success.

ENGINES

A new supplier

When Renault announced last year that they were withdrawing from the Formula One series, a new name appeared in the public eye – Mecachrome.

The Mecachrome company is based in Aubigny sur Nère near Bourges in France – not far from Magny-Cours – and took over from Renault Sport the task of equipping Williams and Benetton with engines. The precision engineering company has been a partner of Renault since 1974 and, in the last three years, has had a 50 per cent responsibility for the maintenance of Renault race engines.

The Mecachrome unit that will be used by Williams and Benetton for this year is the 1997 season RS9 Renault engine. This engine was presented as a totally new design in 1997 and was thought to have further growth potential for this season.

The only question-mark over Mecachrome's involvement is their alleged lack of experience in matters of research and development. Previously, they had only been concerned with maintaining the engines, leaving Renault responsible for all major design work. Now, however, Mecachrome have to take on a brand new role and develop the engine's potential themselves.

Mecachrome have been helped, however, by an influx of engineers from Renault. In the background, furthermore, Renault's sport department has been discreetly supporting Mecachrome's efforts.

Jean Ives Houe, manager of Mecachrome, believes in the work of his talented team: "We want to equip Williams and Benetton with reliable and competitive engines. Whether that is sufficient to win is, in the end, a matter for the team."

REGULATIONS

The new grooved tyres introduced by the FIA, manufactured by the Japanese Bridgestone company and Goodyear of the United States.

Designers get round the rules

Every year since 1906, the International Motorsport Association (FIA) has tried to limit certain aspects of racing car design. For this season the FIA ordered a series of fundamental restrictions intended to reduce speeds. The designers, however, worked hard to get round them and, to the dismay of the FIA, overall speeds were little changed.

Concerned at the growing speeds of racing cars, especially during cornering, the FIA instituted what it saw as a major review of Formula One safety. Tyres were therefore narrowed and grooves were cut into their surfaces. Another means to reduce speed on the corners came with an edict limiting the number of brake callipers per wheel. The authorities hoped that this would make racing not only safer but also more exciting, as it would make overtaking easier to perform.

Stately processions

One of the constant criticisms levelled at Formula One in recent years was the difficulty drivers had in getting past each other. The great overtaking duels that had formerly characterized the sport seemed to be a thing of the past, as cars now followed each other in procession. It was hoped that the new reforms would end this problem.

However, the FIA staff discovered, after the qualifying sessions at the start of the season in Melbourne, that the Formula One designers had more tricks up their sleeves than had been previously assumed. Half of the vehicles improved their times on the previous year and, with top speeds in excess of 300 kmh (186 mph), the drivers were at variance with the wish of the FIA for slower races.

Nevertheless, the FIA staunchly defended its measures, which were intended to deal with a whole range of safety issues. FIA's President Max Mosley was concerned that the authorities should be seen to be doing their utmost to improve the sport. There were four major areas of concern that were troubling the FIA.

The first was the crash test. Before a car could be allowed to race in Formula One, it had to survive a rigorous side impact test. Speed was increased from the previous 5 m/sec (16 ft/sec) to 7 m/sec (23 ft/sec).

Secondly, the FIA ruled on tyre track width. Then, the maximum width of a car was reduced from 200 cm (79 in) to 180 cm (71 in). The object of this measure was to reduce air resistance and, in consequence, lessen contact pressure on the ground. Most of the teams, however, were able to compensate for this ruling before the start of the first race with the addition of extra wing effect.

Thirdly, measures were taken on tyres. Instead of slicks or bald tyres, that had now been forbidden by the FIA, the new regulations were for three longitudinal grooves for the front tyres and four longitudinal grooves for the rear tyres. In comparison to last year's tyres, this change meant a 17 per cent reduction on the contact surface and therefore reduced ground adhesion. Further regulations were issued to ensure that the grooves were sufficiently deep to prevent them wearing away into slicks through normal wear during a race.

Lastly, the FIA regulated on the brakes. Whereas brake discs with a thickness of 32 mm (1.25 in) were permitted in the past, drivers now had to use a disc with a maximum width of 28 mm (1.12 in). In addition, all the drivers had to manage with one brake calliper and brake disc, and were provided with a maximum of two brake linings per wheel. Longer braking distances were now expected.

New camera angles

Other minor modifications were introduced by the FIA. These included improvements to on-board cameras attached to each car. Formula One had always recognized the central importance of television to the commercial health of the sport. And those who run Formula One were determined that new technology should be used, especially with the proposed introduction of digital television.

Mika Hakkinen leapt the first hurdle of the season in Melbourne. With team-mate David Coulthard he dominated the entire race.

Hakkinen victorious – thanks to Coulthard

8 MARCH, MELBOURNE. The early season dominance of the McLarens was confirmed in Australia with a clear double victory for the British team. Coulthard's decision to wave Hakkinen through to take the lead and win the race produced equal amounts of praise and criticism.

By the end of the first lap it was clear to all observers that McLaren-Mercedes had achieved a rare mastery over the rest of the field. The McLaren-Mercedes alliance showed which team had done their winter homework most effectively when both of the Silver Arrows raced away from the rest of the field at the start of the race. The other teams could only watch in astonishment and hope to make improvements that would increase their cars' performance. Heinz Harald Frentzen, in his second year with Williams, made a remarkably prophetic assessment of how the race would proceed. He bet his team-mate Jacques Villeneuve that both the McLarens would lap the field. Frentzen, who finished third in the race, was proved absolutely right.

While McLaren drivers Mika Hakkinen and David Coulthard pursued their solitary race and moved further and further ahead, the remainder of the field provided an uninspiring spectacle. There were few overtaking manoeuvres and no exciting battles for position.

The Australian race showed few signs of what the FIA had hoped to achieve in the 1998 season through their review of the rules. The cars were stuck together and the drivers raced round the Melbourne circuit in much the same lap times as they had the previous season. In effect, the first race of the 1998 World Championship was something of a procession.

The monotony was temporarily broken in the 36th lap when, having lapped Johnny Herbert, Alexander

Mika Hakkinen crosses the line, closely followed by his McLaren team-mate David Coulthard.

Wurz, and World Champion Villeneuve in rapid succession, McLaren's Mika Hakkinen was mistakenly called into the pits before the refuelling team was ready to deal with the car. He was waved right through and returned four laps later for his scheduled refuelling stop. This error, however, cost the Finn the lead to David Coulthard, who had managed to pull some 33 seconds ahead of his team-mate. Despite this setback, Hakkinen pulled himself together and then proceeded to drive the fastest lap of the whole race. Hakkinen's will to win remained undiminished.

Three laps before the end, with Coulthard's fourth Grand Prix victory apparently secure, the leading McLaren suddenly slowed on the main straight. The spectators thought that Coulthard's car must have developed a fault. In reality, the Scot had deliberately slowed to let Hakkinen pass. This seemingly selfless decision mirrored that of the final race of the 1997 season in Jerez. There, Villeneuve had permitted Hakkinen to pass in the last lap.

First to the bend

Coulthard and Hakkinen had agreed before the race that whichever McLaren driver reached the initial bend first would be allowed to go on and win. Coulthard, who had an excellent record of fast starts, was confident of his chances, even though he was second to Hakkinen at the grid. "I was very confident that I would beat Mika to the first corner," Coulthard said, "but he made the best start. I think he deserved to win the race, no question about it. I could think about it clearly and did what I thought was the right thing to do."

Hakkinen was generous in his praise for Coulthard's chivalrous action: "What David did today was remarkable. I have been in Formula One for many years and seen a great deal. What he did was really gentlemanly, unreal, and fantastic."

McLaren, however, were bitterly attacked in the press. The World Council of the FIA agreed with the critics and issued a proclamation forbidding so-called "team orders" with threats of fines and possible exclusion from the World Championship. As far as Melbourne was concerned, however, the new regulations did not affect the British McLaren-Mercedes team. In defence

CIRCUIT

Albert Park

This exciting racecourse, which passes through the city park of Melbourne, replaced the classic Australian track in Adelaide in 1996. A very popular course with the drivers, Melbourne is characterized by a mix of hairpins and fast corners, between which are a series of sweeping curves. Tyre wear can be heavy, and maximum downforce is required.

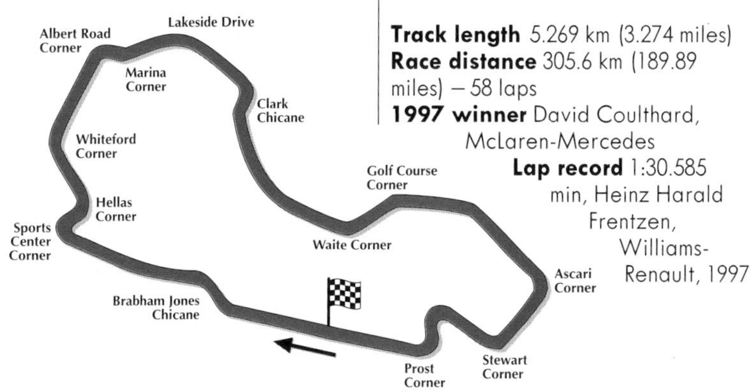

Track length 5.269 km (3.274 miles)
Race distance 305.6 km (189.89 miles) – 58 laps
1997 winner David Coulthard, McLaren-Mercedes
Lap record 1:30.585 min, Heinz Harald Frentzen, Williams-Renault, 1997

PRACTICE

McLaren set the pace

The top qualifying drivers at Albert Park: Coulthard, Hakkinen, and Schumacher.

Qualifying Results

1	Hakkinen	McLaren-Mercedes	1:30.010
2	Coulthard	McLaren-Mercedes	1:30.053
3	M. Schumacher	Ferrari	1:30.767
4	Villeneuve	Williams-Mecachrome	1:30.919
5	Herbert	Sauber-Petronas	1:31.384
6	Frentzen	Williams-Mecachrome	1:31.397
7	Fisichella	Benetton-Mecachrome	1:31.733
8	Irvine	Ferrari	1:31.767
9	R. Schumacher	Jordan-Mugen-Honda	1:32.392
10	Hill	Jordan-Mugen-Honda	1:32.399
11	Wurz	Benetton-Mecachrome	1:32.726
12	Alesi	Sauber-Petronas	1:33.240
13	Takagi	Tyrrell-Ford	1:33.291
14	Barrichello	Stewart-Ford	1:33.383
15	Trulli	Prost-Peugeot	1:33.739
16	Panis	Prost-Peugeot	1:33.851
17	Salo	TWR-Arrows	1:33.927
18	Tuero	Minardi-Ford	1:34.646
19	Magnussen	Stewart-Ford	1:34.906
20	Rosset	Tyrrell-Ford	1:35.119
21	Diniz	TWR-Arrows	1:35.140
22	Nakano	Minardi-Ford	1:35.301

The competition for the best placings at the start of the Australian Grand Prix was the first official trial of strength for the 1998 teams. The McLaren drivers were able to confirm the rumours in the paddock that the team's hard work during the cold winter months was about to pay off handsomely.

Michael Schumacher's Ferrari was immediately behind the two McLarens. Although the Ferrari was no match for the McLarens, Schumacher made it quite clear that his new car had at least sufficient potential to keep pace with the Williams team, last year's adversary.

Williams were obviously disappointed by this development and Heinz Harald Frentzen, in particular, was unhappy with the results of the qualifying session. Frentzen finished in sixth position, two places behind his Canadian team-mate Jacques Villeneuve.

Another team disappointed by their qualifying performance was Jordan who had hoped for better things from its new team that included former World Champion Damon Hill and Ralph Schumacher, Michael's younger brother.

For a so-called "second division" team, the Sauber driven by Johnny Herbert achieved a commendable fifth position on the starting grid, well ahead of team-mate Jean Alesi in a disappointing twelfth place.

AUSTRALIAN GRAND PRIX

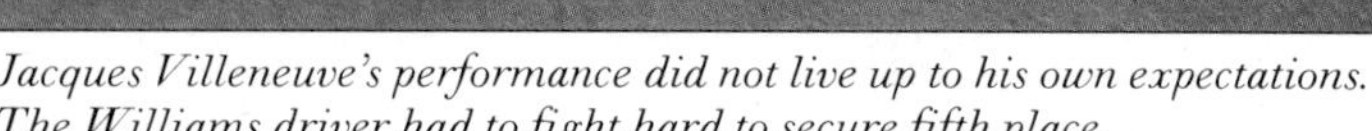

Jacques Villeneuve's performance did not live up to his own expectations. The Williams driver had to fight hard to secure fifth place.

Arriving in hope, departing disappointed. Ferrari driver Michael Schumacher retired with engine failure after only five laps.

of his team's actions, Mercedes motorsport boss Norbert Haug pointed out that Hakkinen's unplanned pit-stop was the fault of the team, and that the Finnish driver should not be punished for the team's error.

Ferrari optimistic

Quite apart from this controversy, the McLaren Silver Arrows' dominance drew comment from the other drivers. Michael Schumacher had travelled to Australia with great hopes but had had to park his Ferrari at the edge of the track with a failed engine after only five laps. At the end of the race, the German driver spoke to the waiting press: "If I had finished the race, I would not have been far behind the McLarens. To avoid any misunderstanding, however, I do not think that I would have had a chance today. But this does not mean that it will always be like this. In my opinion, various factors leading to this superiority acted in conjunction today. One of these was the pitstop strategy. Another is that we have not yet been able to employ the ideal Goodyear."

Heinz Harald Frentzen also had problems with the Goodyear tyre, claiming that the compound used was too hard for the conditions encountered at Albert Park. Overall, the Williams team did not fulfil the high standards expected of a team with such a superb World Championship pedigree. The technical director of Williams, Patrick Head, called his team's disappointing Melbourne result "a pretty weak performance".

Head's criticisms of his own team, however, were not shared by Schumacher's Ferrari team-mate Eddie Irvine who was typically upbeat about Ferrari's chances for the rest of the season: "I don't think the gap between us and McLaren is as big as it looked today. We need to improve the driveability of the engine, but overall I was very happy with the car and think we can beat Williams and challenge McLaren with the improvements we have in the pipeline." Irvine finished fourth, behind Frentzen and in front of Villeneuve and Herbert. Jordan's Damon Hill managed only eighth.

The new Championship leader, Mika Hakkinen, refuted the Ferrari drivers' optimistic estimates of the close performance between McLaren and the rest of the field. He explained: "It would actually have been quite interesting to know just how far in front we would have been if we had utilized our full potential." Although this was only the first race of the season, such confidence did not augur well for the other teams' chances.

Race Result

1	Hakkinen	1:31:45.996
2	Coulthard	1:31:46.698
3	Frentzen	1 lap behind
4	Irvine	1 lap behind
5	Villeneuve	1 lap behind
6	Herbert	1 lap behind

Drivers' Championship

1	Hakkinen	10 points
2	Coulthard	6 points
3	Frentzen	4 points
4	Irvine	3 points
5	Villeneuve	2 points
6	Herbert	1 point

Constructors' Championship

1	McLaren-Mercedes	16 points
2	Williams-Mecachrome	6 points
3	Ferrari	3 points
4	Sauber-Petronas	1 point

BIOGRAPHY

Hakkinen is the "Flying Finn"

Mika Hakkinen (born in 1968) earned his nickname from his exuberant high-speed skills, especially on the straight where he often summons up a speed advantage over his rivals. This ability, however, almost brought a premature end to Hakkinen's career – and life. While racing a McLaren, he crashed during the final meeting of the season in Adelaide in 1995. During qualifying, Hakkinen left the track at high speed after a tyre failure and smashed into the tyre wall. The track doctor had to cut into Hakkinen's windpipe at the scene of the accident to enable him to breathe.

The Finn's serious head injuries initially indicated that he may have to retire prematurely from Formula One. In fact, he made an amazingly swift recovery. After spending only one day at the Royal Adelaide Hospital he was already sitting up on the edge of his sickbed and was looking forward to the next season's racing with the McLaren team.

Early start

Like many other Formula One stars, Hakkinen started his racing career in karting – becoming Finnish champion at the age of 13 – before moving into Formula Ford in 1987. There he proved an immediate success, winning the European title in that same year. He then moved to British Formula Three, where he raced against fellow Finn Mika Salo to win the championship in 1990. In 1991, Hakkinen was given a ride in the Formula One Lotus team, and on the basis of his former successes he predicted that he would win the World Championship within three years at the most. In fact, his Formula One career was far from meteoric, and he needed six years to achieve his first Grand Prix victory.

Spanish victory

This first triumph – his 96th Grand Prix – took place in October 1997 during the final race in Jerez. Hakkinen's victory in Spain was assessed by the majority of the media as a "present" from Jacques Villeneuve, then certain to be World Champion, rather than as a result of Hakkinen's driving ability. But the win provided the Finn with an enormous boost as he at last experienced "how simple victory is once it has been achieved."

After signing full-time with McLaren in 1994, Hakkinen struck up a productive working relationship with Ron Dennis, the McLaren team boss. Dennis was impressed by the way Hakkinen struggled with the uncompetitive McLaren cars of the mid-1990s. During the 1998 season, Hakkinen showed that he had lost none of his speed, regularly out-qualifying his team-mate David Coulthard. He also demonstrated a new-found maturity that saw him convert raw talent into race victories. The new McLaren and the "Flying Finn" were to prove to be a successful and formidable combination.

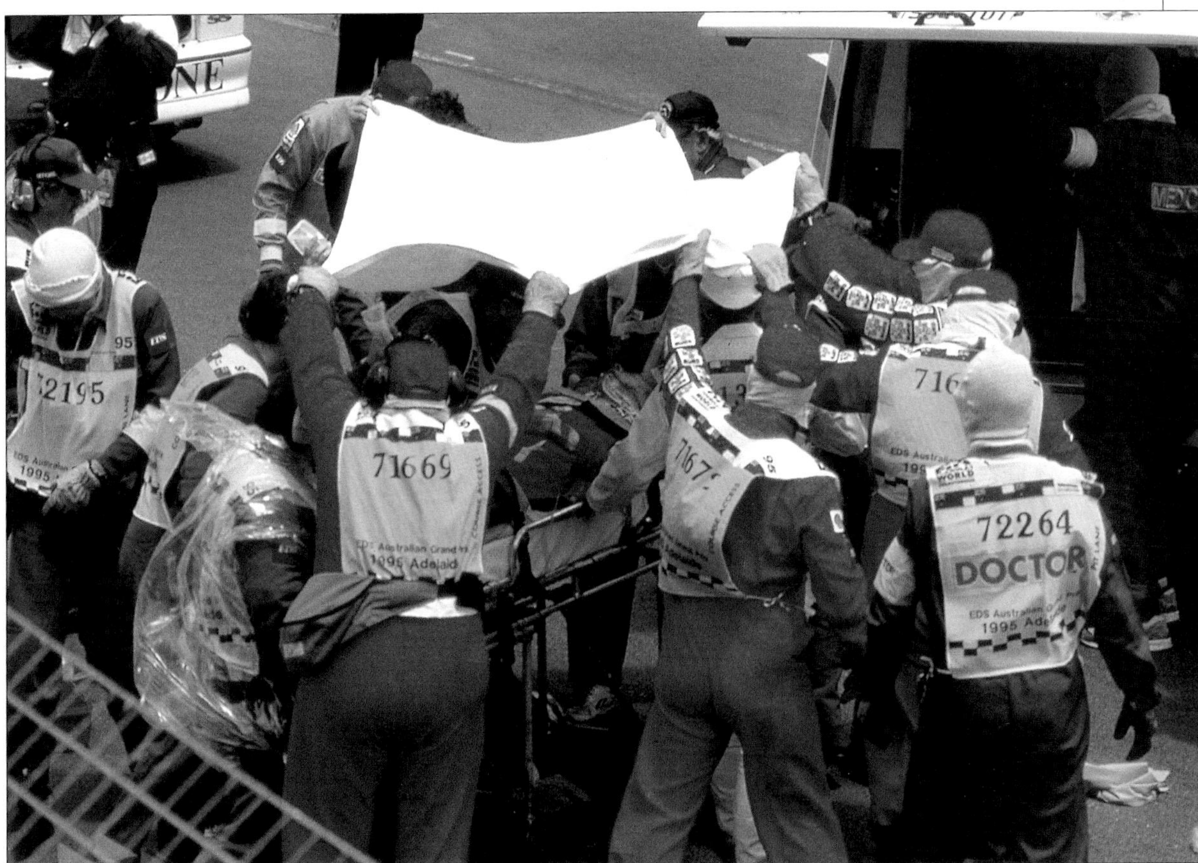

Hakkinen receives emergency treatment on the track after his 1995 accident at Adelaide.

In 1998 Mika Hakkinen benefited from the superb combination of Mercedes engine and McLaren car.

CIRCUIT

Autodromo José Carlos Pace

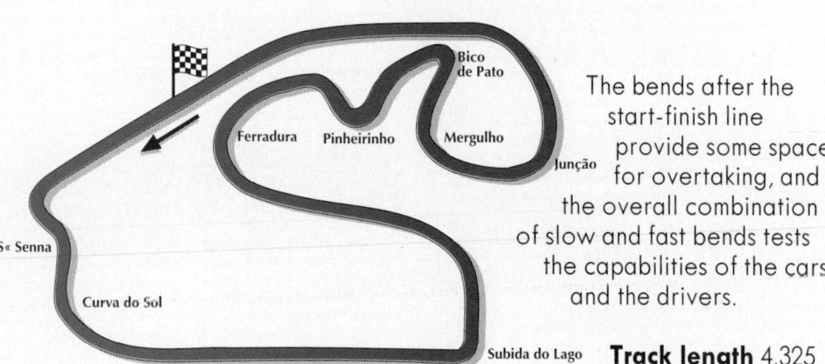

The bends after the start-finish line provide some space for overtaking, and the overall combination of slow and fast bends tests the capabilities of the cars and the drivers.

Track length 4.325 km (2.684 miles)

The Interlagos race track is located to the south of São Paulo. Named after José Carlos Pace – a winner in 1975 – the circuit is very bumpy and tiring for the drivers, despite being re-surfaced for the 1995 season.

Race distance 306.075 km (190.77 miles) – 71 laps
1997 winner Jacques Villeneuve, Williams-Renault
Lap record 1:18.397 min, Jacques Villeneuve, Williams-Renault, 1997

Although frustrated by the McLarens' performance advantage, Michael Schumacher remained optimistic about Ferrari's race chances.

BRAZILIAN GRAND PRIX

McLaren Ahead

29 MARCH, SÃO PAULO. Brazil provided McLaren-Mercedes with their second one-two victory of the season. Meanwhile, the Ferrari team complained about the controversial McLaren brake-steer system which, they claimed, did not conform to Formula One rules.

At times the Brazilian Grand Prix seemed to have relatively little to do with racing – the teams were far too busy attacking McLaren-Mercedes. The dispute, organized by Ferrari, centred on the new brake-steer system. This was a braking system developed by the McLaren team that allowed the driver to brake the rear wheel on the inside of the curve by turning the steering wheel. This method of slowing the car was additional to the main braking system.

When a Formula One team succeeds in gaining a significant advantage over the others through a technical advance, it has always been the practice for the other discomfited teams to protest to the authorities. So it was little surprise that this was exactly the case in São Paulo.

Asked in Melbourne whether Ferrari would make good the ground lost to McLaren by developing a similar brake-steer system, Schumacher replied: "No, something better." In Brazil, however, Ferrari did not appear with a technical innovation. Instead, they brought forward Ferrari lawyer Henry Peter who had a 109-page brief in his luggage. Peter's contention was that the McLaren, Williams, and Jordan systems should be classified as four-wheeled steering – which is forbidden in Formula One. The main target for the Ferrari protest, however, was not Williams or Jordan – whose additional braking had proved more of a hindrance than a help – but McLaren.

Brakes off

The Ferrari team breathed a sigh of relief when the protest succeeded, forcing McLaren and other teams to dismantle their brake-steer systems. According to Ferrari team leader Jean Todt, it would have taken at least another four races for Ferrari to produce a competitive system.

In São Paulo, the most effective response from McLaren came on the track. Even when deprived of their contentious brake-steer systems, Hakkinen and Coulthard raced away from the field at the start of the race. In contrast to the Australian Grand Prix, the struggle for the other places at Interlagos provided some real excitement. Michael Schumacher, in fourth place on the grid, had a bad start and by the first bend had been forced back to sixth place. In typical fashion, however, the gritty German fought his way back up the field.

While Schumacher overhauled Benetton's Alexander Wurz, his Jordan-driving luckless brother Ralf came off the track to achieve his second premature Grand Prix retirement in a row (his team-mate Damon Hill was later disqualified for driving an underweight car).

Race Result

1	Hakkinen	1:37:11.747
2	Coulthard	1:37:12.849
3	M. Schumacher	1:38:12.297
4	Wurz	1:38:19.200
5	Frentzen	1 lap behind
6	Fisichella	1 lap behind

Drivers' Championship

1	Hakkinen	20 points
2	Coulthard	12 points
3	Frentzen	6 points
4	M. Schumacher	4 points
5	Irvine	3 points
	= Wurz	3 points
7	Villeneuve	2 points
8	Herbert	1 point
	= Fisichella	1 point

Constructors' Championship

1	McLaren-Mercedes	32 points
2	Williams-Mecachrome	8 points
3	Ferrari	7 points
4	Benetton-Mecachrome	4 points
5	Sauber-Petronas	1 point

Michael Schumacher now had his own team-mate Eddie Irvine ahead and steadily caught up with him. Irvine had qualified in the row behind Schumacher and had shot past the German driver at the start of the race. Unfortunately for Irvine, Schumacher had the new higher-revving 047D Ferrari engine that gave him a good speed advantage. "In the warm-up," commented Irvine, "I was about 6 mph down without it and had to take off a load of downforce to get the speed back. That made the car pretty critical under braking, which is the main area where I lost out in the race.

"I found that I could still run with Michael and Frentzen, but I ended up flat-spotting the left front tyre, which did me no favours. Add

Silver Arrow drivers Mika Hakkinen (with helmet) and David Coulthard (in background) were cheered by the fans after their double victory.

Mercedes motorsport boss Norbert Haug was philosophical over the brake-steer episode and delighted with the McLaren double victory.

▲ *Principal actors in the brake-steer struggle: FIA President Max Mosley (left) discusses the problem with Ferrari team-leader Jean Todt.*

▶ *McLaren chief designer, Adrian Newey, condemned the brake protesters.*

on, as well, the couple of seconds it cost me to let Michael by and the result of all this was that I came out from my first stop behind Alesi, who was stopping only once, which effectively ended my race."

After passing Irvine, Schumacher had a clear track ahead but there was no way that he could reel in the two McLarens who, in the end, finished a full minute ahead of the Ferrari.

Wurz pressure

As the race was entering lap 51, Alexander Wurz – who had been driving brilliantly anyway – began to turn on the heat. The Benetton driver set about making life difficult for Frentzen who was in fourth place. Two laps later, Frentzen was forced to submit to the pressure exerted by Wurz, who then held fourth place to the end of the race. As Wurz crossed the finishing line he was only one second behind Schumacher.

Apart from Mika Hakkinen, David Coulthard, and Michael Schumacher, Wurz was the only driver who completed the full distance. As in the Melbourne curtain-raiser, all the other drivers were lapped by the McLarens.

Despite the emphatic McLaren victory, the Ferrari team refused to be downcast by the result. After the race, Schumacher expressed his continuing optimism about his and Ferrari's Grand Prix expectations: "I am gradually getting used to being behind the McLarens; the one-second difference is no reason for giving up. When I see how good the Bridgestone tyres are and knowing the developments we have in store, I am sure that we will catch up. Until then, best of the rest has to be our objective."

BACKGROUND

FIA troubled by braking system

Although McLaren accepted the FIA brake judgment announced just one day before the Brazilian Grand Prix, there was much shaking of heads among the McLaren team. Whereas Mercedes motorsport boss Norbert Haug expressed his consternation at the whole situation – "What did we do wrong?" – engine supremo Mario Illien was less diplomatic: "I think the FIA has an internal problem. A protest can strangle any innovation in future." In any event, McLaren were quite certain that they had reported the disputed brake system to the FIA in accordance with the regulations. During the winter months, McLaren had corresponded extensively with the FIA technical spokesman Charlie Whiting who had given the brake system his blessing and ruled that it was in conformity with the rules.

The race commissioners in Brazil did not share this opinion, however, and stated for the record that while Whiting had indeed given the opinion of the FIA, this was not the same as a judgment on site. The whole episode reflected the communication problems between the FIA and the racing teams.

PRACTICE

Frentzen behind McLaren's Silver Arrows

"We have always said that the brake system is not a fundamental constituent of our car." With these words, McLaren's Adrian Newey underlined the superiority of the Silver Arrows in practice. Mika Hakkinen – with a lead of just six-tenths of a second over his team-mate David Coulthard – was once again in pole position. In the second row, Williams driver Heinz Harald Frentzen gained third place in front of Michael Schumacher's Ferrari.

Prost driver Olivier Panis dismantled his car during Sunday's warm-up.

Frentzen's qualifying performance was significantly better than that of his team-mate, Jacques Villeneuve, who only managed tenth place.

Wurz and Fisichella occupied fifth and seventh places respectively, underlining Benetton's determination to make a positive impact this season.

Practice Results

	Driver	Team	Time
1	Hakkinen	McLaren-Mercedes	1:17.092
2	Coulthard	McLaren-Mercedes	1:17.757
3	Frentzen	Williams-Mecachrome	1:18.109
4	M. Schumacher	Ferrari	1:18.250
5	Wurz	Benetton-Mecachrome	1:18.261
6	Irvine	Ferrari	1:18.449
7	Fisichella	Benetton-Mecachrome	1:18.652
8	R. Schumacher	Jordan-Mugen-Honda	1:18.735
9	Panis	Prost-Peugeot	1:18.753
10	Villeneuve	Williams-Mecachrome	1:18.761
11	Hill	Jordan-Mugen-Honda	1:18.988
12	Trulli	Prost-Peugeot	1:19.069
13	Barrichello	Stewart-Ford	1:19.344
14	Herbert	Sauber-Petronas	1:19.375
15	Alesi	Sauber-Petronas	1:19.449
16	Magnussen	Stewart-Ford	1:19.644
17	Takagi	Tyrrell-Ford	1:20.203
18	Nakano	Minardi-Ford	1:20.319
19	Tuero	Minardi-Ford	1:20.459
20	Salo	Arrows-Hart	1:20.481
21	Rosset	Tyrrell-Ford	1:20.748
22	Diniz	Arrows-Hart	1:20.847

CALENDAR

7 April
This is the 30th anniversary of the death of British driver Jim Clark (born 14 March 1936, died 7 April 1968). The greatest racing driver of his age, Clark was World Champion twice – in 1963 and 1965. He died in an accident during a Formula Two race at Hockenheim, Germany.

9 April
Despite an Argentine law banning cigarette advertising, representatives of the Formula One tobacco sponsors are able to negotiate a special deal with the government allowing cars in the Argentine Grand Prix to carry the logos of various cigarette brands as usual.

12 April
Buenos Aires: Michael Schumacher wins the Argentine Grand Prix, ending the sequence of early-season victories by the McLaren-Mercedes team.

24 April
Rumours are spreading in Formula One circles to the effect that Michael Schumacher may have left Ferrari for McLaren-Mercedes by next season. Although the German driver strongly denies this, he makes it clear in the same breath that his agreement with Ferrari does have a clause which permits him to leave if he wishes to do so.

26 April
David Coulthard triumphs in the San Marino Grand Prix at Imola. It is the McLaren driver's first victory of the season – a just reward for a brilliant performance.

The company that operates the Nürburgring announces that it intends to invest large sums of money in upgrading the course over the next three years to keep the circuit up to standard for future Grand Prix events.

29 April
Three days after the San Marino Grand Prix, the FIA bans the use of so-called "X-Wings", apparently for safety reasons.

1–30 April
Stories appear that a Croatian lawyer is attempting to blackmail the Formula One boss Bernie Ecclestone for a million dollars.

Jeremy Fergusson, Dunlop's motorsports chief, denies rumours suggesting that the tyre manufacturer might be planning to return to Formula One.

A new warning-light system is introduced into cockpits for the first time at the Argentine Grand Prix. The arrangement involves three coloured LEDs – yellow signifies "no overtaking", red means "race stopped", blue requires the driver to allow faster cars coming up behind to overtake him.

The one-time Williams test driver Christophe Boulion signs a test contract for the BAR team.

After the row about the McLaren braking system, some team chiefs are asking the FIA to clarify the regulations for 1999.

The first appearance of the Formula One McLaren-Mercedes two-seater is postponed because of manufacturing delays.

After the removal of the Portuguese Grand Prix from this year's racing calendar (because conversion work on the track at Estoril had not been carried out) a start is made on upgrading the track. The Portuguese are now hoping to obtain approval from the FIA for a Formula One Grand Prix in 1999.

The main Williams sponsor, Winfield, invites the four-times motorcycle World Champion Mick Doohan and the double World Rally Champion Tommi Makinen to test-drive the 1997 Williams Formula One car. Both men are impressed. In the process, however, the Williams FW19 racing car is totally written off.

The GPrasa company, the owner of the Autodromo Oscar y Alfredo Galves, is in financial difficulties. "We have invested millions of dollars in the track and have earned too little money," stated Carlos Soriano of GPrasa.

The Motopark company plans to apply for a Formula One Grand Prix to be held at Oschersleben, near Hanover, Germany. It would be timed to coincide with the Expo 2000 World Exhibition in Hanover. Opponents of the scheme argue that there have already been two Grand Prix races held in Germany each season for several years, and that is already one too many.

In the search for a rising new generation of engineers, computer manufacturer Hewlett Packard and the Benetton Formula One team invite entries for an engineering competition. As a prize, the seven best competitors will be invited into the pit lane for the Luxembourg Grand Prix held at the Nürburgring.

A comic book entitled *Our Schumi* appears in Germany. It is by the artist Kim Schmidt and the writer Lutz Mattesdorf and takes a lighthearted and ironic look at the events of last year's Formula One season.

Quotes
"At Ferrari, everything is done to suit Michael Schumacher. What will these people do if Michael ever becomes ill?"
Ex-World Champion Keke Rosberg in *Welt am Sonntag*.

"Easter and Christmas would have to fall on the same day for our drivers to appear on the podium."
Team owner Peter Sauber on the difficulties he faces in 1998.

"If the Labour Party had only accepted my millions! Since they have given them back, any madman can have a bit of them."
Bernie Ecclestone on the demands of the Croatian lawyer who is allegedly attempting to blackmail him.

PORTRAIT

Swiss engine guru

Just as connoisseurs of Formula One are certain that Michael Schumacher is the best racing driver since Ayrton Senna, and that Adrian Newey is the aerodynamics genius of the twentieth century, they are convinced that Mario Illien is number one for engines.

The Swiss-born Illien left the manufacturer Cosworth in 1984 after five years working on their Formula One engines. Together with Paul Morgan, he founded the Illmor company. This gave Illien, a professional mechanical engineer, the facilities for manufacturing his own engines. The two-man company first directed their attention to the American IndyCar series. It was here that Illien designed and built the Chevrolet V8, the first of his own products. This first effort required a development period of almost a year and a half and, before it was finished, it gave the 49-year old Swiss many sleepless nights. Once the engine had overcome all its teething troubles, however, the CART V8 turbo engine became a star. Within four years it had 72 victories under its belt.

Super engine

When, in 1994, Mercedes decided to take part in the Indianapolis 500 event with the Roger Penske team, the Stuttgart company employed the services of Illmor. The result was the 1010hp engine called the 500I, which was produced in only nine months and accelerated the Penske-Mercedes to an amazing 412 km/h (257 mph). On its first – and, in fact, only – appearance, this engine caused a furore. The 500I "one-day flight" produced a pole position followed by victory. For Illien, this success opened the way to full co-operation with Mercedes via the CART series. Mercedes and Illien then moved on to Formula One.

March to success

The Illmor company were already no stranger to Formula One – they had been supplying March with engines since 1991 – but success had eluded them. Even with Mercedes as a new partner, the breakthrough took time. Although the engines produced in the 320-man manufacturing set-up incorporated Illien's philosophy of making the power plant as small, light, and efficient as possible, they frequently failed for lack of endurance. However, Illien did not give up and tackled the various weak points of the engine with the obsessive energy and punctilious attention to detail that have become his trademark.

Illien summed up his working philosophy as follows: "I work best when under pressure. That's the ideal." This attitude was finally rewarded at the end of last year's season. In the last race of the 1997 Formula One World Championship, a Mercedes won its first Formula One Grand Prix in 42 years – with plenty of Illmor horsepower driving it. The 1998 season promised further success for Mario Illien and Mercedes.

Mario Illien (left) has been engine chief of Mercedes since 1994. The Illmor engines are the smallest and lightest in Formula One, and the most powerful.

BACKGROUND

Legal trouble with Europe

'he FIA and its boss, Bernie Ecclestone, have been attracting the nwelcome attention of the European Union (EU) supervisory uthorities ever since it became known that Ecclestone was planning to loat his highly profitable Formula One business on the stock market.

: was Bernie Ecclestone himself who tarted the ball rolling with an nquiry to the EU Commission in 'russels. The British businessman was eeking exemption from a law against cartels that would have blocked a stock market flotation. The EU's response to this approach was to place the matter in the hands of Commissioner Karel van Miert, who was given the job of clarifying the organizational relationships between the FIA and the Formula One Administration (FOA) company controlled by Ecclestone.

As a result of the Commissioner's investigation, the EU sent the FIA and Ecclestone a 15-page letter explaining that they were guilty of blatant infringements of EU laws on free competition. Van Miert accused Bernie Ecclestone in particular of the abuse of a monopoly position. Basing itself firmly on this accusation, the EU sought to initiate an investigation into the way Formula One marketed itself. The EU position was that Ecclestone had had Formula One all to himself for 15 years. They considered this a problem, and said that there might be a variety of ways in which the problem could be resolved.

ulling the strings behind the Formula One circus – Bernie Ecclestone.

Very unusually, the warning letter from the Commissioner, which should have been confidential, was leaked to four British newspapers. Bernie Ecclestone, for his part, was not best pleased by what had taken place, but seemed fairly relaxed and upbeat. He did, however, suggest that Van Miert would have done well to tone down his strong comments, and also accused the EU Commission of an arrogant belief that they could do what they liked.

The FIA President, Max Mosley, reacted in a considerably less relaxed manner. He used Van Miert's "mistake" in letting the press see his letter as a reason for submitting a case against the EU Commission at the European Court in Luxembourg. Mosley claimed that by allowing his colleagues to release confidential written matter to the public, Van Miert had damaged the good reputation of the FIA. Mosley put in a claim for damages set at $300 million.

Van Miert affected to treat this legal action lightly, describing it as

FIA President Max Mosley submitted an action for damages against the EU Commission at the European Court.

"only an attempt to frighten us". He went on with his campaign to, "clean up", as he saw it, Formula One.

Van Miert imposed a heavy defeat on the FOA by blocking a merger between the media groups Kirch and Bertelsmann. This would have linked the Ecclestone/Kirch Formula One station DFI with the flourishing Bertelsmann private channel Premiere.

Ecclestone, who is also Vice President of the FIA, expressed no opposition to this decision by the EU Commission. In contrast, Max Mosley reflected almost nostalgically on the "good old days" when Formula One sport was not yet at the centre of public interest. According to Mosley, it was a problem of scale. He suggested that when Formula One had been a relatively modest and special-interest sport, European bureaucrats had taken no interest in it. But now, when the sport had grown big enough to compete in the same league as the Olympics and football, it had come under attack. However, Mosley asserted that Formula One would survive the current scrutiny.

ARGENTINE GRAND PRIX

The decisive moment of the 1998 Argentine Grand Prix – Michael Schumacher pushes past David Coulthard to take the lead.

Ferrari's new tyres do the trick

12 April, Buenos Aires. In the third race of the 1998 Formula One World Championship – one of the most exciting in recent years – Ferrari's Michael Schumacher ended the series of McLaren-Mercedes victories with a scintillating display of tough and skilful driving.

"That was the nicest Easter present. This win shows that we have already turned the corner and that everything is now possible in the race for the title," was Schumacher's comment on the surprising result of the race. And Ferrari team leader Jean Todt also gushed superlatives in his generous assessment of his highly expensive and successful employee: "Only Michael can win a race like that. Once again, he has shown that he is the best racing driver in the world."

Quite apart from his undisputed driving ability, Schumacher was aided by the improved Goodyear tyres that, for the first time in the present season, were highly competitive. During th previous races, Ferrari had been losin approximately one second per lap t the McLarens, which were equippe with Bridgestone tyres. Goodyear ha promised an improvement for the rac in Buenos Aires, and they kept thei word – in qualifying, Schumache won a front-row starting position, jus behind David Coulthard's McLaren.

Frentzen failure

Schumacher lost his second position a the first bend to Mika Hakkinen wh raced past the Ferrari. Heinz Haral Frentzen also tried to mount an attac on Schumacher, but with relativel little success. Frentzen appeared t have exhausted all his energies i vainly attempting to overtake Schumacher – by the fourth lap he ha been overtaken by three cars.

Schumacher's Ferrari team-mat Eddie Irvine, was the first to pas Frentzen – on the outside in a tigh right-hand bend. A few seconds late Frentzen's own team-mate Jacque Villeneuve slid by, soon to be followe by Sauber's Jean Alesi. Meanwhil Schumacher's Ferrari, which wa

CIRCUIT

Autodromo Ciudad de Buenos Aires

In contrast to the many high-speed circuits where power is essential, the twisty and bumpy Argentinian circuit demands precise control from the drivers. The cars' wing-levels are therefore set to exert the maximum downforce possible. The course is not popular with the majority of drivers who generally find it difficult to maintain a steady driving rhythm.

Track length 4.259 km (2.64 miles)
Race distance 306.654 km (190.08 miles) – 72 laps
1997 winner Jacques Villeneuve, Williams-Renault
Lap record 1:27.981 min, Gerhard Berger, Benetton-Renault, 1997

Curva de Ascari
Mixtos
»S« de Senna
Cajón
Confiteria
Curvón
Horquilla
Curva No. Uno

arrying a lighter fuel load than the McLarens, began to close on Hakkinen, and Schumacher had little lifficulty in passing the Finn. On lap our, the lead changed in a spectacular f disputed manner. Schumacher was ble to exploit a problem Coulthard was having with his gear-change. Schumacher pushed himself on the nside of the bend alongside Coulthard ut in the process collided with the McLaren. The German came off best rom this "shove" as he was able to ake the lead with only a slightly bent rack rod, whereas Coulthard had pun once and had to rejoin the race ight down in sixth place.

This scene raised memories of 997's final race in Jerez where Schumacher had attempted to force Villenueve off the track. His actions in Buenos Aires inevitably caused ontroversy. Coulthard was understandably aggrieved by Schumacher's behaviour, saying: "He is correct that was a little wide, because I was having a problem on the downhange. But I was in front, the next orner was a left-hander, and I don't hink I turned right into him. I think

PRACTICE

Schumacher keeps his eye on the ball

Michael Schumacher, twice World Champion, headed for Buenos Aires with the express intention of challenging McLaren's seemingly unassailable supremacy. He moved towards this objective during the final practice session by winning a valuable first-row position beside David Coulthard's McLaren.

Brother Ralf also found himself towards the front of the field after a long period without much success. Taking fifth place on the grid, he pushed Williams drivers Jacques Villeneuve and Heinz Harald Frentzen back to sixth and seventh places. He also won the on-going duel with team-mate and previous World Champion Damon Hill for the third time in succession. The unfortunate Hill suffered a spin and only managed a relatively poor ninth position on the starting grid.

Away from the race track, Michael Schumacher honed his skills with the Argentinian national football team.

Practice Results

	Driver	Team	Time
1	Coulthard	McLaren-Mercedes	1:25.852
2	M. Schumacher	Ferrari	1:26.251
3	Hakkinen	McLaren-Mercedes	1:26.632
4	Irvine	Ferrari	1:26.780
5	R. Schumacher	Jordan-Mugen-Honda	1:26.827
6	Frentzen	Williams-Mecachrome	1:26.876
7	Villeneuve	Williams-Mecachrome	1:26.941
8	Wurz	Benetton-Mecachrome	1:27.198
9	Hill	Jordan-Mugen-Honda	1:27.483
10	Fisichella	Benetton-Mecachrome	1:27.836
11	Alesi	Sauber-Petronas	1:27.839
12	Herbert	Sauber-Petronas	1:28.016
13	Takagi	Tyrrell-Ford	1:28.811
14	Barrichello	Stewart-Ford	1:29.249
15	Panis	Prost-Peugeot	1:29.320
16	Trulli	Prost-Peugeot	1:29.352
17	Salo	Arrows-Hart	1:29.617
18	Diniz	Arrows-Hart	1:30.022
19	Nakano	Minardi-Ford	1:30.054
20	Tuero	Minardi-Ford	1:30.158
21	Rosset	Tyrrell-Ford	1:30.437
22	Magnussen	Stewart-Ford	1:31.178

ARGENTINE GRAND PRIX

he had a clearer view of whether we were going to touch than I did and he was prepared to take the risk."

Mercedes motorsport boss Norbert Haug and team leader Ron Dennis took a remarkably sanguine view of the unfortunate incident: "The shove did not help us and we were not particularly pleased about it. However, such scenes occur repeatedly in motorsport and for this reason we have not protested."

Needless to say, Schumacher was sure that he had not committed any offence at all: "Coulthard played a similar game with me in Melbourne, where I was on the outside and he forced me out. In this case, the position was the other way round, I was on the inside and had a little bit more speed out of the bend but he closed in and then, in fact, we touched."

Spin survivor

Before Schumacher could cross the line for the first time this season, he had to deal with a worrying few seconds. Four laps before the end, with rain beginning to fall, the Ferrari spun off the track and into a gravel trap. Remarkably, Schumacher kept his nerve and his engine going and got back into the race still in the lead.

Only a few metres separated Schumacher from his 28th Grand Prix victory.

Hakkinen was closing on Schumacher but could not wrest the lead from him, especially after being held up by Frentzen who was then a lap adrift. McLaren's Adrian Newey was infuriated at the turn of events: "Frentzen not moving over cost us the race."

Race Results

1	M. Schumacher	1:48:36.175
2	Hakkinen	1:48:59.073
3	Irvine	1:49:33.920
4	Wurz	1:49:44.309
5	Alesi	1:49:54.461
6	Coulthard	1:49:55.926

Drivers' Championship

1	Hakkinen	26 points
2	M. Schumacher	14 points
3	Coulthard	13 points
4	Irvine	7 points
5	Frentzen	6 points
	= Wurz	6 points
7	Villeneuve	2 points
	= Alesi	2 points
9	Herbert	1 point
	= Fisichella	1 point

Constructors' Championship

1	Williams-Renault	20 points
2	McLaren-Mercedes	19 points
3	Ferrari	14 points
4	Benetton-Mecachrome	11 points
5	Prost-Peugeot	6 points
6	Jordan-Mugen-Honda	4 points
	= Sauber-Petronas	4 points

Happiness for one, disappointment for the other. While Michael Schumacher and his third-placed team-mate Eddie Irvine rejoiced with team leader Jean Todt, an obviously frustrated Ralf Schumacher (right) regretted having spun out of the race.

LOGISTICS

▲ *Four Benettons are prepared for the journey overseas. If necessary, the team mechanics can assemble a fifth car from the accompanying spare parts.*

◀ *For the races in Australia, Brazil, Argentina, Canada, and Japan, the vast trailer trucks are left behind in Europe. Instead, everything is packed away in aluminium crates.*

▼ *After the Formula One Constructors Association (FOCA) has gathered together the teams' equipment, the crates are taken to three waiting freight aircraft that transport the massive load to the next race destination. Every kilo of surplus weight costs the team extra.*

A sixteen-ton circus travels round the world

When the season gets underway, the first job for all the teams is to pack their bags. For European races, this is not such a problem as missing parts and other mechanical items can be secured relatively easily when required. The situation becomes more difficult for races held outside Europe, especially as vast amounts of equipment and spare parts have to be air-freighted around the globe.

Air transport

The Formula One Constructors Association (FOCA) organizes three jumbo freighters for the transfer of all the teams' equipment. On average, the teams manage to pack loads that weigh approximately 16 tonnes apiece. The logistics experts leave nothing to chance and ensure that almost everything comes with them, from drinking water to specialized machinery for the manufacture of spare parts on site. In addition to three or four complete cars, the top teams take six units of each key part. A list published by Jordan for the 1997 season included everything that needed to be transported over distances of approximately 170,000 kilometres (105,000 miles). Just for food and drink, the British-based team took 73 kg (161 lbs) of ham, 60 kg (132 lbs) of sausages, 840 eggs, 6800 packs of cakes, and 768 bottles of wine.

Needless to say, this way of travelling is not cheap. The total travel budget per Grand Prix season is around £10,000,000 – just one of the reasons why Formula One racing is such an expensive sport.

Speed packing

The journey from Brazil to Argentina was a highly complicated operation for team logistics managers such as Jim Vale (Jordan), Jo Ramirez (McLaren), Beat Zender (Sauber), and Stefano Demenicali (Ferrari). Each crew had to gather their equipment together immediately after the race at São Paulo in preparation for FOCA's operatives who would already be ready and waiting to collect the full containers.

The teams' "packing artists" had a mere three hours for packing thousands of valuable individual spare parts and components and for completing the inevitable and time-consuming paperwork. They knew that any delays would result in substantial financial penalties.

The Italian fans have been waiting for a Ferrari victory in the San Marino Grand Prix since Patrick Tambay's win in 1983.

Coulthard thwarts Ferrari ambitions

26 April, Imola. McLaren-Mercedes driver David Coulthard dashed the hopes of the 100,000 Italian *tifosi* (sports fans) for a long-awaited Ferrari victory. Italian fans could take some comfort that the second and third places went to Ferrari drivers Michael Schumacher and Eddie Irvine.

"The assumption that the victory over the Silver Arrows in Argentina would be repeated was over-optimistic," said second-placed Michael Schumacher to the hordes of fans who had been desperate for a Ferrari victory.

From the outset, McLaren made it clear that their defeat in Buenos Aires was not to be repeated and that they were not going to allow Schumacher to deprive them of a win for a second time. As in Melbourne and Brazil, they raced away from the competition. By the third lap, with Coulthard in front, they had gained a comfortable three-second lead.

On the first corner of the race, however, there was drama. Suffering from jammed gears, Alexander Wurz lost speed suddenly, causing Damon Hill to hit Wurz's wheel with his wing. This forced Hill to return to the pits for repairs. Hill's current bad luck was to recur later in the race – he was forced to retire with engine failure three laps from the end.

Hakkinen forced out

During lap 17, second-placed Mika Hakkinen slowed dramatically. His McLaren had also developed gearbox trouble, and he too was forced to retire from the race soon afterwards.

Schumacher's Ferrari was now unexpectedly in second place behind the race leader, and the *tifosi* in the stands scented victory. For the objective observer, however, this change in position did not suggest any change in trend as Coulthard had by then achieved a safe and unassailable 16-second lead over his nearest pursuer.

And, as Schumacher also admitted after the race, third position would have been the best possible result if Hakkinen's McLaren had not broken down. When considering the current relative performance of Ferrari and McLaren, Schumacher took the opportunity to fire a few poisoned darts at Goodyear. "There is still something to come from the car but the major step is now up to Goodyear. The mechanical and aerodynamic improvements open to us will bring us level with the McLarens. But the Bridgestone tyres are certainly worth plus or minus half a second, depending on the track characteristics."

During the race, Schumacher was only once able to get close to the McLarens. When Coulthard returned to the track after his second refuelling stop on lap 44 the difference was down to 1.2 seconds. This gain was temporary as two laps later Schumacher also made his second stop in the pits, thereby allowing Coulthard to regain his safety margin.

Schumacher closes in

Nevertheless, the excitement level rose again during the last 12 laps as Schumacher gained on Coulthard. By the end of the race he had reduced the difference from 16 to 4.5 seconds. But this gain had less to do with Schumacher's driving ability than with some minor problems David Coulthard was experiencing with his car.

After Hakkinen had retired, the engine temperature of Coulthard's McLaren also began to rise sharply – a phenomenon that had preceded the unfortunate Finn's breakdown. Worried team chief Ron Dennis, who does not normally leave the pitwall, made several trips to the garage to analyze Coulthard's telemetry data.

Calculations were made and Coulthard was instructed by radio to change up earlier in order to ease the load on the gearbox. With a substantial lead under his belt, Coulthard selected a less demanding gear and completed the first "start-to-finish" victory of his Formula One career.

The nervous anticipation of the last few laps of the San Marino Grand Prix also affected the nerves of Mercedes director Jürgen Hubbert, who said: "I can manage without this excitement during the next race".

Race Result

1	Coulthard	1:34:24.593
2	M. Schumacher	1:34:29.147
3	Irvine	1:35:16.368
4	Villeneuve	1:35:19.183
5	Frentzen	1:37:14.445
6	Alesi	1 lap behind

Drivers' Championship

1	Hakkinen	26 points
2	Coulthard	23 points
3	M. Schumacher	20 points
4	Irvine	11 points
5	Frentzen	8 points
6	Wurz	6 points
7	Villeneuve	5 points
8	Alesi	3 points
9	Herbert	1 point
	= Fisichella	1 point

Constructors' Championship

1	McLaren-Mercedes	49 points
2	Ferrari	31 points
3	Williams-Mecachrome	13 points
4	Benetton-Mecachrome	7 points
5	Sauber-Petronas	4 points

After the race, Coulthard put Schumacher's spectacular attempt to catch up in perspective: "Is it necessary to win by 20 seconds? Certainly not. A few tenths of a second also suffice, don't they?"

Ferrari could console themselves with the fact that they were in the majority on the victors' podium – Eddie Irvine drove the other Ferrari to third place – and with the hope that they might finally realize their fans' ambition for a Ferrari victory next year (previously celebrated by Patrick Tambay in 1983).

Schumacher to go?

Apart from the anxiety of the race itself, those in charge at Ferrari had other worries – the uncertainties created by rumours of a Schumacher move to another team. The German driver's manager, Willi Weber, was partially responsible for these speculations. In a statement he wrote: "We have always said that we should like to return to Mercedes."

The Silver Arrows of the McLaren-Mercedes team shared the front row, with the Ferraris of Schumacher and Irvine behind.

Immediately after the start, the two McLarens raced away from the rest of the field, Coulthard maintaining his lead.

Coulthard emerged from the pit lane a few metres ahead of Michael Schumacher, who had still to go into the pits.

Coulthard was a worthy winner of the San Marino Grand Prix.

PRACTICE

Ferrari versus McLaren

McLaren-Mercedes and Ferrari again dominated the final practice session at Imola. The struggle for pole position was an exclusively Silver Arrows contest, however, and was won by David Coulthard. Consequently, his Finnish team-mate and main rival Mika Hakkinen started in second place.

Benetton's Alexander Wurz qualified in fifth position behind Ferrari's Michael Schumacher and Eddie Irvine. Wurz gave an outstanding performance and edged ahead of the present World Champion Jacques Villeneuve. Previous World Champion Damon Hill took precedence over Williams driver Heinz Harald Frentzen. Hill's competent performance in qualifying in seventh place was a considerable improvement on his previous efforts.

Qualifying Times

1	Coulthard	McLaren-Mercedes	1:25.973
2	Hakkinen	McLaren-Mercedes	1:26.075
3	M. Schumacher	Ferrari	1:26.437
4	Irvine	Ferrari	1:27.169
5	Wurz	Benetton-Mecachrome	1:27.273
6	Villeneuve	Williams-Mecachrome	1:27.390
7	Hill	Jordan-Mugen-Honda	1:27.592
8	Frentzen	Williams-Mecachrome	1:27.645
9	R. Schumacher	Jordan Mugen-Honda	1:27.866
10	Fisichella	Benetton-Mecachrome	1:27.937
11	Herbert	Sauber-Petronas	1:28.111
12	Alesi	Sauber-Petronas	1:28.191
13	Panis	Prost-Peugeot	1:28.270
14	Salo	Arrows-Hart	1:28.798
15	Takagi	Tyrrell-Ford	1:29.073
16	Trulli	Prost-Peugeot	1:29.584
17	Barrichello	Stewart-Ford	1:29.641
18	Diniz	Arrows-Hart	1:29.932
19	Tuero	Minardi-Ford	1:30.649
20	Magnussen	Stewart-Ford	1:31.017
21	Nakano	Minardi-Ford	1:31.255
22	Rosset	Tyrrell-Ford	1:31.482

Ferrari President Luca di Montezemolo immediately went on the offensive and emphasized that Schumacher was, until further notice, in his team and that he would continue to do everything in his power to keep the German at Ferrari.

After the race, Mercedes' Norbert Haug expressed his pleasure at Coulthard's victory: "I'm delighted for him. He's had criticism from certain quarters about not being quick enough and it's not right. What's happened this year proves to me that we were correct to stay with Mika and David.

"David is a great guy to work with. He listens and he learns. There's absolutely no arrogance at all. To be able to put a car on pole, which he did for the second time, and then compete with a guy like Mika really means something. It was a great race."

CIRCUIT

Autodromo Enzo and Dino Ferrari

Major modifications were made to this circuit in the aftermath of the 1994 race that saw the deaths of Roland Ratzenberger and Ayrton·Senna. The former high-speed circuit was tamed by changes to the Tamburello, Villeneuve, and Variante Bassa curves. The modified circuit now places a premium on heavy braking.

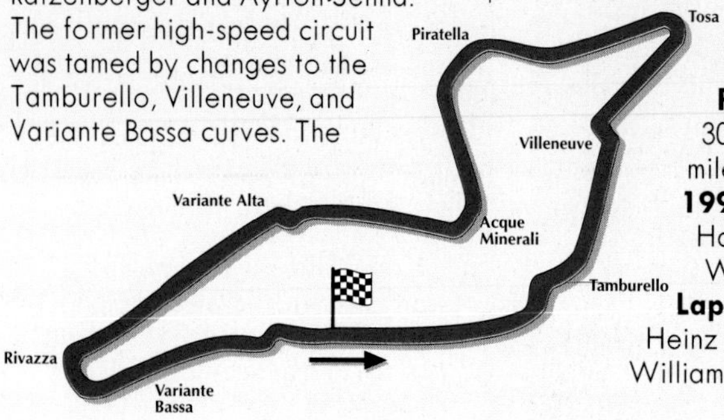

Track length 4.892 km (3.039 miles)
Race distance 303.304 km (188.473 miles) – 62 Laps
1997 winner Heinz Harald Frentzen, Williams-Renault
Lap record 1:25.531 min, Heinz Harald Frentzen, Williams-Renault, 1997

X-WINGS

"Mickey Mouse" invention

As early as 1977, Tyrrell equipped its racing cars with additional wings attached to the right and left of the driving seat that pointed vertically upwards. X-Wings (or Tower Wings, or even Side-Wings) gained further supporters in 1998 when Sauber, Jordan, and Prost also began to use them. Supporters of these bizarre aerodynamic aids claimed that on the straight they provided the cars with an advantage equivalent to two-tenths of a second per lap.

At Imola, Ferrari was the first major team to use these wings. However effective they may have been, some onlookers considered them ugly and described the structures as "Mickey Mouse" ears. Before the race, Michael Schumacher doubted whether they made much of a difference anyway, although he quipped: "If these allow us to win here today, all the Italians will have wings on their cars on Monday."

FIA President Max Mosley found the X-Wing controversy less amusing. At first he tried to engineer an amicable agreement between the teams to ensure that the wings would disappear in future. Mosley's safety worries – that the wings might endanger the driver's head in the event of a side-impact crash – were not accepted by all the teams. In consequence, the X-Wings remained in place for the San Marino Grand Prix, with 11 teams opting to use them. A week after the race, Mosley – in his role as FIA President – declared that the additional structures were a general safety risk and had them banned forthwith. The teams, for their part, were less than pleased by the edict, with Jordan claiming that they had invested £50,000 in developing X-Wings but had nothing to show for it.

Mosley's judgement seemed something of a curiosity to veteran Sauber driver Jean Alesi, who could not understand what all the fuss was about: "Tyrrell has been using these X-Wings since the beginning of 1997. Has it just occurred to the FIA that they are dangerous?"

Imola was considered a potentially easy win for Michael Schumacher. As the race progressed, it became clear that there was no prospect of a Schumacher victory.

FLASHBACK

A golden age of Italian drivers

The very first Formula One World Championship was decided on 3 September 1950 at the Italian Grand Prix. The World Champion was the legendary Giuseppe "Nino" Farina, driving an Alfa Romeo.

Farina began his career in hill climbing, but under the guidance of the Tazio Nuvolari he moved over to road racing in 1933, driving for Maserati. Even in his first year as a racing driver, his utterly determined aggression convinced many of his contemporaries that this was a champion in the making. Nino Farina's early promise was confirmed when he won the Italian drivers' title in 1937, 1938, and 1939.

Success with Alfa Romeo

After the Second World War, Farina found a place with Alfa Romeo – considered at that time to be an unbeatable team. He exploited all the possibilities provided by Alfa Romeo and became one of the best racing drivers in the world.

It was not Farina's taste, however, to spend much time celebrating his victories. The morning after a race he would still go to work at his bodywork factory Stabilmenti Farina. The Italian driver – born on 30 October 1906 – shied away from the publicity and pomp normally associated with a World Champion, an attitude that sometimes led to accusations of arrogance.

On the track, however, the introvert became obsessed. But this obsession had a price tag. No other racing driver of the period was involved in so many accidents as Farina. Of these, the worst happened during the initial race in Argentina on 18 January 1953. In attempting to avoid spectators who had wandered on to the track, Farina ran into a small crowd on the other side. The consequences were tragic: 10 dead and more than 30 severely injured.

Crash and burn

In 1952, Farina joined Ferrari – only to be eclipsed there by his new team-mate Alberto Ascari. Worse was to follow in 1954 when, during a sports car race, his car crashed and was engulfed in flames. The next year he bravely attempted a comeback,

Giuseppe "Nino" Farina (right) won the British, Swiss, and Italian Grand Prix races in 1950. As a result of these three famous victories he became the first Formula One World Champion in the history of motorsport.

'scari takes a refreshment break at the 1953 British Grand Prix.

but despite the heavy use of painkillers, he was unable to continue the season and was eventually forced to retire from Formula One. Farina was killed in a road accident in 1966.

The modest Ascari

In contrast to Farina, Alberto Ascari was idolized by the Italian public. The popularity of this Italian – born on 13 July 1918 – may be largely attributed to his modesty. Wherever the Milan driver appeared, he had a ready smile and a pleasant word for all.

His enthusiasm for motor racing started early. His father Antonio, also an outstanding racing driver, was killed in a fatal accident during the French Grand Prix on 26 July 1925. Despite this tragedy, Alberto Ascari determined to make his name in motorsport. His most famous employer, Enzo Ferrari, once asked him why he did not simply give up motor racing for some occupation that was less dangerous. "Without racing, I do not know how I should live," was his answer.

Competitive instincts

Even as a youngster, Ascari sought out competition. First in bicycle racing and then, as an 18-year-old, in motor cycles. His major objective was to follow in his father's footsteps. Ascari made his first appearance in a racing car in the 1940 Mille Miglia race. There he drew attention to his driving as, until a technical fault caused retirement, he was the undisputed leader in his class.

Alberto Ascari returned to racing in 1947 after the war. Ferrari gradually became aware of this "rough diamond" and gave him his chance in 1950 by enlisting him as team leader. He came fifth overall that year, and was runner-up to the great Juan Manuel Fangio in 1951.

Ascari's skill as a driver was confirmed in 1953 when he won his first World Championship. This was followed by a second consecutive World title in 1954. Over his career, he was to achieve an impressive 13 victories from 32 Grand Prix races.

Monaco ducking

In 1954, Ascari moved briefly to Maserati before returning to drive the Ferrari-run Lancias. Success proved elusive. Monte Carlo, 1955, was not only Ascari's last race but also the most spectacular of his career. Leading Fangio and Moss, Ascari's Lancia raced to the harbour chicane, skidded, and broke through the quay wall at high speed. The car and driver plunged into the sea and disappeared under the waves. A few seconds later, however, shocked onlookers were relieved to see the driver floating on the surface of the water. Ascari, to the delight of his fans, escaped the crash with just a broken nose and slight bruising.

A few days later, on 26 May 1955, Ascari was sitting with friends in the restaurant on the race track in Monza. One of these friends, Eugenio Castellotti, had arrived with a new Ferrari sports car. Ascari climbed into the car with the intention of giving it a thorough test run – and also to try and put the Monaco accident behind him. But, tragically and inexplicably, the car went out of control at a relatively low speed, left the track, and smashed into a tree. Alberto Ascari died of his injuries at the scene of the accident, aged just 26.

.egendary Ferrari driver Ascari races against Stirling Moss.

The wreckage of the Ferrari in which Ascari lost his life.

CALENDAR

7 May
Despite the ban on X-Wings, Prost racing cars are brought to a race acceptance inspection in Barcelona with these additional wings. The FIA announces that the French team only wished to check a technical detail. The wings were taken off during qualifying.

8 May
Barcelona: Three drivers are caught speeding in the pit lane and are fined accordingly: David Coulthard ($750), Olivier Panis ($2750) and Giancarlo Fisichella ($500).

9 May
Barcelona: For the first time this season, a driver has been stopped from taking part in the Grand Prix by the 107 per cent rule (in which all drivers must qualify within 107 per cent of the fastest lap time). Tyrrell driver Ricardo Rosset failed the qualification test for the Spanish Grand Prix by just .066 of a second.

10 May
The FIA states that for safety reasons, only a few photographers will now be admitted to the pit lane during the warm-up. If this rule is not observed, then they will be excluded from the pit lane for the whole season.

The McLaren driver Mika Hakkinen wins the fifth Formula One World Championship race in Barcelona, with David Coulthard and Ferrari's Michael Schumacher second and third.

18 May
Imola: The ex-Formula One driver Ricardo Patresi organizes a football match between Italian singers and racing drivers, including Michael Schumacher, Max Biaggi, the 1997 250cc motor cycle World Champion, and Eros Ramazotti. The proceeds from the match go to aid leukemia sufferers.

21 May
Jacques Villeneuve comes to Monaco with a new variant of his hair colour – platinum blond with blue streaks.

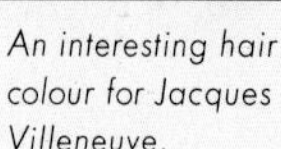
An interesting hair colour for Jacques Villeneuve.

Ricardo Rosset has been warned by the race authorities for a misdemeanour during the the Monaco Grand Prix when he "slammed the door" on Jacques Villeneuve in such a way that both cars ended up hitting the crash barriers.

23 May
The Stewart driver Rubens Barrichello celebrates his twenty-sixth birthday. Engine supplier Ford surprises Barrichello with an engine bearing his name instead of the standard designation of "Zetec-R".

24 May
Mika Hakkinen triumphs in his McLaren-Mercedes on the narrow Monaco street track. Because of an unplanned pitstop, Michael Schumacher only manages to scrape home in a literally pointless 10th place.

1–31 May
A high honour for the Canadian driver Jacques Villeneuve: The province of Quebec has awarded him its "National Order".

The out-of-favour Stewart driver Jan Magnussen keeps his driving seat for the Spanish Grand Prix. The reason for the stay of execution is that negotiations with his replacement, the Dutchman Jos Verstappen, have temporarily been broken off.

Alexander Wurz is being considered as a potential driver by a number of leading teams. In addition to Ferrari, British American Racing (BAR) team manager Craig Pollock has also shown interest in the young Benetton driver

Sauber driver Jean Alesi has a spare-time job. In his home town of Avignon, he is acting as a guide for French President Jacques Chirac and the German Chancellor Helmut Kohl.

Bernie Ecclestone is planning a Grand Prix on the newly built and extremely up-to-date track in Kuala Lumpur, Malaysia, as the second race after Melbourne in the 1999 season.

The former Benetton team manager Flavio Briatore is to become the new commercial director of the French engine manufacturer Mecachrome from 1999.

Flavio Briatore

Unexpected help has been offered to Eddie Irvine from the Stewart sponsor Lear. The firm has offered Irvine a special seat which should ease the painful back condition he has suffered from since the start of the season.

Minardi chief Gabriele Rumi is involved in negotiations with Ferrari team leader Jean Todt to allow Minardi to use the Ferrari V10 power plant from 1999 onwards.

It is probable that three teams will be equipped with new Mecachrome engines in the coming season – Benetton, Williams, and BAR.

For the year 2000, McLaren and Mercedes are looking for a suitable partner team for their home-ground Formula One Juniors. The possibilities are Jordan, Arrows, or the new BAR team, which would be equipped with Mercedes engines for this proposed future junior team.

As Honda prepare to move back into Formula One racing, they are believed to be looking for an existing Formula One team to act as the basis for their own Honda team. As Jordan already use the Mugen-Honda engine, rumours are that Honda will try to buy the British team – but is Eddie Jordan prepared to sell up and lose control over his beloved team?

Quote
"Many people from Formula One have ended in prison. But there are at least as many running around who ought to end up there."
Pat Symmonds, chief technician of Benetton, in the magazine *Sport Auto*.

"Surfing at Sylt in wind strength 9? Much too dangerous! I'm certainly not risking my life...."
McLaren driver David Coulthard, refusing an offer to go windsurfing.

PORTRAIT

Pilgrim's Progress

The junior Mercedes driver, Nick Heidfeld, stood on the victor's podium for the first time, after winning the fifth round of the Formula 3000 series in Monaco.

Despite this first victory for Nick Heidfeld in the Formula 3000 race in Monaco, however, his wish to start in Formula One next year remains unfulfilled for the time being – in part because he has not been able to overcome his main rival for the Formula 3000 title, the Colombian driver Juan-Pablo Montoya.

Nonetheless, Heidfeld's performance over the year has been enough to interest a number of Formula One teams, as well as Mercedes. For years, McLaren and Mercedes have been working with young drivers such as Heidfeld, grooming them for employment in the top class through their "Driver Support Programme".

Talent or cash

"We still believe," said McLaren team chief Ron Dennis, "that talent should be the decisive criterion for a future career in motorsport."

But the other way of securing a seat in Formula One, especially in the smaller teams like Sauber and Arrows, is for a driver to contribute large sums of money to the team from sponsors or other private sources. This can mean that rich playboys get ahead of more naturally skilful drivers, but for many cash-strapped teams this is the only way they can operate within Formula One, with its ever-escalating costs.

Nick Heidfeld hopes to build upon his success at Monaco, and eventually move into Formula One.

While Heidfeld cannot bring in large wads of money, Mercedes are content to develop their protégé slowly over time. "Nick is only 21," explains Mercedes motorsports boss Norbert Haug, "and we do not want to steer him too early into a wrong direction. We want to find a programme with good possibilities and that is not necessarily Formula One." Whatever the route taken, Heidfeld's future looks promising.

COMPARISON

Motor racing – the American way

The film star Paul Newman (inset) has been a successful racing-team owner in the IndyCar series.

t first sight, the vehicles used in Formula One and the American ndyCar series look very similar. Closer examination reveals a number of differences: IndyCars are more powerful but less sophisticated.

tewart driver Jan Magnussen has aced in both Formula One and the ndyCar series – sometimes called ART – and when asked about the ifference between the two ompetitions, he answers simply: "An ndyCar is more fun to drive." lthough other drivers who have riven in both series may offer ifferent opinions, there is something n Magnussen's comment.

In the first place, IndyCar vehicles re heavier than those used in ormula One, and are less hard on river error. The second factor is the hallenge offered by the wide variety f tracks encountered in the Indycar eries. In addition to circuits similar to hose seen in Formula One, races are lso run on ovals, on street circuits, nd airfields. And because the race ars have broadly equal technical apabilities, spectators enjoy many nore dramatic wheel-to-wheel battles han would typically take place in a ormula One season.

xcitement and danger

he IndyCar public favours oval racks – called "noodle pots" – which re not only very fast but allow the pectators to view almost the entire ction at any one time. During the uly US 500 in Brooklyn, Michigan, he lead changed no less than 63 times n what was one of the most exciting races of the year. But at the same time, a serious accident at the race cast a dark shadow over the series. In the 174th of 250 laps, the Reynard-Ford of Adrian Fernandez collided with the wall of the oval. The right-hand front wheel and parts of the rear suspension of Fernandez's car flew into the crowd, killing three spectators and seriously injuring six others. In the area of driver and spectator safety, Formula One racing is well ahead.

Until recently, IndyCar races were limited to the United States, but they are now making some progress internationally. The 19 races are now distributed between Canada, the United States, Brazil, Australia and Japan. In return, it is hoped that Formula One will one day return to the United States, employing one of the excellent IndyCar street circuits.

TECHNOLOGY COMPARISON

	Formula One	CART
Engine	3 litre induction engine	2.65 litre turbo
Power	Approx. 750 hp	Approx. 850 hp
Top speed	Approx. 350 kmh (220 mph)	Approx. 400 kmh (250 mph)
Max. no. of cylinders	12	8
Max. no. of valves	No rule	32
Valve pneumatics	Permitted	Forbidden
Fuel	Unleaded petrol	Methanol
Tank capacity	No rule	Max. 151.4 litres (40 gallons)
Chassis	Carbon fibre	Carbon fibre/aluminium
Gear box	Semi-automatic with gear rocker	Sequential with gear level
Width	180 cm (70.9 in)	199 cm (78.35 in)
Height (rear wing)	95 cm (37.4 in)	91 cm (35.8 in)
Minimum weight	600 kg (1,320 lb, with driver)	704 kg (1,548 lb, without driver)
Carbon brakes	Permitted	Forbidden
Anti-lock system	Forbidden	Forbidden
Traction control	Forbidden	Forbidden
Tyre width front	30.5–38.1 cm (12–15 in)	Max. 30.5 cm (12 in)
Diameter front	Max. 66 cm (26 in)	Max. 65 cm (25.6 in)
Tyre width rear	36.5–38.1 cm (14.4–15 in)	Max. 40.6 cm (16 in)
Diameter rear	Max. 66 cm (26 in)	Max. 68.6 cm (27 in)
Dry tyres	Profiled	Unprofiled
Engine manufacturers	Mercedes, Peugeot, Honda, Ford, Hart, Mecachrome, Ferrari	Mercedes, Ford, Honda, Toyota
Chassis manufacturers	Williams, Ferrari, Benetton, Prost, McLaren, Jordan, Arrows, Sauber, Stewart, Tyrrell, Minardi	Reynard, Penske, Swift, All American Racers, Lola

PREVIEW

No smoke, no money

If it depends on the European Union, the future of Formula One looks decidedly bleak. The prohibition of tobacco advertising will deprive the racing teams of a very substantial source of revenue.

On 4 December 1997, the ministers of the European Union agreed on a timetable to ban the advertising of tobacco products in Formula One. According to this agreement, all forms of Formula One tobacco advertising will come to a phased end from 2001 onwards. In accordance with EU guidelines, names such as Marlboro, Philip Morris, and Winfield will no longer be plastered over Formula One cars from 1 October 2006. This trend is being followed in other parts of the Western world, with Australia joining the EU in its overall ban.

Since 1992, it has already been the case that the tobacco industry can only advertise at sporting events by means of a statutory exemption, which has to be renewed every year.

After the ban, who will fill up the empty spaces on the cars?

The Formula One world has been fighting back. Bernie Ecclestone is engaged in a round of furious lobbying to get the ban lifted. Ron Walker, the organizational chief of the Australian Grand Prix, has issued dire warnings about the gloomy future of Formula One, saying that there was not the slightest doubt that the races would end, with the loss of more than one hundred million dollars.

Michael Schumacher had to sit out his stop-go penalty of 10 seconds, a punishment for excessive speed in the pit lane.

McLaren Ascendant

10 May, Barcelona. McLaren-Mercedes dominated in Spain, and their third "one-two" victory further extended their lead in the World Championship. While Mika Hakkinen and David Coulthard roared off into the distance, a resurgent Benetton struggled hard with Ferrari for a third place on the victor's podium.

The two McLaren-Mercedes started on the front, and both raced away cleanly with Hakkinen in the lead. By lap 16, the Finn was over 13 seconds ahead of David Coulthard, who had to content himself with second place throughout the race.

Michael Schumacher, who had previously been the only driver able to keep in touch with the McLaren-Mercedes team, surprisingly found himself back among the hunted in Barcelona. Eddie Irvine and Benetton's Giancarlo Fisichella got in front of Schumacher at the start of the race and, until his first pitstop, Fisichella had no difficulty in keeping Schumacher at bay. Fisichella even started to make life hard for third-placed Eddie Irvine until they both went into the pits on lap 25 to refuel. Schumacher went into the pits a few laps later. Fortunately for him, he rejoined the race ahead of Irvine and Fisichella.

Caught speeding

Schumacher had got in front of the Benetton and other Ferrari as a result of some very fast driving during his "in-lap" – the lap before entering the pits. But when he entered the pit lane, the speed limiter that should have slowed Schumacher's car to the specified speed limit failed. As a result, he was subjected to a stiff and mandatory 10-second stop-go penalty.

Luckily for Schumacher, he was helped again by his team-mate. At the end of lap 28, Fisichella attempted to drive past Irvine on the start-finish straight. At the end of the straight, however, Fisichella skidded into the Ferrari and both drivers sped into the gravel trap and out of the race. For Fisichella, the Barcelona Grand Prix proved quite expensive. Although he personally felt he was not guilty, this opinion was not shared by the race officials. Having been subjected to a $500 fine in qualifying due to excessive speed in the pit lane, the FIA demanded a further $7,000 from Fisichella for bumping into Irvine.

PRACTICE

Benetton fights for position

Benetton driver Giancarlo Fisichella did well in qualifying.

The McLaren-Mercedes of Mika Hakkinen and David Coulthard once again swept all before them, the only two cars to achieve 1:20s during final qualifying. Hakkinen was considerably faster than Coulthard, a result that the Scot attributed to braking problems: "I was locking up a lot, whereas Mika was on it straight away. I just didn't have the confidence to really attack the circuit."

The two Benettons of Giancarlo Fisichella and Alexander Wurz spent much of the practice session leap-frogging each other in a battle for third position on the grid. In fact, they provided much of the entertainment for the entire practice session. In the end they were pipped to third position by Michael Schumacher. The two Benettons were followed by Eddie Irvine's Ferrari in sixth place.

Practice Results

1	Hakkinen	McLaren-Mercedes	1:20.262
2	Coulthard	McLaren-Mercedes	1:20.996
3	M. Schumacher	Ferrari	1:21.785
4	Fisichella	Benetton-Mecachr.	1:21.894
5	Wurz	Benetton-Mecachr.	1:21.965
6	Irvine	Ferrari	1:22.350
7	Herbert	Sauber-Petronas	1:22.794
8	Hill	Jordan-Mugen-Honda	1:22.835
9	Barrichello	Stewart-Ford	1:22.860
10	Villeneuve	Williams-Mecachr.	1:22.885
11	R. Schumacher	Jordan-Mugen-Honda	1:22.927
12	Panis	Prost-Peugeot	1:22.963
13	Frentzen	Williams-Mecachr.	1:23.197
14	Alesi	Sauber-Petronas	1:23.327
15	Diniz	Arrows-Hart	1:23.704
16	Trulli	Prost-Peugeot	1:23.748
17	Salo	Arrows-Hart	1:23.887
18	Magnussen	Stewart-Ford	1:24.112
19	Tuero	Minardi-Ford	1:24.265
20	Nakano	Minardi-Ford	1:24.538
21	Takagi	Tyrrell-Ford	1:24.722
NON -QUALIFIER			
22	Rosset	Tyrrell-Ford	1:25.946

SPANISH GRAND PRIX

Eddie Irvine blocked Fisichella to help his Ferrari team-mate Michael Schumacher.

Schumacher, however, recognized the performance of the Benetton driver and paid his respects: "I profited from the retirement of Fisichella today because, at the beginning of the race, I could not hold him. And who knows whether I could have done so later."

The other Benetton, driven by Alexander Wurz, also became a problem for Schumacher in the latter part of the race. Wurz tried to hang on to the Ferrari – lap after lap – until the brake wear on his car became excessive. The Benetton driver then abandoned the struggle for third place and contented himself with making sure of a satisfactory fourth position.

Barcelona was another nightmare for the Jordan team. Damon Hill retired on lap 47 with engine failure, and Ralf Schumacher started and ended the race in 11th position.

Williams' point

There were also more problems for Williams. The 1997 World Championship winning team ended the weekend with only a single point. And current Champion Jacques Villeneuve even had to give way to the Stewart of the Brazilian Rubens Barrichello. Despite Williams' best efforts, Villeneuve was forced to acknowledge that things had not been going his way since the start of the season: "I had to work very hard for this single point and it doesn't bring us much closer to the World Championship. I could have beaten Rubens but there was a slight mishap with the tank flap once again during the pitstop. I was a little bit quicker than he was with the second set of tyres.

"We really are at the limits of the car. Everybody in the team works very hard and wants to win. The atmosphere is good. We simply need one improvement more to return to our normal competitiveness."

Heinz Harald Frentzen, Villeneuve's team-mate, was also finding life hard. His experience in Barcelona was particularly bitter. Starting back in 13th place, Frentzen almost immediately locked horns with Jean Alesi. The Frenchman's Sauber ran into and damaged the front of the Williams. Frentzen was only able to resume the race after a frustratingly long repair stop that forced him right back to 20th position.

Race Result

1	Hakkinen	1:33:37.621
2	Coulthard	1:33:47.060
3	M. Schumacher	1:34:24.716
4	Wurz	1:34:40.159
5	Barrichello	1 lap behind
6	Villeneuve	1 lap behind

Drivers' Championship

1	Hakkinen	36 points
2	Coulthard	29 points
3	M. Schumacher	24 points
4	Irvine	11 points
5	Wurz	9 points
6	Frentzen	8 points
7	Villeneuve	6 points
8	Alesi	3 points
9	Barrichello	2 points
10	Herbert	1 point
=	Fisichella	1 point

Constructors' Championship

1	McLaren-Mercedes	65 points
2	Ferrari	35 points
3	Williams-Mecachrome	14 points
4	Benetton-Mecachrome	10 points
5	Sauber-Petronas	4 points
6	Steward-Ford	2 points

Hunting Stewart

The Spanish Grand Prix brought some crumbs of comfort to the hard pressed Stewart-Ford team, with Rubens Barrichello scoring the first points of the season by gaining a well deserved fifth place. Team boss Jackie Stewart was delighted with the performance of both team and drivers: "We've had a tough winter, and everyone has been pretty critical about our choice of gearbox, and so to get both cars to finish was a big deal.

"Rubens made a great start, the new Phase 4 Ford engine that we were using for the first time went well, and the balance was good. It is very satisfying. It was so tense towards the end – we were worried about Jacques [Villeneuve] making a good

)nce again, Alexander Wurz showed that he could hold his own in the top class. He might have had a place on the podium had it not been for technical problems.

'he Barcelona weekend was just one
·ng disappointment for Williams
·river Heinz Harald Frentzen.

pitstop because we had had a slightly slower second one with the right rear [tyre] taking a while."

McLaren optimism

At McLaren-Mercedes, Norbert Haug expressed himself in absolutely euphoric terms after the race: "What these two have demonstrated in Spain recalls the great victory drives of Lauda-Prost or Senna-Prost. Our two drivers help each other along. If we look back to how things were last year, we were then discussing which drivers we should take. Now the two of them are rewarding the whole team for believing in them."

The Circuit de Catalunya confirmed the superiority of the McLaren-Mercedes team over the competition. This was made very clear by an examination of the Constructors' Championship points listing, with a massive 65 out of 80 possible World Championship points being awarded to McLaren – more than twice as many points as at the same time in the previous Grand Prix season. Mika Hakkinen's drive in Spain was particularly noteworthy, a sparkling and dynamic performance that his team-mate David Coulthard did not hesitate to praise generously: "Mika gave me a bit of a driving lesson all this weekend. I gave it everything, but it wasn't quite enough."

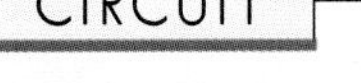

Circuit de Catalunya

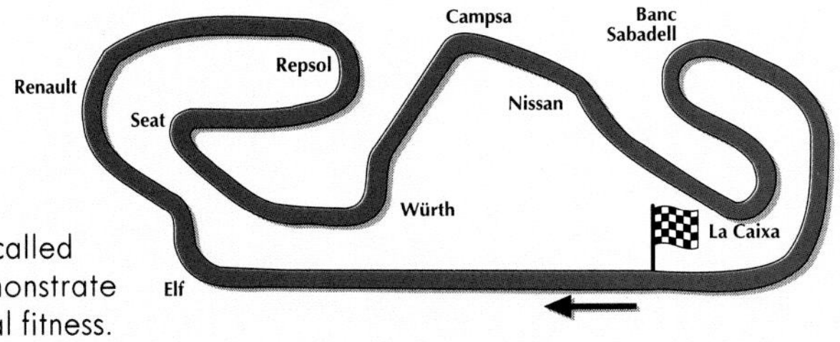

A number of tight bends at this circuit ensure that drivers are called upon to demonstrate their physical fitness. Although a demanding track, Catalunya has good run-off areas, and from a safety point of view it is popular with the drivers. The cars are subject to high levels of fuel consumption and tyre wear, the latter being a consequence of the track's highly abrasive surface.

Track length 4.728 km (2.937 miles)
Race distance 307.32 km (190.969 miles) – 65 laps
1997 winner Jacques Villeneuve, Williams-Renault
Lap record 1:22.242 min, Giancarlo Fisichella, Jordan-Peugeot, 1997

MONACO GRAND PRIX

Unlucky Sauber driver Jean Alesi crashed in qualifying and suffered technical failure during the race.

Complaining of acute understeering problems, Alesi spins into the tyre wall at the swimming pool during qualifying.

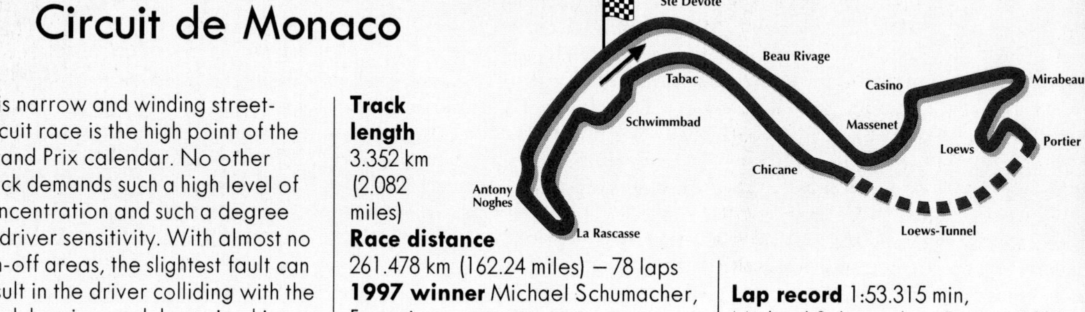

CIRCUIT

Circuit de Monaco

This narrow and winding street-circuit race is the high point of the Grand Prix calendar. No other track demands such a high level of concentration and such a degree of driver sensitivity. With almost no run-off areas, the slightest fault can result in the driver colliding with the crash barriers and damaging his car.

Track length 3.352 km (2.082 miles)
Race distance 261.478 km (162.24 miles) – 78 laps
1997 winner Michael Schumacher, Ferrari

Lap record 1:53.315 min, Michael Schumacher, Ferrari, 1997

McLaren continue to set the standard

'4 MAY, MONACO. Mika Hakkinen's triumph at Monaco was one of the ;reatest moments of his racing career. "I don't see how you get nything better than this," said Hakkinen, celebrating his victory in the amous street circuit. And only engine failure in team-mate David ;oulthard's car prevented the race being another McLaren "one-two".

Blast, I really needed the points. But here is no point in grumbling. My nly chance is to close the gap etween myself and Mika as soon as ossible." Monaco did not make the isibly frustrated David Coulthard ive up his World Championship opes, even though the breakdown ut him 17 points behind Hakkinen.

The disappointment expressed by)avid Coulthard was also felt by 'errari driver Michael Schumacher. 'he Ferrari camp had hoped that heir shorter wheel-base car might ive them an edge over the more owerful McLarens in the twisting Ionaco circuit. But the Ferrari team

Race Result

Hakkinen	1:51:23.595
Fisichella	1:51:35.070
Irvine	1:52:04.973
Salo	1:52:23.958
Villeneuve	1 lap behind
Diniz	1 lap behind

Drivers' Championship

Hakkinen	46 Points
Coulthard	29 Points
M. Schumacher	24 Points
Irvine	15 Points
Wurz	9 Points
Frentzen	8 Points
= Villeneuve	8 Points
Fisichella	7 Points
Salo	3 Points
= Alesi	3 Points

Constructors' Championship

McLaren-Mercedes	75 Points
Ferrari	39 Points
Williams-Mecachrome	16 Points
= Benetton-Mecachrome	16 Points
Sauber-Petronas	4 Points
= Arrows-Hart	4 Points

ad a rude awakening from their reams, as Monaco was very much a epeat of the previous race at arcelona – a pair of Silver Arrows in ront with Schumacher to their rear, vho at the same time was forced to rapple with Fisichella's Benetton.

Although Schumacher tried to put ressure on Fisichella, there was no eal possibility of passing because of he Ferrari's inferior Goodyear tyres. 'he Benetton driver, with the Japa-ese-made Bridgestone tyres, even uilt up a small time buffer between imself and the Ferrari driver.

Schumacher now displayed his actical cunning and came in for an arly pitstop. And the gamble worked. The pit crew dealt with Schumacher in an overall time of only 24.328 seconds. Just one lap later, Fisichella's team needed about three seconds longer in his pitstop, and the Ferrari raced past the Benetton driver.

On lap 18, Coulthard was forced to retire with smoke and flames billowing from his Mercedes engine. This ensured that Schumacher was now third behind the second Benetton of Alexander Wurz – his next target.

When the two drivers came up to lap the trio of Trulli, Herbert, and Diniz on lap 37, Schumacher saw his chance. He pushed inside in the Loews curve and took up position beside Wurz. The Benetton driver, however, held on and thwarted the Ferrari driver. Schumacher tried the manoeuvre once again in the following lap, and ruthlessly forced his way past. This hard-fought duel was, however, costly for Schumacher. Both vehicles had locked wheels, breaking the Ferrari's fragile right-hand rear track rod in the process.

Schumacher hurried back to the pits and, after discussion with Ferrari chief designer Ross Brawn, waited four minutes until the mechanics had repaired the damage. Now three laps behind but still hopeful of being able to gain some valuable points should competitors have to retire, he renewed his assault on the leaders. In the end, these expectations were not fulfilled and an exhausted Schumacher ended the Monaco Grand Prix in 10th place.

Benetton shunt

The Ferrari-Benetton clash probably had unfortunate consequences for Alexander Wurz. In the 42nd lap, after a pitstop, the unlucky Austrian crashed heavily in the tunnel. Both front wheels of his Benetton were torn off before the car subsequently shot forward into the harbour chicane.

Fortunately, Wurz was uninjured and immediately signalled to the race doctors hurrying to his aid that everything was alright. What exactly had failed in his car and led to the accident will remain a mystery for Benetton – the car "survived" the dramatic crash as a pile of scrap.

With Schumacher and Wurz no longer in contention, Fisichella maintained a comfortable second place behind Hakkinen and in front of Eddie Irvine, whose podium position was, at least, some compensation for Schumacher's failure to score any points in the Monaco Grand Prix.

Perhaps the most surprising event of the race was the sudden and spectacular emergence of the Arrows team into the top six. Mika Salo came in fourth, less than 20 seconds behind Irvine, while the once-derided Pedro Diniz followed World Champion Jacques Villeneuve into sixth place. To get both cars into the points was a superb result. Arrows chief Tom Walkinshaw spoke of his delight with obvious enthusiasm: "This is a truly spectacular result for the entire team who have worked tirelessly to improve the performance of our cars."

The former Arrows driver Damon Hill had another literally pointless day in the principality, only managing eighth place – some two laps behind the leaders. To make matters worse for the Jordan team, on lap 44 their other driver, Ralf Schumacher, trundled his car into the garage to end a very disappointing day.

Title contender?

Race winner and championship leader Mika Hakkinen relished the splendour of his victory but added a note of caution towards any outcome to the season: "My recipe for success is simple. I just have to carry on what I am doing at present and then perhaps it will come off. But I would be a fool if I was already thinking too much about the title. As long as even the mathematical chance exists that someone will overtake me, I shall not lean back. I still have a long way to go – ten races, that is half an eternity."

Michael Schumacher used the subject of the World Championship to make known his views on Goodyear,

Giancarlo Fisichella was delighted with his surprising second place.

MONACO GRAND PRIX

the Ferrari team's tyre suppliers: "Fundamentally, all I can say on the subject of the World Championship title is that either we make a giant step forward with respect to the tyres or we can forget the title. This does not mean that I have given up all hope. On the contrary, we have carried out tests before Monaco in Magny-Cours and have sorted out some very promising mixtures for Canada. I have criticized Goodyear severely in the past but now I can see positive signs. If things continue like that, the McLaren-Mercedes cars can be held."

In the same breath, however, he also modified this forecast: "If I cannot even hold an Arrow in check coming out of the bends, that gives me something to think about. There is no doubt that the Japanese tyres offer better traction out of the bends. We simply do not have enough grip."

Goodyear stung

The continuous criticisms in Monaco certainly got on the nerves of the Italian Goodyear chief Antonio Corsi. He answered the accusations with unusual sharpness: "Schumacher is spitting in the plate he eats from." Nonetheless, Schumacher's words had their almost inevitable effect and Goodyear redoubled their efforts to provide the Ferrari team – and their other clients – with new tyres for the forthcoming battle with Bridgestone at the Canadian Grand Prix in Montreal.

Schumacher hit the barrier on the last lap, losing his nose cone in the process.

PRACTICE

Fisichella pushes the McLarens

There are few places on the course where the spectators can see the Formula One drivers at such close quarters as in the bar at Rascasse – but it is an expensive luxury.

The third row was taken up by the Williams of Heinz Harald Frentzen and the Benetton of Alexander Wurz. Frentzen's fifth position compared favourably with the poor 13th place gained by his team-mate Jacques Villeneuve. At the rear of the field, the Tyrrell driver Ricardo Rosset achieved a small record – once again he failed to qualify for the race.

In qualifying for the Monaco Grand Prix, Italian Giancarlo Fisichella showed that recent improvements were no coincidence. He even managed to steal the show from McLaren for one moment when he set a best time of 1:20.368 minutes.

Mika Hakkinen and David Coulthard, who led in the overall classification, soon recovered from the shock of this result. Both McLaren drivers bettered Fisichella's time to share the front row – with Hakkinen holding pole position.

Michael Schumacher had to be content with starting on the second row of the grid. Having crashed his car at Casino in the pre-qualifying sessions, further mechanical trouble forced the German to use the spare car for qualifying on Saturday. Given these setbacks, he was fairly satisfied with his overall position.

Qualifying Times

1	Hakkinen	McLaren-Mercedes	1:19.798
2	Coulthard	McLaren-Mercedes	1:20.137
3	Fisichella	Benetton-Mecachrome	1:20.368
4	M. Schumacher	Ferrari	1:20.702
5	Frentzen	Williams-Mecachrome	1:20.729
6	Wurz	Benetton-Mecachrome	1:20.955
7	Irvine	Ferrari	1:21.712
8	Salo	Arrows-Hart	1:22.144
9	Herbert	Sauber-Petronas	1:22.157
10	Trulli	Prost-Peugeot	1:22.238
11	Alesi	Sauber-Petronas	1:22.257
12	Diniz	Arrows-Hart	1:22.355
13	Villeneuve	Williams-Mecachrome	1:22.468
14	Barrichello	Stewart-Ford	1:22.540
15	Hill	Jordan-Mugen-Honda	1:23.151
16	R. Schumacher	Jordan-Mugen-Honda	1:23.263
17	Magnussen	Stewart-Ford	1:23.411
18	Panis	Prost-Peugeot	1:23.536
19	Nakano	Minardi-Ford	1:23.957
20	Takagi	Tyrrell-Ford	1:24.024
21	Tuero	Minardi-Ford	1:24.031
NON-QUALIFIER			
22	Rosset	Tyrrell-Ford	1:25.737

disappointed David Coulthard after his McLaren's breakdown on lap 18.

Alexander Wurz climbs uninjured from the wreck of his Benetton.

CALENDAR

7 June
Canadian Grand Prix: After one restart, two multiple pile-ups, three safety-car phases, and the total failure of the McLarens, Michael Schumacher is able to celebrate his third victory on the Gilles Villeneuve circuit. The previous ones were in 1994 and 1997.

Canadian Grand Prix: The Williams team protests about Schumacher's irresponsible overtaking of Heinz Harald Frentzen, who ended up in the gravel. The protest is rejected by the FIA stewards.

17 June
Brandenburg: Construction officially begins on the Lausitzring, which is intended to become the fourth Formula One circuit in Germany by the year 2000. The others are the Nürburgring, Hockenheim, and the Oschersleben circuit.

19 June
During a test run at Magny-Cours, France, Williams driver Heinz Harald Frentzen drives at high speed into a pile of tyres that bury him. Frentzen is rescued from his almost completely wrecked car and taken to a hospital in Nevers. However, he is discharged from the hospital on the same evening.

20 June
Jordan driver Damon Hill changes his job at short notice. He travels to Southampton this weekend to take part in the "Round the Island" yacht race in the Solent.

27 June
Doping tests: After the final practice for the French Grand Prix, six drivers have to provide urine samples – Mika Hakkinen, Damon Hill, Jean Alesi, Olivier Panis, Esteban Tuero, and Ralf Schumacher.

Damon Hill

28 June
French Grand Prix: On the Magny-Cours circuit, Michael Schumacher and Eddie Irvine celebrate the first Ferrari double victory for eight years – since Alain Prost led Nigel Mansell over the line at Jerez in 1990.

Formula One takes on football: Half an hour after the end of the French Grand Prix, the France-Paraguay match kicks off in the World Cup finals. The French race organizers react promptly by showing the match on all the track's giant TV screens.

30 June
The Stewart Building is officially opened in Milton Keynes, in the presence of Princess Anne. It will be the headquarters of both the Grand Prix team and Paul Stewart Racing.

1–30 June
Rumours from the United States suggest that Jordan driver Damon Hill has been offered a place in Bobby Rahal's CART team for next season. The triple CART champion Rahal intends to end his career as a driver in 1999.

The Mobil oil company is the main sponsor for this year's German Grand Prix, which takes place on 2 August at Hockenheim. One of the bends will be renamed "Mobil Bend".

BAR team chief Craig Pollock has confirmed that, from 1999, his team will race for the next two Formula One seasons with Supertec engines. The engine has been designed and developed by Renault Sport, but it is being assembled and maintained by Mecachrome.

Hollywood movie star Sylvester Stallone is considering employing Formula One drivers, including Jacques Villeneuve and Michael Schumacher, in support roles in a motor-racing film planned for the year 2000.

Ferrari race manager Jean Todt is awarded the Gino Palumbo trophy, in recognition of his achievement in making the Ferrari team World Championship contenders after years in the wilderness. The trophy is named after a former editor-in-chief of the Italian sports newspaper *Gazetto dello Sport*.

Ralf Schumacher is criticized by his employer, Eddie Jordan. In the current season, the young German driver has failed to win a single World Championship point for his team. He has only finished in two races so far this season, at Imola and Barcelona.

Sylvester Stallone, a familiar figure at Formula One races.

Because of the clash between the FIA and FOA on one side and the European Union Commissioner Karel van Miert on the other, the stock market flotation of Formula One boss Bernie Ecclestone's business has to be postponed.

Benetton driver Alexander Wurz has signed a contract with Swiss watchmaker SMH for a new limited edition of Swatch watches to appear under the name "Wurz edition". The Austrian driver has been busy in the marketing area, as he already promotes a brand of iced tea.

Relations between Olivier Panis and his team boss Alain Prost deteriorate after comments made by Prost to a French newspaper. Rumours abound that Panis will not be driving for the Prost team next year, and that he is now looking for a new employer.

Sayings and quotations

"Whether you believe it or not, there is another major event in France apart from the football World Cup."
From a Williams press release

"My neck feels as if I have been sucking a Viagra pill."
Heinz Harald Frentzen on the swellings after the Magny-Cours accident.

"If it involved animals, they would be put to sleep. In any event, I am not sure whether it is possible to call them people at all."
Michael Schumacher on football hooligans.

"Of course these are not football fans. However, whoever suggests putting people to sleep makes a shocking contribution to coarsening language and society."
German politician Volker Beck criticizing Michael Schumacher's statement about football hooligans.

CHANGE OF DRIVER

Hire and fire

Jos Verstappen, the Dutch driver who made a Formula One comeback this year, has found out just how brutal the Grand Prix world can be for drivers who are not in the spotlight.

Jos Verstappen is certainly no greenhorn. He was tenth in the 1994 season, and has 48 Grand Prix races under his belt. But it was a surprise when the Dutchman was taken on by the Stewart team as number two to Rubens Barrichello after the poor showing of Danish driver Jan Magnussen. "Jos the Boss" took his place in the driving seat for the French Grand Prix.

However, the 26-year-old's happiness was to prove shortlived. Apparently his efforts did not satisfy Jackie Stewart, and before the start of the Monza Grand Prix, Stewart announced that Johnny Herbert was being taken on for the next season. Since Barrichello was staying in the team, Verstappen had to go. The Dutch driver consoled himself with the idea of trying his luck in the American IndyCar series.

Jos Verstappen, seen here at the Argentine Grand Prix in 1996, twice achieved third place in Formula One.

BACKGROUND

Fittipaldi challenge

Brazilian Emerson Fittipaldi, Formula One World Champion in 1972 and 1974, is planning to set up his own Formula One team.

Since driving into a concrete wall during the Michigan 500 in 1996 – and almost killing himself in the process – 51-year-old Fittipaldi has withdrawn from racing. But he wants to prove himself in the next few years as manager of his own Formula One team. For some time now he has been in negotiation with Bernie Ecclestone, who is trying to help him achieve his ambition.

The Brazilian has already had one attempt at being a team owner. In 1980, he combined the functions of team chief and number one driver, taking on the Finn Keke Rosberg as his second driver and employing Harvey Postlethwaite as designer. However, the ambitious project failed after only a year due to a lack of success on the track and the absence of the necessary financial backing from his sponsors. In the years that followed, Fittipaldi tried his luck in the American IndyCar series, but he has now turned his back on racing in the United States in favour of his earlier passion for Formula One.

In a good mood as he considers a return to Formula One, ex-World Champion Emerson Fittipaldi.

UPDATE

Honda plan Formula One comeback in 2000

When Honda announced their retirement from Formula One at the end of 1992, the other teams breathed a sigh of relief. Between 1987 and 1991, the Japanese had been considered unbeatable. During this period, they won the Drivers' and Constructors' Championships four times.

The success story of the Japanese company began 11 years ago. In 1987, Honda won the Constructors' Championship with an engine installed in the Williams car, and won the Drivers' Championship with Nelson Piquet. Despite this double success and 20 victories with Williams, the Japanese company then moved to McLaren. They were enticed by McLaren's recent signing of drivers Ayrton Senna and twice World Champion Alain Prost. These two were regarded as the leading Formula One drivers of their time.

Triumphant alliance

Even during the first year – the last in which the turbo engines was used – the alliance between McLaren and Honda demonstrated its superiority. At the end of the season, Ayrton Senna was firmly in place as World Champion with 90 points after 13 pole positions and eight victories. His team-mate Prost completed the success story with second place in the Championship, achieving two pole positions, seven victories, and a total of 87 points. Between them the two drivers won every race except Monza, and even in Italy victory was within their grasp – Senna was in the lead when he was forced to retire after colliding with a Williams that he was trying to lap.

Some hoped that the McLaren-Honda dominance would be broken when turbo engines were banned for the 1989 season. But the World Championship again turned into an internal team duel between Prost and Senna. This time the Frenchman, known as the "professor" because of his unspectacular but precise driving, kept his nose in front.

The sequence of Formula One successes continued for McLaren-Honda in the years that followed. They won the World Championship title again in 1990 and 1991, both times through Ayrton Senna. It was only from the start of the 1992 season that problems began to creep in as McLaren's competitors began to improve. Neither Ayrton Senna's driving skill nor Honda horsepower was enough to make up for the McLaren's lack of competitiveness.

Honda pulls out

After five triumphant years, Honda largely withdrew from Formula One. They did not cut their links with Formula One entirely, however. Mugen-Honda supplied the Prost team with engines for the 1997 season, for example, and provided Jordan with a completely new engine design in the same year.

At the beginning of this year, there were widespread rumours that Honda were planning a comeback as a works team. However, the Japanese consistently denied these stories. It was only on 4 October, when the company was celebrating its 50th anniversary, that the Japanese stunned the Formula One world with the announcement that they intended to enter the competition in the year 2000 with their own engines. Apparently, Honda had considered returning in 1999 but had called the venture off because of the uncertain state of the Japanese economy.

Let there be no doubt that Honda are entirely serious about this exciting new start in Formula One. Having reflected on the consequences of depending on others in years gone by, the management at Honda now fully intend to set up their own team.

Honda will exploit the time between now and their comeback to try to ensure a top-class performance from the first Grand Prix of the 2000 season. The company intend to build a factory in England to manufacture Formula One cars. Johnny Herbert, now with Sauber, has been seen as a possible test driver, although he looks likely to choose to drive for Stewart next season. Honda are also interested in Japanese driver Toranosuki Tagaki, now driving for Tyrrell.

The great Ayrton Senna in action. The Brazilian always co-operated closely with the mechanics to try to improve the McLaren-Honda's performance.

CANADIAN GRAND PRIX

A multiple somersault ended Alexander Wurz's attempt to move up on the first bend. The crash was spectacular but Wurz was unhurt.

Schumacher livens up World Championship

7 June, Montreal. After two starts, three safety car phases, and a 10-second stop-go penalty, Michael Schumacher achieved his second victory of the season at the Gilles Villeneuve circuit. A succession of crashes and near misses renewed old controversies within the pit lane.

This year's Canadian Grand Prix once again lived up to its reputation as the racing circuit with the greatest potential to provide a spectacular race. Just after the first bend – and after a near perfect start had allowed Michael Schumacher to overtake Mika Hakkinen and slip into second position behind David Coulthard – the race ground to a halt after a spectacular first-corner pile-up.

Demolition derby

The stoppage was primarily caused by Alexander Wurz. When turning into the chicane after the start-finish line, Wurz firstly demolished Jean Alesi's Sauber before taking Johnny Herbert and Jarno Trulli with him into the gravel trap. His Benetton then spun over three times before finally coming to a dramatic rest – upside down.

The main victim of this unfortunate fracas was Herbert as, on this particular weekend, his replacement car had been reserved for his French team-mate, Jean Alesi. Although Herbert's technicians did succeed in repairing the car before the restart, he was forced to restart in last place.

The field formed up again at the start-finish line. But to the amazement of the spectators, bodywork parts were once again seen flying through the air at exactly the same spot. This time it was Ralf Schumacher who was responsible for the chaos. His spin on the track caused Irvine to cut off the nose of Alesi's Sauber. To add insult to injury, Alesi's car was then mounted by Trulli's. Not surprisingly, Alesi lost his cool and later condemned the "youngsters" in the race as "madmen who will not realize that no race is decided in the first bend." The veteran's criticism, however, fell on deaf ears. In fact, Alexander Wurz thought he was in the right: "Of course I could have braked earlier. But I am a racing driver."

After the second collision, the race management decided against a second restart. Instead, the safety car was sent on. Such was the length of time taken to clear up the debris that it remained on the track until the fifth lap.

McLaren disaster

Coulthard took the lead, followed by Schumacher and Giancarlo Fisichella. To the dismay of McLaren, Mika Hakkinen dropped out in the first lap of the restart with gearbox problems. Worse was to follow. While the safety car was on the track for the second time – to clean up after a spin by Pedro Diniz – Coulthard's throttle linkage began to fail, and on lap 19 he went into the pits. For the first time in the season, both McLarens had dropped out due to mechanical failure.

Schumacher now took over the lead. In lap 20, a crash by Mika Salo brought out the safety car yet again. Schumacher brilliantly exploited the delay by diving into the pits to carry out a routine stop. As always, the Ferrari team's work was near faultless, and Schumacher was back on the track after only 9.1 seconds.

But now, however, the German revealed the darker side of his character. As Schumacher emerged from the pit lane, Williams driver Heinz-Harald Frentzen passed by at high speed. Instead of slowing down and remaining on the inside of the track, Schumacher forced Frentzen into the gravel trap and out of the race. Schumacher, after a substantial delay, received a 10-second stop-go penalty for this action. Frentzen seemed completely frustrated when he spoke to the media. The Williams driver gave full rein to his considerable anger: "I am so disappointed. What do I think of Schumacher's manoeuvre? The TV pictures show it all."

Although Schumacher said that he had only seen his countryman at the last moment, he nevertheless later apologized to Frentzen: "If I made a mistake, I am very sorry. I did not see you. When I drove out of the pits, Diniz and Villeneuve came past and then there was a gap."

In this statement, however, Schumacher avoids two key points. At the time of the incident, the race was under blue flag conditions in which no driver is allowed to overtake. Furthermore, during the drivers' pre-race briefing he had specifically proposed that particular attention should be paid to the on-coming traffic when driving out of the pit. Many seasoned race observers considered Schumacher's pronouncements to be yet another example of the driver's breathtaking arrogance.

Race Result

1	M. Schumacher	1:40:57.355
2	Fisichella	1:41:14.017
3	Irvine	1:41:57.414
4	Wurz	1:42:00.587
5	Barrichello	1:42:18.868
6	Magnussen	1 lap behind

Drivers' Championship

1	Hakkinen	46 points
2	M. Schumacher	34 points
3	Coulthard	29 points
4	Irvine	19 points
5	Fisichella	13 points
6	Wurz	12 points
7	Frentzen	8 points
	= Villeneuve	8 points
9	Barrichello	4 points
10	Salo	3 points
	= Alesi	3 points

Constructors' Championship

1	McLaren-Mercedes	75 points
2	Ferrari	53 points
3	Benetton-Mecachrome	25 points
4	Williams-Mecachrome	16 points
5	Stewart-Ford	5 points
6	Arrows-Hart	4 points

Wheel-to-wheel

On lap 38, Schumacher almost fell victim to a defensive action by his old rival Damon Hill. After the Ferrari driver had sat out his time penalty and rapidly advanced to third place, he attempted to pass Hill on the straight before reaching the start-finish line. At this moment, Hill zigzagged in front of Schumacher and there was almost wheel contact. Schumacher countered and passed Hill, but was not pleased by the incident. He said: "At that point, we were doing 200 mph and somebody moving line three times is not on. I was so angry. If someone wants to kill you, they can do it in a different way. I was lucky to get through the chicane. I can't handle an experienced man doing something like that. I will be having big words with him."

As might be expected, the 1996 World Champion saw the situation somewhat differently to Schumacher. He later spoke to the press: "Look, we were racing for second place and I wasn't going to give it to him. He's obviously got this massive problem and overstates the case to try and defend himself. He can't claim that anybody drives badly when you look at the things he's been up to. I mean, he just took Frentzen out completely. He's got nothing to complain about. He should be happy he won the race and forget all about it."

Fisichella pressed

Schumacher set about catching Fisichella to gain the lead. Both drivers knew, however, that they would have

When Jarno Trulli landed on Alesi's Sauber after the second start, his engine caught fire but was successfully extinguished.

CIRCUIT

Circuit Gilles Villeneuve

Long, high-speed straights alternate with slow chicanes and hairpin bends on the island track in Montreal. This shape of racing circuit puts a heavy strain on the brakes and transmission. However, the long straights before the bends offer excellent possibilities for overtaking manoeuvres.

Track length 4.421 km (2.747 miles)
Race distance 305.049 km (189.543 miles) – 69 laps
1997 winner Michael Schumacher, Ferrari
Lap record 1:19.635 min, David Coulthard, McLaren-Mercedes, 1997

to pit again. Fisichella was first in on lap 44, allowing the German to take first place. Schumacher built up his slender lead until his pitstop on lap 50.

Schumacher ahead

The Ferrari mechanics did not fail their lead driver, and Schumacher raced out on to the track just ahead of Fisichella. Schumacher even gained an extra few seconds as a safety margin to ensure victory. Fisichella later claimed he had been slowed down by a sticky third gear; and his slower lap times seemed to bear this out. In the end, Fisichella had to be content with second, with Eddie Irvine third – making it two Ferrari drivers on the podium.

PRACTICE

McLarens in qualifying duel

The final practice session in Canada was dominated by the McLaren-Mercedes drivers. Even Schumacher, who was driving with improved Goodyear tyres, could not disturb the private battle between the McLarens. For a long time, it looked as if Mika Hakkinen, leading the Formula One series, would maintain his superiority over team-mate David Coulthard. In fact, the Scot repeatedly failed to match the time of his Finnish rival during almost the entire one-hour session. But when Coulthard demanded everything from his car in the last lap, in the last minute he scraped ahead of Hakkinen with a lead of just 69-thousandths of a second. Giancarlo Fisichella demonstrated his driving skill with a qualifying time which was just behind that of third-placed Michael Schumacher.

Qualifying Times

1	Coulthard	McLaren-Mercedes	1:18.213
2	Hakkinen	McLaren-Mercedes	1:18.282
3	M. Schumacher	Ferrari	1:18.497
4	Fisichella	Benetton-Mecachrome	1:18.826
5	R. Schumacher	Jordan-Mugen-Honda	1:19.242
6	Villeneuve	Williams-Mecachrome	1:19.588
7	Frentzen	Williams-Mecachrome	1:19.614
8	Irvine	Ferrari	1:19.616
9	Alesi	Sauber-Petronas	1:19.693
10	Hill	Jordan-Mugen-Honda	1:19.717
11	Wurz	Benetton-Mecachrome	1:19.765
12	Herbert	Sauber-Petronas	1:19.845
13	Barrichello	Stewart-Ford	1:19.953
14	Trulli	Prost-Peugeot	1:20.188
15	Panis	Prost-Peugeot	1:20.303
16	Takagi	Tyrrell-Ford	1:20.328
17	Salo	Arrows-Hart	1:20.536
18	Nakano	Minardi-Ford	1:21.230
19	Diniz	Arrows-Hart	1:21.301
20	Magnussen	Stewart-Ford	1:21.629
21	Tuero	Minardi-Ford	1:21.822
22	Rosset	Tyrrell-Ford	1:21.824

A second victory in Canada brought Michael Schumacher to second place in the overall championship classifications.

Asprey

Asprey
Asprey

FRENCH GRAND PRIX

Ferrari fightback under way

28 June, Magny-Cours. For the first time this season, Ferrari managed to overwhelm the formerly dominant McLarens. Superb driving, good teamwork and improved tyres lay behind the Ferrari renaissance.

The first Ferrari double victory since 1990 was of great significance, not least for Michael Schumacher. His victory meant that he was only six points behind leader Mika Hakkinen in the World Championship, and justified realistic hopes that he may still gain the Championship title.

At the start of the race, the new Stewart driver Jos Verstappen (who had replaced the unconvincing Jan Magnussen) unintentionally made himself the centre of attention. His car stalled just as the front of the field sped away. The race management decided to restart the race.

Ferraris in front

Michael Schumacher was the main beneficiary of this decision. On the restart, Schumacher got away extremely well – in contrast to Hakkinen. The Finnish driver showed such poor concentration on restarting that Eddie Irvine in the second Ferrari passed him without difficulty.

What the McLarens had achieved in the previous races – getting in front immediately and staying there – was now emulated perfectly by the Ferrari drivers. Schumacher drove faultlessly and, aided by Eddie Irvine, he was never in danger of losing the race – his third victory of the season.

An emotional and very happy Schumacher – who made this his fourth win at the Magny-Cours circuit in five years – found new confidence for his World Championship hopes: "For the first time, we are in a position to beat McLaren by our own efforts. Their dominance is broken."

Schumacher did not stint in giving credit where he thought it was due: "I have criticized Goodyear severely in recent months but I must now say that the Americans have done some outstandingly good work. In high temperature conditions, I believe the Goodyear tyres are now better than those of Bridgestone."

The developments made by the American Goodyear company were not equally appreciated by all their customers, which included the Swiss Sauber team. A week before the race, Johnny Herbert and Jean Alesi had had their best qualifying times with the advanced version of the racing tyres. When Ferrari, which had played a major part in the development of the new tyres, decided on the tyre mixture for France, Sauber trailed behind the field because they had matching problems with the new compounds. A resigned Alesi concluded: "We shall have to accept whatever is worked out by Ferrari."

Irish support

The tyres and Schumacher's victory were not the only matters of interest. Ferrari driver Eddie Irvine put up a brilliant show in the battle for second place. From the outset, the Irishman had the edge over Mika Hakkinen and kept him at bay right to the end of the race. To achieve this, Irvine drove his Ferrari to the limit and did not make a mistake throughout the race.

Formula One supremo Bernie Ecclestone found praise for Irvine's performance: "The best Number Two in the field. It is not everyone in his class who would serve the cause in this way." Irvine himself was relatively uninterested in the attention that his performance had attracted. Instead he

Although the McLaren driver David Coulthard (above) drove well and achieved the fastest lap, he finished in sixth place because of a defective refuelling system. Michael Schumacher (left) and Eddie Irvine, on the other hand, provided Ferrari with their first double victory since that of Nigel Mansell and Alain Prost in 1990.

PRACTICE

Pressure on McLaren increases

McLaren driver Mika Hakkinen rejoices over his fifth pole position of the season.

Even though Mika Hakkinen achieved pole position for the fifth time during qualifying in Magny-Cours, Ferrari showed McLaren that their star was very much in the ascendant. Michael Schumacher earned a prized second place on the starting grid, being only 0.2 seconds behind the Finnish driver. Schumacher was highly satisfied with this result: "For the first time, I was in a position to fight for the pole position. We are so close that it is good enough for the race."

Just a few minutes after the beginning of qualifying, the German went on to the track and achieved an initial best time of 1:16.227 minutes. Shortly after that, his team-mate Eddie Irvine took provisional lead and underlined the Ferraris' strong performance. However, the Silver Arrows of McLaren countered as a pair. Hakkinen went away from the field, in fact, with a lead of more than half a second; Coulthard was behind him but had to be satisfied – for the time being – with a second place.

Then, however, Schumacher produced a super-fast lap. He came very close to the leader and placed himself between the two McLarens.

After qualifying, Hakkinen was sure of his chances for victory: "I am self-confident because my McLaren is faster on the straight and overtaking here is extremely risky." He would find out, however, that such predictions are not always to be relied upon.

Qualifying Times

1	Hakkinen	McLaren-Mercedes	1:14.929
2	M. Schumacher	Ferrari	1:15.159
3	Coulthard	McLaren-Mercedes	1:15.333
4	Irvine	Ferrari	1:15.527
5	Villeneuve	Williams-Mecachrome	1:15.630
6	R. Schumacher	Jordan-Mugen-Honda	1:15.925
7	Hill	Jordan-Mugen-Honda	1:16.245
8	Frentzen	Williams-Mecachrome	1:16.319
9	Fisichella	Benetton-Mecachrome	1:16.375
10	Wurz	Benetton-Mecachrome	1:16.460
11	Alesi	Sauber-Petronas	1:16.627
12	Trulli	Prost-Peugeot	1:16.892
13	Herbert	Sauber-Petronas	1:16.977
14	Barrichello	Stewart-Ford	1:17.024
15	Verstappen	Stewart-Ford	1:17.604
16	Panis	Prost-Peugeot	1:17.671
17	Diniz	Arrows-Hart	1:17.880
18	Rosset	Tyrrell-Ford	1:17.908
19	Salo	Arrows-Hart	1:17.970
20	Takagi	Tyrrell-Ford	1:18.221

CIRCUIT

Circuit de Nevers, Magny-Cours

The home track of World Champion Alain Prost's team is located between Paris and Lyons. The newly resurfaced course is characterized by its smooth surface and a general lack of grip. The circuit is also known for its combination of high- and slow-speed corners. As in Monaco, overtaking is very difficult when the race gets under way.

Estoril
Lycée
Chicane
Grande Courbe
Golf
Imola
Château d'Eau

Track length 4.25 km (2.64 miles)
Race distance 306.029 km (190.08 miles) – 72 laps
1997 winner Michael Schumacher, Ferrari
Lap record 1:17.070 min, Nigel Mansell, Williams-Renault, 1992

FRENCH GRAND PRIX

intimated that in future he did want to restrict himself to the role of assistant to Schumacher.

Despite a podium finish for Hakkinen – which helped defend the leadership position in the World Championship – there was little jubilation to be heard coming from the McLaren-Mercedes team. Apart from the obvious irritation caused by Ferrari's victory, the team knew they had failed David Coulthard during one of the refuelling stops.

When Coulthard drove into the pits to fill up for the second time, the refuelling connection failed to work. After waiting more than 30 seconds, the team decided to send him back on to the track for another lap so that the refuelling system could be remedied or at least replaced.

Fading hopes

This next stop, however, lasted an "infinitely long" 14 seconds in the pits. And because Coulthard had to come in for a fourth time for petrol in the 63rd lap, he only managed a very poor sixth place. Although Coulthard was typically phlegmatic over the McLaren foul-up, the single point from this race (and none from the previous race at Monaco) was little short of a ruinous disaster for his hopes of ultimate victory.

With the Championship at the half-way stage, the "minor" teams of Jordan, Prost, Tyrrell, and Minardi left the race track at Magny-Cours without a single point. The Prost team was particularly disappointed, this being their home Grand Prix. A new longer wheel-based car had to be returned to the garage as its handling proved too nervous for the Magny-Cours circuit. A poor qualifying session was followed by a race retirement for Jarno Trulli (who spun off the track) and an 11th-place finish for Olivier Panis. Clearly, swift improvements were now essential.

Race Result

1	M. Schumacher	1:34:45.206
2	Irvine	1:35:04.601
3	Hakkinen	1:35:04.773
4	Villeneuve	1:35:51.991
5	Wurz	1 lap behind
6	Coulthard	1 lap behind

Drivers' Championship

1	Hakkinen	50 points
2	M. Schumacher	44 points
3	Coulthard	30 points
4	Irvine	25 points
5	Wurz	14 points
6	Fisichella	13 points
7	Villeneuve	11 points
8	Frentzen	8 points
9	Barrichello	4 points
10	Salo	3 points
	= Alesi	3 points

Constructors' Championship

1	McLaren-Mercedes	80 points
2	Ferrari	69 points
3	Benetton-Mecachrome	27 points
4	Williams-Mecachrome	19 points
5	Stewart-Ford	5 points
6	Arrows-Hart	4 points
	= Sauber-Petronas	4 points

Thanks to Eddie Irvine's protection, Michael Schumacher (front) was able to extend his lead over the McLarens of Hakkinen and Coulthard.

TEAM TALK

Ralf Schumacher did not come up to the expectations of his team manager in Canada, and catapulted out of the race after a spin.

What's gone wrong for Jordan and Williams at the halfway point?

Vhen the half-time whistle sounded or the current Formula One season, ordan and Williams shared the same roblem – they had not met the bjectives they had clearly defined or 1998. Frank Williams wanted to lefend the titles in the driver and onstructor tables. Halfway through ne season, this objective had ecome merely a dream. Eddie ordan had not aimed quite so high – e hoped for one Grand Prix victory n the present year. This was not an nrealistic hope when looking back o 1997. At the same time last year, ordan had 13 World Championship oints, and they ended a respectable fth in the Constructors' Champion-nip at the end of the 1997 racing eason – just behind McLaren.

No points, no money

t Magny-Cours, if not earlier, Eddie ordan has realized what a sharp ifference there is between wish and eality. After eight races – with an x-World Champion on board – the eam had still not gained a single oint. Even worse, in the Grand Prix aces that had taken place, the total umber of times that either driver ad seen the finishing flag was only even. This was reason enough for ne sponsors to restrict the flow of oney to the team. The normally heerful Jordan crew had already ost cohesion before Magny-Cours, fact made obvious by the sudden eparture of three engineers.

Another difficulty was the redesign of the car – thought necessary at the start of the season. The high cost of this was in no way justified, however, and engine partner Mugen-Honda immediately began to fear that all was not quite right. Although Eddie Jordan continued to secure the services of Mugen-Honda, the agreement now included a clause that the leasing price for the engines would possibly be raised by 50 per cent in the coming year.

The main cause of this "increase in price" was thought to be Ralf Schumacher. Because of his indifferent performances in the first half of the season, the younger Schumacher became Eddie Jordan's prime target – "For his current performance, Ralf is too expensive." Against this background, Ralf Schumacher attempted to make a better showing, particularly in France, and despite a collision with Alexander Wurz, he did actually reach the finishing line for once – but again without any Championship points to justify the interest and approval of the sponsors.

Williams behind

Things did not look much better for the high-flying Williams team, even though those at the top did not have to worry about financial conditions in quite the same way as those at Jordan. The main worry was star designer Adrian Newey's departure, someone Williams could never really replace. Work on the Williams FW-20 car during the current races did not produce any worthwhile results. The Williams cars were well behind the leaders. Although Heinz Harald Frentzen had made it on to the podium at the Melbourne Grand Prix, Williams had still not achieved another top-three placing as the half-way point passed.

Retention problems

Everything indicated that team chief Frank Williams would not hold on to his current drivers, who could have helped him develop the current Mecachrome engine before the anticipated alliance with BMW in the year 2000 got underway. As early as May, the current World Champion Jacques Villeneuve indicated that the Championship train had already left as far as he was concerned, and that he was open to new (and realistic) offers from other teams.

Frentzen also appeared to lack enthusiasm, an attitude that was reciprocated by a growing lack of interest expressed by the Williams team in the German driver. Rumours abounded that Frentzen might rejoin Sauber, which had given him a place in 1994 and facilitated his entry into Formula One – although they remained only rumours. A talented driver, Frentzen probably lacked the temperament needed to survive in a cut-and thrust team like Williams.

Such had been the success of Williams in the past, that few could dismiss the team in its entirety.

Jacques Villeneuve knows there is no chance of a World title in 1998.

CALENDAR

6 July
Gerhard Berger, who ended his Formula One career last year, is appointed the new motor-sport director of BMW. This move completes the management team for the company's return to Formula One in the year 2000.

9 July
Jacques Villeneuve likes it very bright. At Silverstone, the Canadian again appears with a new hair colour – violet. "There's no particular reason for it. I just wanted a change," said the Williams driver.

10 July
Both David Coulthard (96.1 kmh/60 mph, $8,000 fine) and Mika Hakkinen (92.9 kmh/58 mph, $3,250 fine) are caught speeding in the pit lane during qualifying for the British Grand Prix. The permitted maximum speed is 80 kmh (50 mph).

12 July
Controversial Ferrari victory at Silverstone: Michael Schumacher wins the British Grand Prix – in spite of a 10-second penalty in the pits – in front of Mika Hakkinen.

The McLaren team submit an objection to the result of the British Grand Prix. But it will not be until 28 July that the FIA appeal court will finally decide whether Michael Schumacher should retain his points from Silverstone.

23 July
Contract concluded: Jacques Villeneuve will be in the driving seat for the new British American Racing (BAR) team in 1999.

An honour is awarded to Bernie Ecclestone. The Formula One boss has received the "AVL Technology Award" for 1998 from the Austrian company AVL for his services to automobile research and development.

26 July
The McLaren Silver Arrows pair succeed again on the Austrian A1 ring – with Mika Hakkinen taking 10 points.

28 July
An important victory for Schumacher away from the track. He is confirmed as the Silverstone winner and is therefore still in the running for the World Championship.

31 July
New high-speed record: McLaren driver David Coulthard reaches an official speed of 356.4 kmh (221 mph) during practice for the German Grand Prix at Hockenheim.

1–31 July
The FIA motorsport association is considering specifying transverse grooves in addition to the longitudinal grooves for Grand Prix tyres from 1999 onwards. This is another means to cut down on high speeds in the corners.

British designer Mike Gascoyne is taken on by Jordan, where he will support technical manager Gary Anderson as chief designer.

Arrows team manager Tom Walkinshaw intends to procure the Mecachrome V10 engines, supported by his sponsor Parmalat. He is currently negotiating with Mecachrome engine distributor Flavio Briatore.

World Champion Jacques Villeneuve is awarded the "Hawthorne Memorial Trophy". The prize is in honour of Mike Hawthorne, the famous British Grand Prix driver.

The ex-Stewart driver Jan Magnussen is seeking a place with the Benetton team as a test and reserve driver.

David Coulthard is put in an embarrassing position on the "Anything You Want" TV programme, on which he was a guest. A female member of the audience admitted that she would leave her husband on the spot for the racing driver. The husband, who accompanied her to the show, did not look very pleased.

Sauber driver Johnny Herbert has become a hit in his team's home country of Switzerland. He is now a regular guest on chat shows, and on other popular television programmes including the lottery show "Bennissima".

The conversion and modernization work on the Hungaroring has been concluded.

Team manager Jackie Stewart is awarded the honourary title of Doctor of Science by the University of Cranfield.

Working with the Katatga company, Benetton driver Alexander Wurz has designed a bicycle that will be marketed by specialist dealers from September onwards under the name of "Alexander Wurz mountain bike edition".

Quotes
"I am just about fed up listening to the complaints about Michael's driving style."
Bernie Ecclestone in the *Stuttgarter Zeitung*

"Alright then, I have just bought a Mercedes."
Heinz Harald Frentzen in *Sonntag Actuell*, when questioned about his relationship to the Mercedes company.

"Look, we are trying to do some business here on the site. You don't take a snack with you to the opera."
The Austrian A1 Ring managing director Hans Geist, defending the new ban on bringing food and drink on to the circuit.

Mercedes motorsports manager Norbert Haug (left) and David Coulthard in typical local headgear at the Austrian Grand Prix.

Craig Pollock: a new manager for a new team – BAR.

NEW TEAM

BAR aim high

When, in November last year, Ken Tyrrell revealed his decision to sell his team – after running it for 30 years – a new team appeared on the scene with great ambitions for the next season. This was British American Racing (BAR), led by Craig Pollock.

Supported by sponsorship wealth from the major tobacco giant British American Tobacco (BAT), a new racing concern has taken over the old Tyrrell team at a rumoured cost of 30 million dollars. Craig Pollock has been appointed the team manager of British American Racing (BAR), an organization that has taken over the Tyrrell Formula One licence. A brand new factory is being built near Silverstone that will employ 160 people from November 1998 onwards.

There is some uncertainty about the holdings in the new team. BAT holds the lion's share of 51 per cent, and Adrian Reynard, responsible for the technical side of the team, has a 13-15 per cent participation. The rest is supposed to be in the hands of Gerald R. Forsythe, the head of the American CART team of the same name, who was brought in by Pollock in recent months. Pollock himself, who indicated during an interview in April that he would be the second largest shareholder, has not been able to raise the money for his own direct participation, but he has negotiated a management contract for five years.

The Reynard factor

Much of the optimism at BAR is based on the success of Adrian Reynard, who has a proven record in many different types of motor racing – most recently in the IndyCar series. Among his many claims to fame is a noted record – that each time he has entered a new class of racing, one of his vehicles has immediately won the first race.

NOVELTY

McLaren two-seater

McLaren introduced a newly-developed two-seat version of their successful race car. The ex-Formula One driver Martin Brundle used it to chauffeur the FIA President Max Mosley round five laps of the Silverstone track.

McLaren had demonstrated a model version of the two-seater car in Melbourne at the beginning of the season. The full-scale MP4-98T was produced under the direction of chief designer Barry Lett and is equipped with standard Formula One technology, including a Mercedes engine. The passenger sits behind the driver in the fuselage – a space where the fuel tank is normally installed.

Intended primarily as a marketing tool to promote McLaren-Mercedes, the target group envisaged taking a ride in the tandem are newspaper reporters, TV presenters, and other media people. VIPs will also be able to enjoy the thrill of a Formula One drive, but at a price (the proceeds will go to charity).

Most of the people who had enjoyed a run in the new McLaren two-seater clambered out of the car suitably ashen-faced. But they all agreed that it really was an experience of a lifetime.

Brundle and Mosley in the two-seater.

LEGAL MATTERS

Ferrari win again

The appeal court of the Automobile World Association, that met in Paris on 29 July, rejected the McLaren objection to Schumacher's victory in the British Grand Prix.

During the British Grand Prix, Michael Schumacher overtook when the yellow flag was in operation, an illegal action which would normally attract a 10-second penalty in the pit lane. But as a result of the numerous errors made by Silverstone race officials, the appeal court judged that Schumacher should not have had to fulfil the obligatory time penalty in the box.

Instead, the penalty time was merely added to the total time and this meant that Schumacher had a better time than his nearest rival, McLaren's Mika Hakkinen.

acques Villeneuve: leaving Williams or the challenge of BAR.

Having found a top car designer in eynard, BAR has negotiated with lecachrome for engines that will go nder the name of "Supertec Sport". he last component in the overall ackage is the driver. And as Jacques illeneuve's manager, Pollock did not ave much difficulty in persuading e Canadian to come over to his am. BAR is now ready for the acid st – success on the race track.

FINANCE

Schumacher signs super-contract

Twice World Champion Michael Schumacher signed what was almost certainly the most highly lucrative contract in the entire history of Formula One.

At the Ferrari headquarters in Maranello, Schumacher extended his contract – that would have run out in 1999 – for a further three years. According to unconfirmed press reports, this will earn him an incredible £81.5 million ($135 million). Distributing this over 16 World Championship races, Schumacher will be enjoying a fee of more than £1.63 million ($2.7 million) per Grand Prix race. This incredible sum did not seem to unduly worry Ferrari. On the contrary, the Ferrari President Luca di Montezemolo was happy to justify the deal: "We want the World Championship title, we want the best racing driver, and Michael is the best. Only he can win back success, he is worth every mark."

The total turnover of "Schumacher Limited" may well be increased by numerous associated activities. Beside private sponsor money (£3.62 million/$6 million), Schumacher has a 15 per cent participation deal in the sale of merchandise (approximately £36.2 million/$60 million in 1998). In addition, Schumacher will be allowed to use the Ferrari logo for his own marketing purposes in the future.

Before Schumacher made his agreement with Ferrari, his astute personal manager Willi Weber had signalled that Schumacher might be interested in a move to McLaren-Mercedes. The talks failed, according to Mercedes board member Jürgen Hubbert, because of the "extreme demands which could not have been justified to the team". But, of course, these negotiations will have helped Schumacher and Weber in the final stages of their deal with Ferrari.

A successful trio. From the left, Jean Todt, Michael Schumacher, and Luca di Montezemolo.

BRITISH GRAND PRIX

Michael Schumacher demonstrates his mastery of wet conditions during the British Grand Prix.

Rain Meister runs rings round FIA

12 JULY, SILVERSTONE. Rain poured down at the British Grand Prix, a race marred by poor stewarding and conflicting interpretations of the FIA rules. As ever, Michael Schumacher made the most of his legendary good fortune.

For once, it was not a driver but the FIA who controversially occupied centre stage at the British Grand Prix. The whole sorry business started with an overtaking manoeuvre by Michael Schumacher during the safety car phase of the race (when the yellow flag was in operation). The standard punishment for this infringement is a ten-second stop-go penalty in the pit lane. This otherwise straightforward procedure turned into farce, however when the race stewards did not follow the race rules in the correct manner.

According to the FIA rules, the announcement of the penalty is subject to a strict time schedule. If the race stewards decide that there has been an infringement, this must be made known in writing to the relevant team within a maximum of 25 minutes. This is acknowledged by the respective team leader, whereupon the stewards, for their part, indicate the time penalty to all the other teams through their monitors.

Time-penalty bungle

At Silverstone, those responsible obviously had a time problem. A full 31 minutes had passed before the document was acknowledged by Ferrari, and was thus six minutes too late. In addition, the stewards applied the incorrect paragraph (57e) to Schumacher's infringement. This paragraph exclusively applies to events that occur during the last 12 laps. In such a case, the time penalty is added to the driving time at the end.

Schumacher, however, overtook Alexander Wurz's Benetton in the 43rd lap, with 17 laps still to go. Accordingly, the stewards should have dealt with the matter in accordance with Paragraph 57c, resulting in the Ferrari having to come into the pits within the next three laps. The chaos was made absolute because the stop-go penalty was only made known to

)ne spectator performs the age-old British sporting ritual of streaking – wisely conducted before the start of the race.

l the other teams in the 59th of 60 ace laps and, therefore, only then ecame official.

Ferrari used the confusion to its dvantage. Michael Schumacher was rdered into the pits in the last lap. At nat moment, he was leading and was echnically the first to cross the nishing line – even if in the pit lane. Vhen Mika Hakkinen also crossed ne finishing line 22.4 seconds later – lbeit on the track – all the spectators elieved that he had achieved a fifth rand Prix victory. This turned out to be wrong, however, because of the oddly phrased FIA rule that states: "The chequered flag falls at the start-finish line as soon as the leading car has completed the full race distance." Whether the leading car was on the track or in the pit lane was thus deemed to be irrelevant.

The result of the race – even after the addition of the ten-second penalty – was that Schumacher had passed the line in front of Mika Hakkinen. To complicate matters further, the FIA also withdrew the time penalty after the race, justifying this by stating that the statutory 25-minute period had not been properly observed by the Silverstone race stewards.

McLaren incensed

Not surprisingly, the McLaren team was furious at the decision. They immediately lodged a protest and team manager Ron Dennis even accused the FIA of protecting Ferrari in order to keep some excitement in the World Championship. The Ferrari team leader Jean Todt laughed off the allegations: "Some of the Silver Arrows people must be suffering from paranoia. I know some doctors who can cure such persecution mania."

Apart from the FIA drama, there was actually some good racing at Silverstone. Heavy rain fell for the first time this year, forcing the drivers to demonstrate their capability in the wet. Would Hakkinen, who was in pole position after the qualifying session, be able to match Michael Schumacher, the acknowledged rain expert? The McLaren driver answered the question by taking the lead after a superb start and, in increasingly heavy rain, he bettered Schumacher's time by an average of six seconds per lap.

The fact that this was insufficient in the end was mainly due to the presence of the safety car. This was sent on for six circuits on lap 43 because of the floods of water and the continually worsening visibility. It was now possible for the spread-out field to close up, and Schumacher was able to make up about 35 seconds.

When the safety car exited into the pit lane, Schumacher was close behind the McLaren. Hakkinen then showed evidence of nerves and made an error that cost him the lead. He over-braked and, just for a moment, left the track and crossed the grass verge. The Ferrari driver capitalized on this error and passed Hakkinen. Schumacher, however, knew that he could not ascribe his 31st victory to his driving skill alone: "I did not expect a

CIRCUIT

The Silverstone Circuit

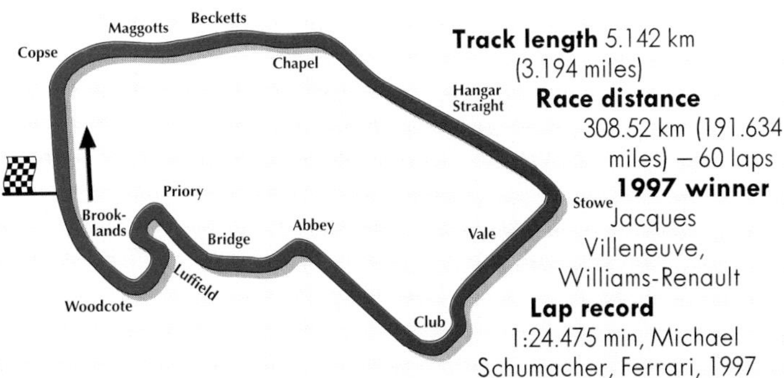

Built on an old airfield, Silverstone remains one of the most demanding high-speed tracks in Formula One. It was at Silverstone that the first British Grand Prix was held in 1926. While the track has lost some of its former character due to the construction of chicanes on many bends, each corner demands everything from drivers and cars, particularly since Copse Corner, at the end of the start-finish straight, has been made faster again. The generally good grip encourages the teams to opt for a middle-range set-up to maximize speed. In addition, the enthusiastic home fans help to make this one of the most spectacular and eagerly awaited events in the world motor racing calendar.

PRACTICE

Villeneuve up with the leaders

Against all expectations, Jacques Villeneuve fought his way on to the second row of the grid. Even the McLaren driver David Coulthard was unable to match Villeneuve's time and had to be satisfied with fourth place. "The car is running really well for the first time," Villeneuve said after the session ended.

As in France, the struggle for pole position was between World Championship leader Mika Hakkinen and the second-placed Michael Schumacher. Despite Schumacher's best efforts, the Finnish driver again secured pole position.

On the third row of the grid, Eddie Irvine's Ferrari was in fifth place followed by Heinz Harald Frentzen's Williams. Damon Hill's seventh position suggested that the Jordan might do well in the race. Benetton, however, were very disappointed with their placings.

Qualifying Times

1	Hakkinen	McLaren-Mercedes	1:23.271
2	M. Schumacher	Ferrari	1:23.720
3	Villeneuve	Williams-Mecachrome	1:24.102
4	Coulthard	McLaren-Mercedes	1:24.310
5	Irvine	Ferrari	1:24.436
6	Frentzen	Williams-Mecachrome	1:24.442
7	Hill	Jordan-Mugen-Honda	1:24.542
8	Alesi	Sauber-Petronas	1:25.081
9	Herbert	Sauber-Petronas	1:25.084
10	Fisichella	Benetton-Mecachrome	1:25.654
11	Wurz	Benetton-Mecachrome	1:25.760
12	Diniz	Arrows-Yamaha	1:26.376
13	Salo	Arrows-Yamaha	1:26.487
14	Trulli	Prost-Peugeot	1:26.808
15	Verstappen	Stewart-Ford	1:26.948
16	Barrichello	Stewart-Ford	1:26.990
17	Takagi	Tyrrell-Ford	1:27.061
18	Tuero	Minardi-Ford	1:28.051
19	Nakano	Minardi-Ford	1:28.123
20	Rosset	Tyrrell-Ford	1:28.608
21	R. Schumacher	Jordan-Mugen-Honda	1:25.461 *
22	Panis	Prost-Peugeot	1:26.847 *

* The qualifying times of drivers Ralf Schumacher (10) and Olivier Panis (16) were cancelled because they did not pass the knee test.

IN THE PRESS

"Schumi won in the pit lane"

The Guardian "Steward's inquiry leaves Ferrari in first place."

The Times "It was a first victory for Schumacher at Silverstone. However, it will be one that is remembered not for his skill, but for a finish that owed more to Keystone Cops than a leading international sport."

The Independent "Cynics concluded God had once more cast his light on the Italian team. Schumacher admitted he had been beaten up to the introduction of the safety car."

The Telegraph "This was a race to support the feeling that Formula One is increasingly being influenced, if not decided, by events beyond the control of the drivers and the teams."

Corriere della Sera "Schumacher remains the sorcerer in rain."

Die Presse "Everything ran smoothly for Germany's Formula One pride. Once again, the luck – or whatever description may be given to the decision of the race authorities to send the safety car on to the track after 45 laps – was on Schumacher's side."

Kronenzeitung "Hellish weather! And Schumi won in the pit lane."

SAFETY RULES

Knees up

Olivier Panis and Ralf Schumacher failed the so-called "knee test" in the qualifying session – both were driving the team replacement cars (often known as T-cars) in place of their regular race vehicles. The test, that is specified in Article 13 of the "Cockpit" rule, states: "Sitting normally with the belt fastened and with the steering wheel pulled down, the driver must be able to pull up both legs in such a way that the knees can be withdrawn under the level of the steering wheel. This action must not be prevented by any part of the car." Because the drivers did not satisfy these strict requirements, they were forced to start the race from the last row, Ralf Schumacher in 21st position and Panis taking up last place.

BRITISH GRAND PRIX

Michael Schumacher (left) and Mika Hakkinen race wheel-to-wheel at Silverstone. A driving error by Hakkinen gave Schumacher the lead.

The safety car played an important part in Schumacher's victory.

result like this at Silverstone. Unde normal circumstances, I would no have won this Grand Prix race."

As for the other major contender in the race, Villeneuve's seventh plac was a poor reflection of his second-row grid position. Before the race he ha said that the Williams would not g well in the wet – and in this he wa proved absolutely right.

David Coulthard also had his own weather problems, especially whe the McLaren team sent him out o intermediate tyres when condition demanded wets – a significant facto in his spin off the sodden track on la 37. After the race, an angry Coulthar said: "I seemed to have a differen weather forecaster than Hakkinen."

Of the other teams, Jordan gaine some hope, and their first point of th season, when Ralf Schumacher fough his way from the back of the grid t sixth position. By contrast, team-mat Damon Hill spun out on lap 13, most unfortunate occurrence for th former World Champion on his hom Grand Prix. Hill's apt commen afterwards: "I felt a bit of a twit."

A study in concentration – Hakkinen examines the computer display.

Michael Schumacher celebrates a lucky – and confused – victory.

Race Result

1	M. Schumacher	1:47:02.45
2	Hakkinen	1:47:24.91
3	Irvine	1:47:31.64
4	Wurz	1 lap behin
5	Fisichella	1 lap behin
6	R. Schumacher	1 lap behin

Drivers' Championship

1	Hakkinen	56 poin
2	M. Schumacher	54 poin
3	Coulthard	30 poin
4	Irvine	29 poin
5	Wurz	17 poin
6	Fisichella	15 poin
7	Villeneuve	11 poin
8	Frentzen	8 poin
9	Barrichello	4 poin
10	Salo	3 poin
	= Alesi	3 poin

Constructors' Championship

1	McLaren-Mercedes	86 points
2	Ferrari	83 points
3	Benetton-Mecachrome	32 points
4	Williams-Mecachrome	19 points
5	Stewart-Ford	5 points
6	Arrows-Hart	4 points
	= Sauber-Petronas	4 points
8	Jordan-Mugen-Honda	1 poin

Ralf Schumacher is surrounded by his pit crew during the race, his car displaying the Benson & Hedges tobacco-ban "Buzzin Hornets" logos.

FLASHBACK

Lotus: An Unforgettable Legend

The Lotus engineering company was formed in 1952 by famous innovator Colin Chapman, who ran the racing outfit until his death in 1982. Even to this day, the pioneering inventions of Colin Chapman can be found in the design and construction of many Formula One cars.

Chapman built his first single-seat racing car in 1957, and two years later an uprated variant ran in Formula One. In 1960, Lotus introduced a completely new design that incorporated the most extreme forms of lightweight construction. The Lotus 18, with a Climax power unit, weighed 45 kg (100 lbs) less than the highly regarded Cooper, and a whole 170 kg (375 lbs) less than the contemporary Ferrari, considered by many to be one of the best cars of the day.

The golden years

The first Grand Prix victory took place at Monaco in 1961 in a car driven by Stirling Moss – although the team had to wait until 1963 before winning their first Constructors' title. Drivers were fascinated by Chapman's innovative enthusiasm. The best of them took the helm for Lotus – and won. The great Scottish driver Jim Clark, in particular, complemented Chapman. He was World Champion twice (1963 and 1965) and, until his death, the pair were considered unbeatable.

Clark was killed during a Formula Two race on the Hockenheim circuit in 1968 and was succeeded by Graham Hill. Known for his fighting spirit, Hill was taken on as No. 2 by Chapman in 1967, and he found no difficulty in providing Clark with some tough competition inside the team. Nevertheless, Clark's death seemed to knock Hill off course. He found being the team No. 1 difficult, but he pulled himself together in good time and secured the World Championship for Lotus in 1968. This was a memorable event because Hill had also taken part in the first race for Lotus just ten years previously.

During the sixties and seventies, Chapman's urge to develop the technology seemed to know few bounds. He invented the monocoque (chassis-less construction) in 1962 and set new standards with the Lotus Type 72 in 1970. In developing a wedge-shaped vehicle with an extremely low frontal area, Colin Chapman succeeded in simultaneously increasing the pressure on the road and improving the streamlining effect needed for the straights. This car, however, also exhibited mechanical faults and these had dramatic and fateful results for the new Lotus driver, the Austrian Jochen Rindt.

During a training run in Monza on 5 September 1970, a hollow brake shaft fractured on Rindt's Lotus. The Austrian driver careered off the track at the Parabolica bend. Help came too late for the 28-year old driver. When the accident happened, Rindt had 45 points, which gave him an unbeatable lead in the World Championship. As a consequence, Rindt was posthumously declared Formula One World Champion.

Rindt's tragic death, and the resulting criticism of the lightweight construction of Formula One cars, did not stop Chapman from trying to find out just what was really possible. In 1977, he again succeeded in revolutionizing racing car technology with the so-called "Wing Cars". These vehicles had aerodynamically shaped bodies in the form of inverted aircraft wing sections mounted to the side between the rear and the front axles. Chapman had discovered the so-called ground effect or, as it is now called, negative lift (ground adhesion). In 1978, the Lotus cars were dealing so effectively with the

Graham Hill: the only driver to win the Formula One World Championship, the Indy 500, and Le Mans.

im Clark won two World Championships for Lotus during his short but brilliant career.

olin Chapman (left) with Jim Clark, one of the most highly regarded drivers of all time.

Posthumous World Champion Jochen Rindt.

hysical laws of negative lift that the eam's rivals had no chance against Aario Andretti, who easily won that ear's World Championship.

Although the Lotus construction nethods were copied by all of the ther teams, it was forbidden in 1981 y the FISA who objected to the ars' dangerously excessive speeds n the bends. In future, they stated, ll the cars had to have a minimum round clearance of at least 60 mm ($2\frac{1}{2}$ in). These new and restricting FISA rules were sufficient reason for Colin Chapman to dig deeply into his bag of Formula One tricks again.

A last throw

He built a racing car with a chassis that consisted of two independent assemblies. The front assembly was designed in such a way that when the car was in motion, the outer part could be lowered so as to bring it below the specified 60 mm mark and thus restore the negative lift effect. This technical finesse, however, was quickly discovered and the Lotus Type 88 was banned. A furious Chapman threatened to leave Formula One for good. Despite the threats he carried on, and gave Nigel Mansell his start in Grand Prix racing. The pressure on Chapman began to intensify and in 1982 he was fatally struck down by a heart attack.

After Chapman's death the Lotus team began to lose its way. Even when it secured the services of emerging talent Ayrton Senna, and access to the powerful Renault and Honda turbo engines, Grand Prix victories were few and far between. In 1990, former Lotus manager Peter Collins bought the company. Financial problems followed, however, and Lotus was finally wound up in 1994.

Mika Hakkinen achieved his fifth Grand Prix victory at the Austrian Grand Prix and extended his lead in the Drivers' Championship.

Hakkinen stays cool

26 JULY, ZELTWEG. McLaren drivers Mika Hakkinen and David Coulthard returned to form with their fourth double victory of the season, while Ferrari had to be content with third and fourth places.

Only 55,000 spectators were present at the track to watch the Austrian Grand Prix. Could this lack of home interest have been due to the departure of Gerhard Berger from Formula One? Whatever the reason, after the golden years of Lauda and Berger, Austrian hopes now had to focus on Benetton's young driver, Alexander Wurz.

The McLaren team's usual positive outlook did not seem to be unduly influenced by the half-empty terraces. When the race began, Mika Hakkinen – starting from a third grid position – catapulted past Giancarlo Fisichella and Jean Alesi to take the lead. Michael Schumacher, also starting from the second row, overtook Alesi and, at the end of the first lap, overtook Fisichella's Benetton.

Multiple pile-up

The conditions were now set for an exciting duel between Hakkinen and Schumacher, the two genuine World Championship rivals. But before the battle could get underway, multiple collisions occurred further down the field. As a consequence, the safety car was ordered out on to the track.

David Coulthard was involved in the accident, although through no fault of his own. In the attempt to fight his way forward from his poor 14th place on the starting grid, Coulthard was hit by both the Arrows cars in quick succession, causing the McLaren to lose its front wing. Although the McLaren team were able to repair the damage in the pits, the accident left Coulthard at the back of the field. Fortunately, the safety car allowed him to close-up with the rest of the pack before the racing resumed. Back on the track, his fighting spirit showed through and, after only eight laps, he had fought his way into 12th position. By the end of the race, he had achieved a superb second place.

"I must say that all the drivers were absolutely fair when I overtook them," said Coulthard after the race, thanking his fellow competitors for their good behaviour. Coulthard's performance in Austria underlined his suitability for a place in the McLaren-Mercedes team next season.

His team-mate Mika Hakkinen also showed his abilities when fending off a series of furious attacks by Michael Schumacher that began immediately after the return of the safety car to the pits. The reason for Schumacher's haste in attempting to gain the lead lay in the different racing strategies adopted by the two teams – whereas Ferrari planned two stops, McLaren opted for just one. Despite the heavier fuel load carried by the McLaren, the Ferrari driver experienced the greatest difficulty when trying to get past Hakkinen.

Pushing to the limit

Michael Schumacher was continually pushing his car to the limits to put the McLaren driver under pressure – in the hope that the Finn would make mistakes. When asked whether Hakkinen allowed himself to be made nervous by Schumacher, the Mercedes sports manager Norbert Haug answered dryly: "We do not bother to translate German newspapers for Mika, so none of this reaches him. And even if it did, his Scandinavian ancestry gives him the advantage of the right genes. He is cool and stays cool." Haug's estimate was impressively confirmed in the race. The Finnish driver skilfully countered every one of Schumacher's attacks, not once making a mistake.

In fact, any errors that were made were made by Schumacher himself. He flew off the track during his first attempt to take Hakkinen, temporarily losing second place to Fisichella who had been patiently lurking behind the two sparring partners.

Race Results

1	Hakkinen	1:30:44.086
2	Coulthard	1:30:49.375
3	M. Schumacher	1:31:23.176
4	Irvine	1:31:28.062
5	R. Schumacher	1:31:34.740
6	Villeneuve	1:31:37.288

Drivers' Championship

1	Hakkinen	66 points
2	M. Schumacher	58 points
3	Coulthard	36 points
4	Irvine	32 points
5	Wurz	17 points
6	Fisichella	15 points
7	Villeneuve	12 points
8	Frentzen	8 points
9	Barrichello	4 points
10	Salo	3 points
	= Alesi	3 points
	= R. Schumacher	3 points

Constructors' Championship

1	McLaren-Mercedes	102 points
2	Ferrari	90 points
3	Benetton-Mecachrome	32 points
4	Williams-Mecachrome	20 points
5	Stewart-Ford	5 points
6	Arrows-Hart	4 points
	= Sauber-Petronas	4 points
8	Jordan-Mugen-Honda	3 points

After Austria, the World Championship seemed possible for Hakkinen.

AUSTRIAN GRAND PRIX

Ferrari driver Michael Schumacher left the track at speed in the 17th lap . . . and his car suffered substantial damage as a consequence.

After his trip across the gravel, Schumacher drove his Ferrari back to the pits to repair the damage.

Fisichella was unable to hold his position for very long, however. Schumacher outbraked and then overtook Fisichella, and resumed the relentless pressure on Hakkinen.

During lap 17, when approaching the right-hand bend after the start-finish line, Schumacher pushed his car over the limit. He lost control and hurtled his Ferrari into the gravel, causing damage to its nose and barge board. This forced him to make an unplanned pitstop for repairs and for early refuelling, thus putting paid to any chance of a Ferrari victory.

Speaking of the accident later, Schumacher conceded that he had made a driving error: "It was a stupid mistake. I came in too fast, the car ran on to the marbles – and I was off. That cost a lot of time. The nose of the car had vanished and the left-hand guide panel had been torn off. Something happened to the underbody as well. Considering the force with which I skidded off, I was pleasantly surprised by the car's handling after the stop in the pit."

Ralf versus Michael

Schumacher reacted to the setback in a characteristically positive manner, and began the fight back for a place in the points. On the 54th lap, the German came up behind his brother Ralf, then in fifth place. The Jordan driver used the opportunity to show the racing community that he was "a genuine racing driver." He skilfully countered three attacks by his brother before the latter finally dealt with him in the Gösser curve. Ralf was praised by Michael: "Ralf was not easy to beat. I only narrowly missed ramming him once. No one can suggest that he did not fight hard."

Not surprisingly, Schumacher had few problems with his team-mate Eddie Irvine, then lying in third place. Ferrari's number two driver demonstrated how to follow team orders without infringing FIA rules. When Schumacher was behind him, Irvine's lap time slowed by two seconds. Schumacher had no real difficulty in passing Irvine, even though Irvine attempted to explain his sudden loss of speed as a technical problem. "I had trouble with the brakes," stated Irvine to the press after the race. But this explanation only produced amused looks from the other teams – particularly since he suddenly and seemingly effortlessly resumed his previous speed after Schumacher's overtaking manoeuvre.

Hakkinen's ire

The McLaren-Mercedes team – who had provoked the FIA into forbidding "team orders" after their "gentlemen's agreement" during the first Grand Prix in Australia – did not make an official protest in Austria. Nevertheless, the result of the controversial Silverstone race was still sticking in Mika Hakkinen's throat. Before driving over the finishing line, he ironically radioed to his team colleagues in the pits to enquire whether, like Schumacher in Britain, he should finish in the pit lane.

While the four top places were held by McLaren and Ferrari, Ralf Schumacher came in fifth to bring in some more Championship points for the still under-achieving Jordan team. Ralf's team-mate, Damon Hill, came in seventh, a reflection of his poor 15th place on the grid. Hill had found the qualifying session highly frustrating, and tacitly criticized the team for their failure to get him out for the last five minutes of the session: "We really do need to be getting these things right," he said.

In Austria, a good grid position is almost essential for success in the race, a hard fact underlined by the unexceptional performance of local Austrian hero Alexander Wurz. In marked contrast to the success of Benetton's Fisichella, who gained pole position, Wurz only managed to qualify in an undeniably poor 17th place. As a consequence, he was held up by traffic throughout the race and only achieved ninth position. The small Austrian crowd at the A1-Ring went home with little to rejoice about. Maybe next year Wurz will put on a victorious show for the fans.

Ralf Schumacher (left) did not make things easy for his brother Michael when the Ferrari pressed hard to take the lead from the Jordan.

PRACTICE

All a question of timing

Qualification for the Austrian Grand Prix was a race against the weather as well as the clock. The heavens opened at the very start of the session, forcing the drivers to tip-toe their way around the track.

The rain stopped during the final 20 minutes of the hour-long session, allowing the track to begin drying. Business then began in earnest. The Schumacher brothers tried first, followed by Frentzen. Their performance at that point gave every indication that the first three starting places would be occupied by German-speaking drivers.

Ultimately, the best times were achieved by Sauber driver Jean Alesi and Benetton's Giancarlo Fisichella. Just 12 seconds before the end of the session, Alesi passed the finishing line with a time of 1:30.317 min and seemed sure to have achieved pole position. But only five seconds before the flag fell at the end of qualifying, Fisichella bettered the Frenchman's time with 1:29.598 min. "I don't believe it!", cried the Italian.

Mika Hakkinen was third and Michael Schumacher fourth, while Coulthard only managed to secure a surprisingly poor 14th place.

Benetton driver Giancarlo Fisichella achieved his first pole position.

Practice Results

1	Fisichella	Benetton-Mecachrome	1:29.598
2	Alesi	Sauber-Petronas	1:30.317
3	Hakkinen	McLaren-Mercedes	1:30.517
4	M. Schumacher	Ferrari	1:30.551
5	Barrichello	Stewart-Ford	1:31.005
6	Salo	Arrows-Hart	1:31.028
7	Frentzen	Williams-Mecachrome	1:31.515
8	Irvine	Ferrari	1:31.651
9	R. Schumacher	Jordan-Mugen-Honda	1:31.917
10	Panis	Prost-Peugeot	1:32.081
11	Villeneuve	Williams-Mecachrome	1:32.083
12	Verstappen	Stewart-Ford	1:32.099
13	Diniz	Arrows-Hart	1:32.206
14	Coulthard	McLaren-Mercedes	1:32.399
15	Hill	Jordan-Mugen-Honda	1:32.718
16	Trulli	Prost-Peugeot	1:32.906
17	Wurz	Benetton-Mecachrome	1:33.185
18	Herbert	Sauber-Petronas	1:33.205
19	Tuero	Minardi-Ford	1:33.399
20	Takagi	Tyrrell-Ford	1:34.090
21	Nakano	Minardi-Ford	1:34.536
22	Rosset	Tyrrell-Ford	1:34.910

CIRCUIT

The A1-Ring

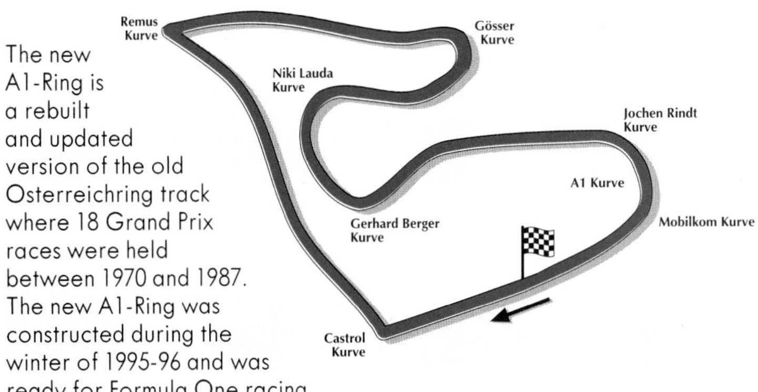

The new A1-Ring is a rebuilt and updated version of the old Osterreichring track where 18 Grand Prix races were held between 1970 and 1987. The new A1-Ring was constructed during the winter of 1995-96 and was ready for Formula One racing in the following year.

The exhilarating high-speed character of the previous track has been retained in the new A1-Ring. Its long, sweeping corners always prove to be a test for both man and machine, although the drivers can experience difficulties in overtaking.

Track length 4.321 km (2.684 miles)
Race distance 306.808 km (190.564 miles) – 71 laps
1997 winner Jacques Villeneuve, Williams-Renault
Lap record 1:11.814 min, Jacques Villeneuve, Williams-Renault, 1997

CALENDAR

1 August
The Grand Prix calendar for next year is presented to the team chiefs in Hockenheim. The only change from the 1998 season is the introduction of a Malaysian Grand Prix, which will take place in October 1999.

Mercedes announce that Mika Hakkinen and David Coulthard are having their contracts renewed for another year.

After an accident, Tyrrell driver Ricardo Rosset follows the recommendation of race doctor Professor Sid Watkins and withdraws from the final practice for the German Grand Prix. According to the regulations, a driver who does not participate in the final practice day cannot start in the Grand Prix.

2 August
McLaren triumph in the German Grand Prix. Mika Hakkinen and David Coulthard celebrate their fifth double victory in the current season.

13 August
At the Hungaroring, Williams driver Jacques Villeneuve once more turns up in the drivers' paddock with a new hair colour. This time his hair is brown.

14 August
A mass is celebrated in Maranello in memory of Enzo Ferrari, who died 10 years ago today.

16 August
Michael Schumacher wins the Hungarian Grand Prix at the Hungaroring, followed by David Coulthard and Jacques Villeneuve.

Four hours after the Hungarian Grand Prix, Williams driver Heinz Harald Frentzen is flown to a Vienna hospital suffering from exhaustion. Before the race, Frentzen had been fed intravenously. Even so, he continued to suffer from diarrhoea and feverish shivering.

Exhausted: Heinz Harald Frentzen

19 August
Vienna: Heinz Harald Frentzen is improving and can leave the hospital after his problems in Hungary. The diagnosis is gastro-enteritis.

The South African head of state Nelson Mandela meets Formula One boss Bernie Ecclestone in an attempt to secure a Grand Prix race for South Africa. But Kyalami is not included in a first draft of the 1999 season.

28 August
Spa-Francorchamps: The Arrows driver Mika Salo and World Champion Jacques Villeneuve survive uninjured after serious accidents during Friday's practice session.

30 August
Belgian Grand Prix: The most serious multiple collision in the history of Formula One takes place, although there are no serious injuries, except perhaps to Michael Schumacher's pride. The eventual victor of the race was Jordan driver Damon Hill, closely followed by his team-mate Ralf Schumacher, with Sauber driver Jean Alesi taking third spot.

1–31 August
Gary Anderson, the Jordan chief technician, accepts an offer of a job from the Arrows chief Tom Walkinshaw. A disagreement between Eddie Jordan and Anderson, and the engagement of the designer Mike Gascoyne, leads to the change of personnel.

The Jordan test driver Pedro de la Rosa, the Nippon Formula One champion in 1997, is hoping to compete in his first Formula One season. He is currently conducting negotiations with the Stewart team.

The course in Zandvoort in the Netherlands will undergo extension and improvement during November. The Dutch racing authorities want to bring Formula One back to Zandvoort from the year 2000 onwards. The last Grand Prix on this track took place in 1985.

The race in Jerez, Spain, planned to take place in October, between the Luxembourg Grand Prix and the Japanese Grand Prix, has been crossed off this year's racing calendar.

Former Formula One World Champions and new administrators of the Jacarepagua race track in Rio de Janeiro, Emerson Fittipaldi and Nelson Piquet, wish to hold the Brazilian Grand Prix at Jacarepagua from as early as 1999. The Brazilian Grand Prix took place on this circuit from 1978 to 1989.

McLaren-Mercedes drivers Mika Hakkinen and David Coulthard star in a commercial for the Mercedes A-Class hatchback.

There are rumours that Honda may return to Formula One as early as next year. The Honda President Hiroyuki Yoshino has confirmed that a Formula One car is to be tested in November.

Hopes that a Grand Prix would be held in China next year are dashed. The main reasons given for the cancellation are an inadequate infrastructure and the possibility of oppressive reporting restrictions.

Swansea's Institute of Higher Education is offering students a degree course in motorsport engineering and design.

According to information from a German magazine, leading Russian politicians and businessmen are planning the construction of a circuit near Moscow.

Despite rumours to the contrary, there will be no change of drivers at Prost-Peugeot: Olivier Panis and Jarno Trulli will continue to drive for the French team in 1999.

Quotes
"I am praying that Ferrari will win the World Championship title this year because whenever they win a title, they fall into a deep sleep."
Benetton driver Alexander Wurz looking forward to 1999 in *Bild am Sonntag*.

"... Eddie Irvine, whom Schumacher treats at times in the same way that Don Quixote treats his page Sancho Panza."
From *Stern* magazine.

"I thought, oh dear, this is going to hurt."
Jacques Villeneuve recalling his spectacular crash during Friday's qualifying session for the Belgian Grand Prix.

BACKGROUND

A waste of bubbly?

The "champagne shower" on the winner's podium has become a familiar ritual at the end of every Grand Prix. But is it simply a waste of an excellent drink?

If the historians of motorsport are to be believed, the champagne ritual became one of the sport's traditions by pure chance. When the Swiss racing driver Jo Siffert topped the performance figures for the Le Mans 24-Hour race in 1966, he was given a magnum of champagne in recognition of the feat. Siffert shook the bottle joyously until the cork popped and the contents sprayed out. Carried away by the excitement of the occasion, the Swiss driver sprayed the fans with the bubbly – and the champagne shower had been born.

The champagne ritual found more and more adherents over the year, until champagne manufacturers Louis-Vuitton-Moët-Hennessy decided to turn this frivolous closing ceremony into an advertising stunt.

When it turned out that the association of the Moët et Chandon brand with Formula One was capable of boosting sales of the drink to a substantial extent, the Formula One authorities naturally wanted to take a cut for themselves. The FIA now charges Moët et Chandon some three million dollars for the privilege of having their champagne shaken up at Formula One events.

It is regrettable that a gesture of joyous spontaneity should have become, in the end, just another sign of the commercialization of sport.

Mika Hakkinen and Heinz Harald Frentzen in the champagne shower.

NEWSFLASH

Bomb threat

Reports of a plan to carry out a bomb attack caused a stir before the Belgian Grand Prix. The police in Spa took the bomb threat seriously and established a high-profile presence at the race circuit.

An anonymous letter was sent to local newspaper *Le Jour-Le Courrier* demanding that Formula One boss Bernie Ecclestone pay 10 million Belgian francs to the French charity Médecins sans Frontieres, currently working to aid famine victims in the Sudan. Otherwise, according to the letter, a bomb would be exploded at the circuit before the start of the race.

Other letters, sent to a variety of locations, specifically threatened attacks on Ferrari and on Ecclestone himself. The Belgian authorities set up a special commission to investigate the threats and intensified security at the circuit. Plainclothes police officers patrolled the drivers' paddock and the pits.

Fortunately, the spectre of a terrorist attack evaporated as it had in 1996, when a bomb threat received at Hockenheim turned out to be a hoax. The Belgian police eventually dismissed this year's threats as being "simply mischievous".

HISTORY

For many years, Jackie Stewart (left and above) and Ken Tyrrell (inset above) were unbeatable. In 1999, the Tyrrell name will be lost to Formula One.

Tyrrell bows out

Team boss Ken Tyrrell retired from Formula One this year, after playing a starring role for more than 30 years. The 73-year-old will be remembered as one of the great legends of Grand Prix.

The rise of Ken Tyrrell began with French aerospace company Matra's entry into Formula One in 1968. Matra had already been involved in the construction of Formula Two and Formula Three vehicles since 1964. In 1967, the French government gave it a subsidy of six million francs for a major Formula One project. The French were determined to make their mark in the world's most prestigious racing series. With additional sponsorship from French oil company Elf, two Matra teams were created simultaneously – the works team Matra-Elf and Matra International, which was handed over to former timber merchant Ken Tyrrell to run.

Tyrrell had already managed Formula Two and Formula Three teams that had earned a reputation for outstanding professionalism. In addition, Tyrrell was able to bring with him to Formula One an exceptionally talented principal driver, Scotsman Jackie Stewart.

Tyrrell and Stewart demonstrated their ability immediately in their first Formula One season. Long-established teams were astonished at the precisely organized manner in which the crew worked. On the track, an enthusiastic public applauded Stewart's bold driving style, reminiscent of Jim Clark. At the end of the first season, the Scot had three Grand Prix victories to his name and was second in the World Championship with 36 points. The following year, the Tyrrell team set out to go one better. A perfectly tuned Matra MS 80, with the superb Jackie Stewart at the wheel, won the Drivers' and Constructors' Championships.

Going it alone

Matra and Tyrrell split up in 1970. The French company joined up with Simca and Chrysler. Tyrrell had to manage without the Ford V8 Cosworth engines he had used previously. But because he considered Ford engines to be the best power units, he bought from March Type 701 racing cars, which had the engines he wanted. His team soon discovered, however, that the rest of the March vehicle was out of date. So Tyrrell decided to have his own vehicle built while the season was still in progress. The Tyrrell 01 was equipped with a Ford engine and was based on a design by Derek Gardner. It immediately proved to be a great success. Stewart and the Tyrrell team were on a high again and once more won the World Championship.

On the way out

Jackie Stewart won the title for a third time in 1973, but this was the last high point for Tyrrell. Stewart retired as a Grand Prix driver and the team's fortunes went downhill. Like many teams in the mid-1970s, Tyrrell lost out as the sport became increasingly dependent on finance from rich and powerful sponsors. Lacking adequate financial backing, the team became more and more mediocre. Year in and year out, it struggled to keep pace with the richest teams.

Ken Tyrrell finally gave up the fight at the end of 1997, selling his team to British American Tobacco (BAT) for $29 million. His final departure from Formula One took place in 1998. After a dispute with the team's new owner, it became clear that there was no further place for Tyrrell in Formula One.

Reflecting Hakkinen's growing popularity in Germany, the banner states: "Masterly, Intelligent, Knowledgeable, Athletic". Meanwhile, Schumacher (below right) seeks divine inspiration.

Black
grüßen

The German Grand Prix gave World Champion Jacques Villeneuve his first podium finish of the season.

German requiem for Schumi

2 August, Hockenheim. The home crowd wanted Schumacher to win, but instead they had to content themselves with a "one-two" from McLaren-Mercedes.

From the outset, Mika Hakkinen and David Coulthard were determined to provide engine-supplier Mercedes with their first home victory since 1954. The two drivers raced into the first bend, and then kept the lead throughout the entire race.

This decisive McLaren victory was sufficient reason for Mercedes director Jürgen Hubbert to adopt a surprisingly upbeat approach towards the season's prospects: "The drivers and the team now know that they can manage it. It is not only individual victories we want now, it's the title."

Scottish support act?

The German Grand Prix also produced a reply to the frequently asked question – whether David Coulthard would be allowed to drive without team orders and go for the title himself? From the incidents during the course of the race, the answer seemed to be in the negative.

As the two Silver Arrows entered the 36th lap, Hakkinen began to slow. His car was leaking oil, and although it did not prove a major problem for the Finn, it unfortunately coated Coulthard's car in oil by the end of the race. Hakkinen was also concerned that he had not taken on sufficient fuel during his pit-stop. His team told him to reduce his fuel-air mixture, which in turn had the effect of reducing the power of his McLaren.

As a result, Coulthard was able to come up right behind Hakkinen, although he gave little appearance of trying to attack his team-mate. Asked the reason for his reserved driving style and his failure to overtake Hakkinen, Coulthard commented: "That's just not possible with a car which is almost identical in set-up, engine power, and braking capability." It was a nicely diplomatic reply, but it fooled no one in the pit-lane.

If the McLaren performance at Hockenheim was yet another confirmation of their dominance on fast circuits, then the race also provided an opportunity for another team to make a good impression

Iuch had been expected of Jordan at ıe start of the season, but until now ıat promise had not been fulfiled.

After a successful start, Jordan river Ralf Schumacher pushed up ehind the McLarens hoping to get ast Coulthard. But unlike most of ıe other drivers, Ralf had decided on two-stop strategy. It was a risky ption that, in the end, did not work. Ie was unable to pass the McLarens nd had to come into the pits and efuel early on the 14th lap.

The thinking behind the Jordan ecision was not so much tactical as ommercial. Team boss Eddie Jordan easoned that if Ralf started with a ghter fuel load, he could get ahead f the McLarens and lead the race for few laps. This would then provide ıain sponsors Benson & Hedges with xtended television coverage.

Despite this setback, the Jordan river – who had been gaining points ince the British Grand Prix – ıanaged sixth place. Although pleased rith the result, Ralf Schumacher claimed that a technical fault had prevented him from gaining a higher placing: "After the first stop I had a problem, probably a defective damper, and then things did not go well. I believe that without this defect and even with two stops, a fourth place would have been possible."

Over to Hill

The fourth place was, instead, taken by his team-mate Damon Hill. After a succession of problems in previous races, the result at Hockenheim came as a great relief for Hill. Bad luck had dogged him throughout the first half of the season, and some observers began to question his motivation. Championship points proved to be the best answer to his critics.

The good placings of his drivers certainly improved Eddie Jordan's mood. In the middle of the season there had been rumours that Jordan planned to replace one or both drivers. At Hockenheim, Jordan informed the press that he saw no reason for a

IcLaren's two-seater gave boxer Henry Maske a ride.

PRACTICE

A monument to despair, Michael Schumacher contemplates the double whammy of being out-qualified by his team-mate and by his younger brother.

Schumacher fails to cut the mustard

While the two McLarens maintained their traditional good form in qualifying at the front row of the grid, it was interesting to see the different racing styles and set-ups employed by each driver.

David Coulthard's car ran with a smaller wing than his team-mate. This enabled him to reach a speed of 357 km/h (222 mph) on the straight immediately before the Jim Clark chicane. Although Mika Hakkinen was not able to achieve this speed, the higher downforce that came with a bigger wing allowed him to negotiate the slower Stadium section more quickly. As a result, Hakkinen gained half-a-second overall.

Michael Schumacher had hoped to come close alongside the McLarens, but a series of misfortunes and mistakes sent him back to the fifth row of the grid. To make matters worse, he was easily out-qualified by his team-mate Eddie Irvine.

If Michael Schumacher failed to impress, then the German fans gained some consolation from the fine performance of Schumacher junior. He pipped team-mate Damon Hill and secured a place on the second row beside Jacques Villeneuve. The Canadian, who had already been written off for the season, was only a fraction of a second behind Coulthard. Villeneuve exploited his good qualifying result by taking a good-natured swipe at Michael Schumacher: "It seems to me that Michael is getting a bit nervous. He drives out and in, hither and thither – something is not quite right."

Practice Results

1	Hakkinen	McLaren-Mercedes	1:41.838
2	Coulthard	McLaren-Mercedes	1:42.347
3	Villeneuve	Williams-Mecachrome	1:42.365
4	R. Schumacher	Jordan-Mugen-Honda	1:42.994
5	Hill	Jordan-Mugen-Honda	1:43.183
6	Irvine	Ferrari	1:43.270
7	Wurz	Benetton-Mecachrome	1:43.341
8	Fisichella	Benetton-Mecachrome	1:43.369
9	M. Schumacher	Ferrari	1:43.459
10	Frentzen	Williams-Mecachrome	1:43.467
11	Alesi	Sauber-Petronas	1:43.663
12	Herbert	Sauber-Petronas	1:44.599
13	Barrichello	Stewart-Ford	1:44.776
14	Trulli	Prost-Peugeot	1:44.844
15	Takagi	Tyrrell-Ford	1:44.961
16	Panis	Prost-Peugeot	1:45.197
17	Salo	Arrows-Hart	1:45.276
18	Diniz	Arrows-Hart	1:45.588
19	Verstappen	Stewart-Ford	1:45.623
20	Nakano	Minardi-Ford	1:46.713
21	Tuero	Minardi-Ford	1:47.265
NON QUALIFIER			
22	Rosset	Tyrrell-Ford	untimed

Mika Hakkinen spins his McLaren during a practice session at Hockenheim.

replacement of any kind. And yet some uncertainty remained, with doubts raised by Schumacher's manager Willi Weber, who wanted to see his protégé with BAR (British-American Racing) in the coming year. In this team, Ralf Schumacher would find himself beside another ex-champion – Jacques Villeneuve.

Podium finish

Villeneuve, who had been repeatedly sidelined before Hockenheim, re-emerged as a major player in Grand Prix racing when he took third place. Villeneuve demonstrated that he had lost neither his technique nor his enjoyment of racing. During the final stages of the race, when the McLarens began to slow, it seemed for a time that he might get past Coulthard.

"I had a poor start," observed Villeneuve, "but then it went quite well. I was even able to put some pressure on the McLarens and I hung in there very well. When Mika had problems, I wanted to attack once again but something broke on my car and I had to slow down myself."

Despite Villeneuve's claim that he was forced to ease the pressure, this was not how it seemed to the two McLaren drivers. Coulthard was trying to protect Hakkinen from the Williams driver, but because his mirrors were covered by oil from Hakkinen's car he had difficulty in seeing the Williams bearing down on him. "I knew Jacques was closing," said Coulthard later, "and I knew he'd have a go if it got to within a second. They were a long last few laps."

Ferrari failure

Michael Schumacher had a wretched race on his home turf. After a badly bungled qualifying session, that saw him start from ninth place, Schumacher was barely able to fight his way up to fifth place by the end of the race – and gain a mere two points. Although it did look as if he could make life difficult for his old rival Damon Hill, Schumacher played this down: "It is quite true that I came closer to Damon for a while. But then I demanded too much from the tyres. Hill certainly had reserves still. I am very sorry that I was not able to do a bit better for my fans."

While Mika Hakkinen had gained maximum points from the races in Austria and Germany, Schumacher had collected just six, leaving an overall gap of 16 points. Yet Schumacher remained optimistic: "The World Championship result is obviously pretty poor up until now. However, the Ferrari should be more competitive in Hungary. And we should also look better in Belgium."

Savouring the moment of victory: David Coulthard (left) and Mika Hakkinen.

Even this worn-for-a-dare headgear could not save Schumacher from failure in his home country.

Race Results

1	Hakkinen	1:20:47.984
2	Coulthard	1:20:48.410
3	Villeneuve	1:20:50.561
4	Hill	1:20:55.169
5	M. Schumacher	1:21:00.597
6	R. Schumacher	1:21:17.722

Drivers' Championship

1	Hakkinen	76 points
2	M. Schumacher	60 points
3	Coulthard	42 points
4	Irvine	32 points
5	Wurz	17 points
6	Villeneuve	16 points
7	Fisichella	15 points
8	Frentzen	8 points
9	Barrichello	4 points
	= R. Schumacher	4 points

Constructors' Championship

1	McLaren-Mercedes	118 points
2	Ferrari	92 points
3	Benetton-Mecachrome	32 points
4	Williams-Mecachrome	24 points
5	Jordan-Mugen-Honda	7 points
6	Stewart-Ford	5 points
7	Arrows-Hart	4 points
	= Sauber-Petronas	4 points

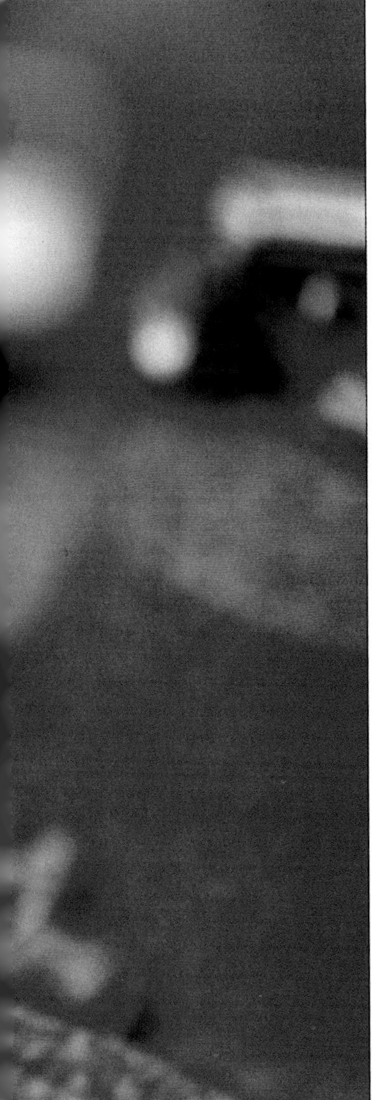

BACKGROUND

"We do not need Schumacher"

Even before the start of the 1998 season, rumours were rife that Michael Schumacher would move over from Ferrari to join the McLaren team. These rumours were fuelled by the belief that Mercedes wanted a German driver on board, someone who would be better able to promote the Mercedes brand name than a non-German. Of course, there was also the added fact that a driver of Schumacher's ability would be in the running to win a World Championship for his team!

Mercedes boss Dr Jürgen Schremp (left) and motorsport Manager Norbert Haug appear suitably satisfied with Hakkinen and Coulthard's performance.

Drivers confirmed

However, speculation about the switch to a new driver ended in Hockenheim. Those responsible at Mercedes let it be known that drivers Mika Hakkinen and David Coulthard would remain in the McLaren team for the next season's Championship.

McLaren team boss Ron Dennis was thought to be less than keen to have Schumacher as part of the team. During the 1980s he had built up one of the great racing teams within Formula One. Dennis had worked with some of the best and most difficult drivers on the Grand Prix circuit, including Niki Lauda, Alain Prost, and Ayrton Senna. While admiring their driving skills, Dennis believed that they and the motor racing public did not fully appreciate the role the McLaren team and the car had played in their many successes. Consequently, he was concerned that employing such a high profile driver might affect the balance of the team.

Nevertheless, the wishes of the engine partner had persuaded McLaren-Mercedes to take part in preliminary negotiations with Schumacher – but without success. It may have been the statement by Mercedes boss Jürgen Schremp – "We do not need Schumacher" – or the lack of enthusiasm from Ron Dennis, but in July 1998 Michael Schumacher extended his contract with Ferrari to the year 2002.

BAR on Villeneuve

McLaren also flirted briefly with the 1997 World Champion Jacques Villeneuve, but again the tentative negotiations led nowhere. The new BAR team was co-owned by Villeneuve's manager Craig Pollack, and so it was not surprising that the Canadian driver should leave Williams for BAR.

Another factor influencing McLaren-Mercedes were opinion poll results that revealed that Mika Hakkinen was becoming increasingly popular in Germany. This fact was highly influential in Mercedes' marketing strategy for their consumer cars.

The confirmation that the Hakkinen/Coulthard line-up would continue into 1999 boosted morale in the McLaren camp where both drivers were proving very popular. Certainly, the two drivers showed their worth at Hockenheim. They dominated qualifying, set the fastest lap of the race, and ensured a maximum-points victory for the team. McLaren were now moving ever nearer to winning the Constructors' Championship and Mika Hakkinen the Drivers' Championship.

CIRCUIT

Hockenheim Ring

One of the longest of the Grand Prix circuits, Hockenheim is divided into two distinct sections with different racing characteristics. The main part of the track comprises a series of fast straights and corners. These are set against the much slower stadium complex with its very tight corners before the start-finish line.

As a result, car set-up is very difficult to manage correctly. Sufficient downforce is needed for the stadium complex, yet this will slow the car down on the long straights. Ultimately, the car set-up will have to be a compromise to suit the individual driver's racing style.

Track length 6.829 km (4.239 miles)
Race distance 307.035 km (190.755 miles) – 45 laps
1997 winner Gerhard Berger, Benetton-Renault
Lap record 1:41.590 min, Riccardo Patrese, Williams-Renault

HUNGARIAN GRAND PRIX

Ferrari win it with brains and Brawn

16 August, Budapest. Ferrari had to wait almost ten years before the Italian team could again celebrate victory at the Hungaroring. Success was made possible by an ingenious pitstop strategy conceived by Ross Brawn, the Ferrari technical director. Meanwhile, Schumacher drove the race of his life to make sure the strategy worked for Ferrari.

The tension was apparent in the Ferrari camp before the start of the race – McLaren had to be stopped from walking away with the World Championship. After the bungled Hockenheim weekend, Ferrari had been testing their cars around the clock at their home base in Fiorano. They even went so far as to put the track under water in blazing sunshine to practise for a possible downpour during the race in Hungary.

During the early stages of the race, it seemed that Ferrari's Michael Schumacher would be no match for the Silver Arrows. Even before the first right-hand bend, Schumacher had been forced to battle with Damon Hill to avoid losing contact with the McLarens. In the event, Schumacher was able to push Hill aside before proceeding to chase down the leading pair. Schumacher was shielded by team-mate Eddie Irvine, who had passed Hill early on in the race.

The Hungarian circuit does not lend itself to easy overtaking manoeuvres. The combination of narrow track and short straights had led the Hungaroring to be called "Monaco without the houses". In such a race, the drivers needed to be patient and to trust their instincts. For their part, the spectators had to be content with watching a procession.

Crossing the Jordan

Damon Hill inherited fourth place from Eddie Irvine during lap 14 when Irvine was forced to retire with a defective gearbox. Hill – who had sensationally taken second place in the previous year when driving a completely inferior Arrow – followed up his success at Hockenheim with a second successive fourth place.

After a terrible start to the year, things were suddenly looking up for Hill and Jordan. When transmission problems slowed Mika Hakkinen's car towards the end of the race, Hill had hoped to climb even further up the ladder, but he was overhauled by the Williams of Jacques Villeneuve who confirmed his great performance in Germany with a fine third place.

"It would have been fantastic to keep Villeneuve behind me and finish on the podium," said Hill, "but there was nothing I could do. He was on the harder tyre and every time I pulled away he caught up as my rubber began to go off. I could see Frentzen closing at the end too, but managed to hold him off by putting in my fastest lap just two laps before the finish. If we keep on going like this we should end up with a podium finish."

Heinz Harald Frentzen, though still weakened by the stomach bug that had affected him at Hockenheim, was fifth. Thus, the third and fifth places gained at the Hungaroring represented another step in the long and painful Williams revival. It had been a long time coming.

Ferrari masterstroke

At the head of the race, events seemed to be taking a predictable course, with the two McLarens safely in the lead, followed by Schumacher's Ferrari. Schumacher, who had made a first pitstop in the 26th lap, suddenly and unexpectedly made an extremely short second stop in the 43rd lap. It suddenly dawned on the other teams – who were all employing a two-stop strategy – that Ferrari's tactic was based on taking three pitstops.

In Schumacher's hands, at least, the advantages of lighter fuel loads and improved tyre performance just about outweighed the time disadvantage of a third pitstop. But it was always a risky decision, especially as Schumacher had to drive at, and sometimes beyond, the limit.

Spinning to disaster?

On lap 52 Schumacher came dangerously close to disaster when his Ferrari spun off the track on the very last corner of the circuit. "At that moment, I was driving at qualifying speed, and may well have overdone things somewhat," admitted Schumacher at the end of the race. But with fortune seemingly favouring the bold, he managed to control the Ferrari and get back on the track, having lost only five seconds to the McLarens.

After Schumacher had taken the lead – when the McLarens made their pitstops – the moment of truth arrived on the 62nd lap. It was then that Schumacher, who at this point had a time buffer of 26.9 seconds over David Coulthard, raced into the pit lane for the third time. Would Schumacher have enough time to return to the track ahead of his McLaren rival?

The pitstop was quick and faultless. Schumacher shot out on to the

Michael Schumacher uplifted by the joy of victory over McLaren.

Schumacher matches the speed of Coulthard's McLaren.

Schumacher in the lead after Hakkinen's second stop.

rack in the lead. Coulthard was five econds down and had no hope of atching the speeding Ferrari, which rossed the finish line a full ten econds clear of Coulthard's McLaren.

Schumacher was delighted with is victory in Hungary: "You dream bout the ideal results, and the naximum I thought I could achieve vas a win, with Mika second. It was n emotional situation down here. It as been a while since Ferrari won ere, and it's fantastic to do it in front f so many fans. It's one of the nicest vins I've had, to be honest."

Schumacher certainly drove a rilliant race. But, arguably, the reater glory belonged to Ross Brawn, errari technical director. Brawn was the man who had worked out the successful pitstop strategy – although he had thought long and hard before taking the risk. It was only when Schumacher had got stuck behind David Coulthard that Brawn decided to bring his driver into the pits for the unscheduled stop – a decision that gave Ferrari victory.

McLaren's failings

Ferrari, of course, benefited from the problems affecting Hakkinen's McLaren. After his second pitstop the Finn began to slow, losing two to three seconds a lap to Schumacher. After the race, the McLaren mechanics found that the problem had been caused by a failure of the control system in the front suspension. "The auto was sliding around like a raw egg on ice. It is a miracle that Mika brought the car to the finish at all and saved one point," stated a visibly disappointed Norbert Haug, who was not even to be consoled by David Coulthard's second place.

Another factor that helped Ferrari were the Goodyear tyres, here clearly superior to McLaren's Bridgestones. Of his tyres Coulthard complained: "Under braking I was locking up the fronts on entry, then when I went on the power I was sliding the rear through lack of traction. It was the maximum we could get from the car, which made it physically hard. I just couldn't get the car plugged in, and it was very uncomfortable. There's a bit of work to do on the tyre front." In contrast, Ross Brawn sang the praises of his tyres: "The Goodyear was durable. The compounds are now superb. Those who wrote us off after Hockenheim were a little premature."

The balance shifts

Hakkinen's failure and Schumacher's success opened up the World Championship once again. The Finn's lead had been reduced to a mere seven points and the ball was now back in McLaren's court. Schumacher eagerly anticipated the remaining races: "Seven points behind with four races to go, that is practically nothing. The struggle for the title is fully open."

David Coulthard: "We should also have used three stops".

Mika Hakkinen rues the failure of his McLaren in Hungary.

HUNGARIAN GRAND PRIX

Race Results

1	M. Schumacher	1:45:25.550
2	Coulthard	1:45:34.983
3	Villeneuve	1:46:09.994
4	Hill	1:46:20.626
5	Frentzen	1:46:22.060
6	Hakkinen	1 lap behind

Drivers' Championship

1	Hakkinen	77 points
2	M. Schumacher	70 points
3	Coulthard	48 points
4	Irvine	32 points
5	Villeneuve	20 points
6	Wurz	17 points
7	Fisichella	15 points
8	Frentzen	10 points
9	Hill	6 points
10	Barichello	4 points
	= R. Schumacher	4 points

Constructors' Championship

1	McLaren-Mercedes	125 points
2	Ferrari	102 points
3	Benetton-Mecachrome	32 points
4	Williams-Mecachrome	30 points
5	Jordan-Mugen-Honda	10 points
6	Stewart-Ford	5 points
7	Arrows-Hart	4 points
	= Sauber-Petronas	4 points

The Ferrari pit crew congratulate Schumacher for his superb win over the McLarens.

The two McLarens raced away in first and second, but Schumacher's Ferrari refused to give up the fight.

CIRCUIT

The Hungaroring

The track near Budapest is one of the slower tracks in Formula One. Built in 1986 especially for Grand Prix racing, the track can be both bumpy and slippery. Victory or defeat is decided by good or bad pit and race strategy, as well as a good starting position on the grid. Overtaking manoeuvres are very difficult, and only those who are clearly faster than their rivals have a chance of getting past on the straights.

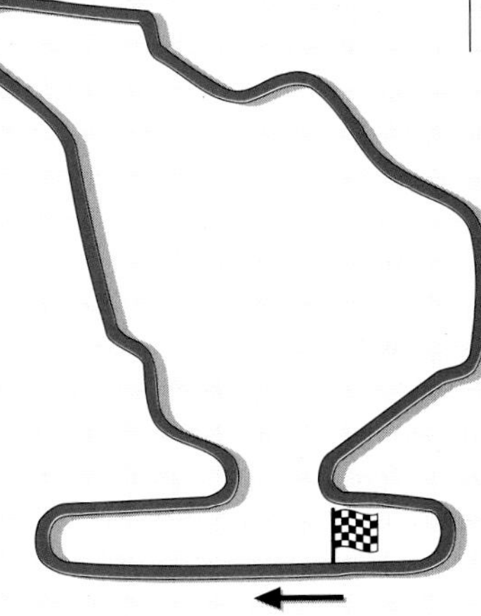

Track length 3.968 km (2.465 miles)
Race distance 305.586 km (189.805 miles) – 77 laps
1997 winner Jacques Villeneuve, Williams-Renault
Lap record 1:18.308 min, Nigel Mansell, Williams-Renault, 1992

The Hungaroring circuit has no bend names.

PRACTICE

Schumi's second-row springboard

During the qualifying session for the Hungarian Grand Prix, the McLaren-Mercedes again burnt the best times into the tarmac. Mika Hakkinen secured pole position in front of his team-mate David Coulthard. For the eleventh time this season, a McLaren had secured pole position.

For Michael Schumacher, who made his effort with hard Goodyear tyres, the best he could achieve was third place. Despite this, Schumacher remained highly optimistic about the forthcoming race: "The pole position was not really to be expected. We have a realistic chance of winning and I think we'll use it."

Damon Hill demonstrated his commitment to Jordan by securing fourth place, although team-mate Ralf Schumacher was only able to manage a distant 10th place.

Practice Results

	Driver	Team	Time
1	Hakkinen	McLaren-Mercedes	1:16.973
2	Coulthard	McLaren-Mercedes	1:17.131
3	M. Schumacher	Ferrari	1:17.366
4	Hill	Jordan-Mugen-Honda	1:18.214
5	Irvine	Ferrari	1:18.325
6	Villeneuve	Williams-Mecachrome	1:18.337
7	Frentzen	Williams-Mecachrome	1:19.029
8	Fisichella	Benetton-Mecachrome	1:19.050
9	Wurz	Benetton-Mecachrome	1:19.063
10	R. Schumacher	Jordan-Mugen-Honda	1:19.171
11	Alesi	Sauber-Petronas	1:19.210
12	Diniz	Arrows-Hart	1:19.706
13	Salo	Arrows-Hart	1:19.712
14	Barrichello	Stewart-Ford	1:19.876
15	Herbert	Sauber-Petronas	1:19.878
16	Trulli	Prost-Peugeot	1:20.042
17	Verstappen	Stewart-Ford	1:20.198
18	Takagi	Tyrrell-Ford	1:20.354
19	Nakano	Minardi-Ford	1:20.635
20	Panis	Prost-Peugeot	1:20.663
21	Tuero	Minardi-Ford	1:21.725
NON-QUALIFIER			
22	Rosset	Tyrrell-Ford	1:23.361

Hill wins first race for Jordan despite collisions

30 AUGUST, SPA. A series of extraordinary multiple collisions made the Belgian Grand Prix one of the most memorable for years. Heavy rain turned into a deluge, as car after car lost control on the track. Tempers flared but Damon Hill won his first race for Jordan.

The most spectacular collision of the season took place only a few seconds into the race. Out of the 22 starters, 12 were converted into piles of scrap. Eddie Irvine tangled with David Coulthard who, when accelerating out of the first bend, lost control of his car and started the chain reaction.

Luckily, with the exception of Rubens Barrichello who received a bruised shoulder, all the drivers clambered out of their cars without real injury. That injuries were so few was a tribute to the high safety standards to be found in Formula One. It could, however, have been very different as many of the wheels flying around as a result of the crash missed members of the public and drivers' helmets by a matter of inches.

Mika out, Hill ahead

When, after an hour or so, the debris had been removed, the drivers who had spare vehicles formed up for a new start. But even the second attempt had its problems. Damon Hill's Jordan got away best and tore into the lead with Mika Hakkinen and Michael Schumacher fighting side by side at the first bend.

Schumacher was on the outside and tried to force past Hakkinen. The McLaren driver resisted but skidded close to the Ferrari. Hakkinen's front tyre touched the side of Schumacher's car. The McLaren then spun about its axis before Johnny Herbert crashed into it and finally put an end to the unfortunate Hakkinen's race.

The new start was also unlucky for the other McLaren driver. After a spot of bother with the Benetton of Alexander Wurz, David Coulthard ran wide into the gravel. Although he

Hakkinen could only hope that his chief rival, Michael Schumacher, would also have problems.

Michael Schumacher approaches David Coulthard's McLaren just before their fateful encounter.

A "three-legged" Schumacher trundles into the pits followed by Coulthard's McLaren.

Surrounded by the press, Schumacher records his unique view of the events.

managed to free himself, he was well behind the field in 14th place. The safety car was ordered on to the track to minimize further accidents.

Later, however, it became clear that this spectacular opening scene was only the curtain-raiser for an even more dramatic afternoon at Spa. When overtaking restrictions were removed, with the return of the safety car to the pits, Hill was leading the two Ferraris and Jacques Villeneuve's Williams. Hill initially defended himself against Schumacher's attacks but the German driver took the lead after a skilful braking manoeuvre before the bus-stop chicane. Schumacher then gave impressive evidence of his driving capabilities in the rain. He raced away from the second-placed Hill and was more than 12 seconds ahead of him by lap 16 when he left the track to make his first pitstop. Hill followed Schumacher into the pits in the same lap.

Race Results

1	Hill	1:43:47.407
2	R. Schumacher	1:43:48.339
3	Alesi	1:43:54.647
4	Frentzen	1:44:19.650
5	Diniz	1:44:39.089
6	Trulli	2 laps behind

Drivers' Championship

1	Hakkinen	77 points
2	M. Schumacher	70 points
3	Coulthard	48 points
4	Irvine	32 points
5	Villeneuve	20 points
6	Wurz	17 points
7	Hill	16 points
8	Fisichella	15 points
9	Frentzen	13 points
10	R. Schumacher	10 points

Constructors' Championship

1	McLaren-Mercedes	125 points
2	Ferrari	102 points
3	Williams-Mecachrome	33 points
4	Benetton-Mecachrome	32 points
5	Jordan-Mugen-Honda	26 points
6	Sauber-Petronas	8 points
7	Arrows-Hart	6 points
8	Stewart-Ford	5 points
9	Prost-Peugeot	1 point

Back on the drenched track, the Ferrari driver increased the tempo still further and, within a few laps, had increased his lead to 30 seconds. Schumacher seemed to be driving towards a certain victory that would have placed him at the top of the World Championship table.

Schumacher's expectation of victory was dashed on lap 25. At that point, the Ferrari caught up with David Coulthard with the intention of lapping him, but the Scotsman did not immediately give way. Instead of waiting for a favourable opportunity to get past, Schumacher became impatient. Amidst plumes of spray,

BELGIAN GRAND PRIX

The victors' podium was dominated by Jordan yellow after the triumph by Damon Hill and Ralf Schumacher.

PRACTICE

Hill outperforms Schumacher

After their modest performance in Budapest, the McLarens showed that they had lost nothing of their power. Mika Hakkinen secured the best lap time, followed by his team-mate David Coulthard who took second place just two-tenths behind him.

To the surprise of the many spectators who turned up for qualifying, Damon Hill's Jordan comprehensively beat Michael Schumacher's Ferrari into fourth place. It was a fine performance from the British driver, and reflected the new-found confidence of Hill and the Jordan team.

Schumacher characteristically dismissed any suggestions that he might face problems from Hill and Jordan, preferring to concentrate on the threat posed by the two menacing McLaren-Mercedes.

Qualifying Results

	Driver	Team	Time
1	Hakkinen	McLaren-Mercedes	1:48.682
2	Coulthard	McLaren-Mercedes	1:48.845
3	Hill	Jordan-Mugen-Honda	1:49.728
4	M. Schumacher	Ferrari	1:50.027
5	Irvine	Ferrari	1:50.189
6	Villeneuve	Williams-Mecachrome	1:50.204
7	Fisichella	Benetton-Mecachrome	1:50.462
8	R. Schumacher	Jordan-Mugen-Honda	1:50.501
9	Frentzen	Williams-Mecachrome	1:50.686
10	Alesi	Sauber-Petronas	1:51.189
11	Wurz	Benetton-Mecachrome	1:51.648
12	Herbert	Sauber-Petronas	1:51.851
13	Trulli	Prost-Peugeot	1:52.572
14	Barrichello	Stewart-Ford	1:52.670
15	Panis	Prost-Peugeot	1:52.784
16	Diniz	Arrows-Hart	1:53.037
17	Verstappen	Stewart-Ford	1:53.149
18	Salo	Arrows-Hart	1:53.207
19	Takagi	Tyrrell-Ford	1:53.237
20	Rosset	Tyrrell-Ford	1:54.850
21	Nakano	Minardi-Ford	1:55.084
22	Rosset	Minardi-Ford	1:55.520

CIRCUIT

Circuit de Spa-Francorchamps

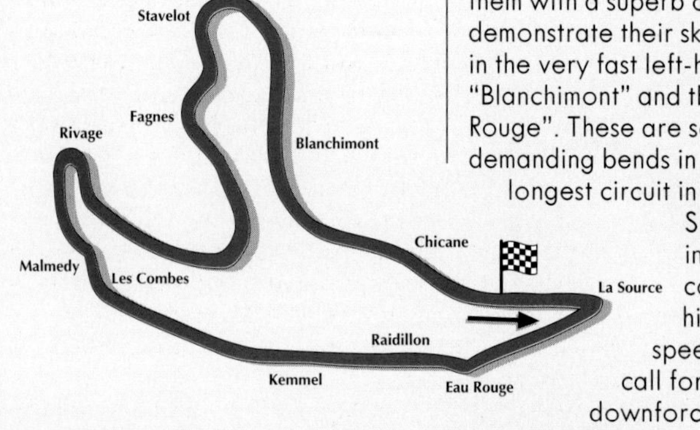

Situated in the hilly and wooded Ardennes region of Belgium, Spa-Francorchamps held its first Formula One race in 1985. The track, which was once a country road, is both winding and undulating. It is popular with the drivers because it presents them with a superb opportunity to demonstrate their skills, particularly in the very fast left-hand bend "Blanchimont" and the downhill "Eau Rouge". These are some of the most demanding bends in motorsport. The longest circuit in Formula One, Spa has an interesting combination of high- and low-speed sections that call for low-to-medium downforce on the cars.

Track length 6.971 km (4.33 miles)
Race distance 306.737 km (190.527 miles) – 44 laps
1997 winner Michael Schumacher, Ferrari
Lap record 1:51.095 minutes, Alain Prost, Williams-Renault, 1993

Fisichella leaps from his flaming Benetton after colliding with Nakano.

The mangled remains of Coulthard's McLaren and Irvine's Ferrari are transported from the track after the aborted first start.

A track marshal attends to Villeneuve's smoking Williams.

Schumacher drove straight into the back of the McLaren. The Ferrari lost its right-hand front wheel and all the associated suspension components. The McLaren, for its part, suffered damage to its rear. Driving in a "funeral procession", Schumacher and Coulthard managed to limp their cars through as far as the pits.

Teutonic fury

An enraged Schumacher leapt out of his car and immediately ran in the direction of the McLaren-Mercedes garage. It was only with difficulty that the McLaren mechanics stopped him from going for Coulthard's throat. Schumacher accused Coulthard of deliberately causing the accident: "The fact that a Formula One driver should take his foot off the accelerator at a speed of 200 is incomprehensible to me.... I must assume that he took his foot off the accelerator and I suspect that it was deliberate."

David Coulthard's reaction to Schumacher's accusations was one of barely controlled anger: "I kept well to the right in bend 9. The next thing I knew was that there was a bang at the back of my car. I don't know whether he saw me at all because of the poor visibility. Schumacher came like an animal into the pit, swearing and calling me a f***ing killer. I am not standing for that."

McLaren-Mercedes sports chief Norbert Haug confirmed that Coulthard had received specific instructions from the pit lane to let Schumacher past. As to Schumacher's "deceleration theory", he commented: "We have looked at the data record. There is no break in the accelerator curve." While the incident was raging between the main protagonists, it was business as usual for the McLaren mechanics who quickly got on with the important job of repairing Coulthard's car.

In lap 31, Coulthard returned to the track with a new rear to the car, but five laps behind the rest of the field. As the race finished he was still five laps behind and in seventh place, leaving him just out of the points.

The spat between Schumacher and Coulthard was only a part of the race. More pleasing for British fans was Damon Hill's victory. With his twenty-second Grand Prix victory, Hill not only demonstrated his own ability as a top-class racing driver but also presented the Jordan team with their first Grand Prix victory since they entered Formula One.

"I did say that I would provide Jordan with their first victory and I have done that," said a jubilant Hill after the race. Yet his win at Spa was by no means a formality following Michael Schumacher's exit. Hill's own team-mate, Ralf Schumacher, who was in second place, pressed him hard in the last third of the race.

Jordan orders

Team manager Eddie Jordan sensibly insisted that no duel should occur between the Jordan drivers. This, however, did not please Ralf Schumacher. On the podium, there were no smiles when he took the cup for second place. He said later: "Of course I wanted to win, but I obeyed the orders given by radio."

In reality, it would have been madness for Schumacher to fight with Hill, especially in such dreadful weather conditions. In all probability, both cars would have left the track, depriving Jordan of their all-important first victory. More to the point, Hill had been well clear of Schumacher before a second safety-car phase closed the gap between the two drivers. In the end, Ralf was prepared to acknowledge Hill's victory: "Damon was quicker all weekend and deserved to win." The Jordan team, who now had 26 points, were closing in on fourth-placed Benetton. Eddie Jordan was delighted: "It's been an unbelievable turnaround for us and a great testament to everyone's hard work."

The continuing downpour at Spa contributed to accidents throughout the race. On lap 27, Fisichella's Benetton went straight into the back of Nakano's Minardi, another spectacular collision that brought out the safety car for the second time. Eddie Irvine's Ferrari spun off, and Jacques Villeneuve ended up in the tyre wall. By any Grand Prix standards, this was really an extraordinary race.

CALENDAR

10 September
Successful peace talks are held between David Coulthard and Michael Schumacher at the premises of the Williams sponsor, Winfield. They discuss their crash in the Belgian Grand Prix and agree to bury their differences, dropping accusations and counter-accusations.

12 September
In a look-alike competition put on by the McLaren sponsor, West, six Mika Hakkinens and three David Coulthards appear before the specialist jury – Erja Hakkinen and Coulthard's girlfriend Heidi Wichlinski.

Mika Hakkinen and his double – the original is on the right and the ringer on the left.

The alliance between the Minardi team and the engine manufacturer Ford is renewed for a further year.

13 September
Another Ferrari double victory: Michael Schumacher and Eddie Irvine triumph before tens of thousands of enthusiastic *tifosi* in the Italian Grand Prix at Monza.

14 September
Johnny Herbert, though still a Sauber driver, has signed a contract with Stewart that will last to the end of the year 2000. As Rubens Barrichello is staying with the Stewart team, the Dutchman Jos Verstappen will be unemployed next year.

Representatives of European Green parties, the World Wildlife Fund (WWF), the Park Committee, and the Committee Against Noise meet in the Parco di Monza to assess the damage that the race has, in their opinion, caused. For years, they have been asking for the Formula One race to be banned from the royal park.

15 September
A gambling game in which bets are placed on the results of Formula One races is being introduced in Italy under the name "101". The game has the blessing of the FIA and will be marketed in Europe and South America.

From today, the Cosworth Racing engine factory is no longer the property of Audi. It has been bought by Ford.

17 September
Damon Hill's 38th birthday passes without much ceremony – he carries out test drives at Magny-Cours. Nevertheless, his team surprises him with a tasty chocolate cake.

24 September
The "chameleon" Jacques Villeneuve again appears with a new hair colour at the Nürburgring. This time Villeneuve's hair has turned black.

27 September
Mika Hakkinen wins the Luxembourg Grand Prix on the Nürburgring, ahead of his World Championship rival Michael Schumacher.

Sauber driver Jean Alesi completes his 150th Grand Prix on the Nürburgring. He becomes only the 15th driver in the history of Formula One to reach this total.

1–30 September
It is now revealed that Damon Hill almost failed to reach the finishing flag in the Belgian Grand Prix at Spa on 30 August. A fault was found on a tyre after the race – the pressure was dangerously low.

The US tyre manufacturer Goodyear announces it is definitely retiring from Formula One racing.

Is the Arrows team out of Formula One? Because team manager Tom Walkinshaw has not managed to land a factory engine contract (for example, Mecachrome), Arrows will have to use Hart V10 engines again in 1999. As a consequence, the team will still lag behind the rest of the field as it has this year.

The Hockenheim Internet page will feature the chance of a virtual racing lap on the track.

Veteran British motorsports commentator Murray Walker is given massive public approval for his unique vocal delivery. In a recent Teletext poll, over three-quarters of the survey begged Walker to carry on for the next season. ITV say they are keen to keep Walker on their books.

The tyre regulations for 1999 have been specified by the FIA. There will be four longitudinal grooves in the rear wheels, as in the present season. The number of grooves in the front tyres must be raised from three to four. The idea of equipping the front tyres with additional transverse grooves has been rejected for the time being.

Arrows chief Tom Walkinshaw is awarded a doctorate by Oxford Brookes University for his services in the design, development, construction, and use of vehicles for road and race track.

Brazilian Ricardo Zonta signs up to be a team-mate of Jacques Villeneuve at BAR for the coming season.

Quotes
"I don't want a kindergarten any longer."
Eddie Jordan on his selection of drivers for the coming season.

"It's all the same to me whether he has violet hair or is bald or wears a nose ring. The main point is that he is fast."
BAR team chief Craig Pollock on Jacques Villeneuve in *Sport Auto*.

"Jordan is becoming an old people's home for ex-Williams drivers."
Damon Hill on Heinz Harald Frentzen signing with Jordan.

"Ferrari does not really exist. Although the team is registered under that name, it is Schumacher who controls everything."
Jacques Villeneuve in *Blick*.

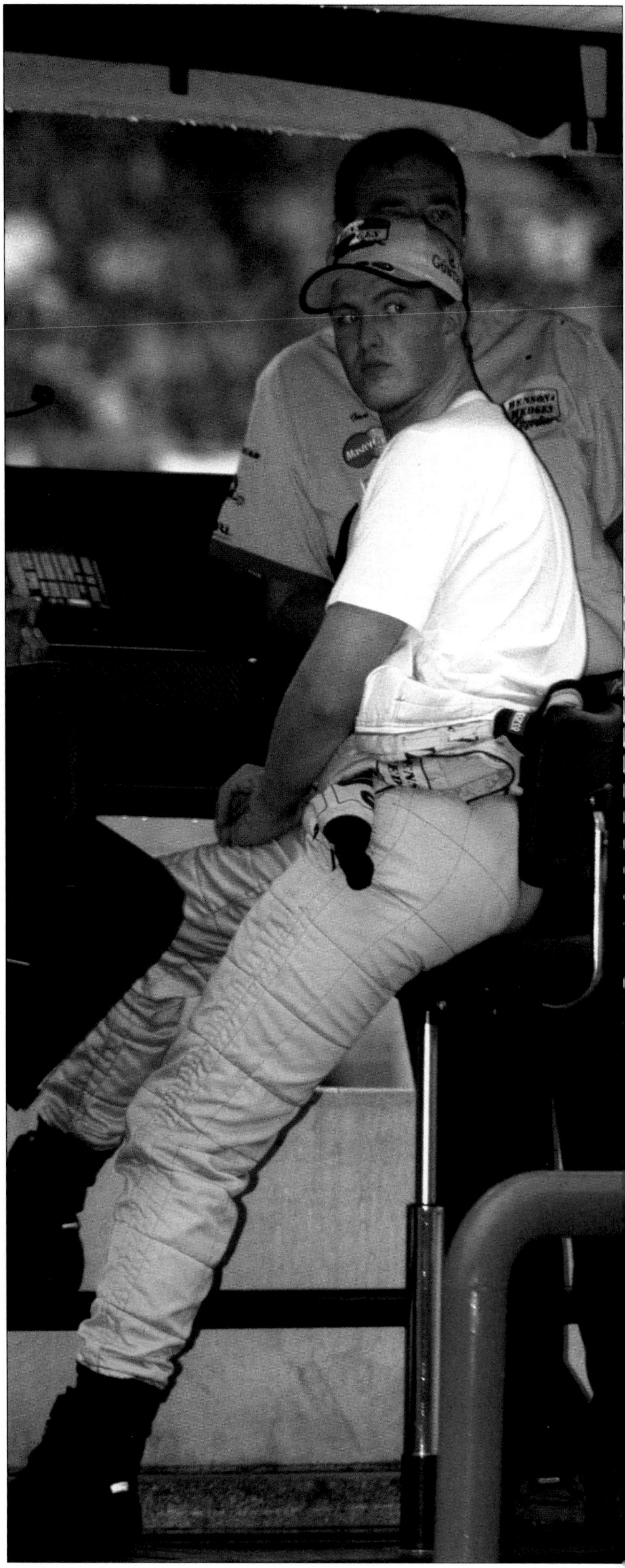

Ralf Schumacher, still wearing the yellow Jordan gear for the 1998 season.

BACKGROUND

Williams and Jordan swap drivers

By the middle of the season, the drivers' roundabout was well underway. Two German drivers, about whom the press had been speculating wildly for months, played the major roles in the most intriguing swap-around – Ralf Schumacher and Heinz Harald Frentzen.

Taking a risk with the new BAR stable: Jacques Villeneuve.

Pedro Diniz: His advertising millions secured him a place with Sauber.

Eddie Jordan, the chief of the team of the same name, is regarded as a mentor of young drivers on the motorsport scene. The Irishman impressively demonstrated his nose for rising talent with the signing up of Michael Schumacher, whom he helped make his debut in Formula One in 1991, of his brother Ralf in 1997, and of Giancarlo Fisichella, also in 1997. Jordan also, however, has the reputation of holding on to employees who want to move, if necessary resorting to the law to keep them – or else negotiating big release fees when a move cannot be avoided.

On the occasion of Michael Schumacher's transfer to Benetton, Jordan received a huge sum in an out-of-court settlement in 1996, seven years after the move occurred. When Fisichella moved to Benetton before the current season, Jordan is reported to have again received a substantial payment. And now yet another Jordan driver wishes to move on – Ralf Schumacher, whose services Jordan allegedly wishes to retain.

Contract opener

Jordan opened the contract game in July with a plain statement that Ralf Schumacher did not figure in his plans for 1999. At this point, the German had retired prematurely five times in eight races and had remained without points in the other three Grand Prix races. Jordan joined the critics who had already decided that Ralf's talent was not a match for his prominent surname. He was already being dismissed as "no longer the golden boy", as his failure to score World Championship points became increasingly embarrassing. Jordan proposed to deal with Schumacher junior's problem in the following season by cutting his pay by a half and paying him the rest as a bonus for points scored. This move put Ralf Schumacher on the defensive.

However, a good fifth place at Silverstone was the curtain-raiser to a successful series of races for Schumacher, culminating in a second place at Spa. He seemed to have turned the corner. Williams and the BAR team, involved for the first time in Formula One in 1999, announced their interest in him, but were warned in writing by Jordan not to enter into any negotiations with the German driver. Schumacher, according to Jordan, had made a verbal agreement to stay with them for a further year and would stick to it.

This created the classic situation for a game of "release poker". Schumacher's manager, Willi Weber, made efforts at the beginning of September to take legal action to check the disputed facts, but he was stopped at the last moment after the intervention of Bernie Ecclestone. Instead, the parties concerned made an out-of-court agreement, the terms of which were kept a closely guarded secret by all sides. By virtue of the large sum that Ralf Schumacher presumably has agreed to pay to his present employer, the German has removed the last obstacle preventing him from taking the Williams driving seat. There he will take the place of Heinz Harald Frentzen, who is making the counter-move to Jordan.

Merry-go-round

Frentzen has had three rather mixed years at Williams. He diplomatically said: "I have been able to learn a lot here." But he wanted to move on in 1999. A new place for Frentzen in Formula One, however, remained doubtful for months. After a good beginning with a third place in Australia, he never really got going this season. He had to say goodbye to his ambitious target of becoming World Champion – not least because Williams were not able to put a competitive car into action during the first half of the season.

Meanwhile, Williams' interest in Frentzen decreased with every poor placing and an extension to his contract seemed to be increasingly unlikely. There were rumours that Frentzen wanted to withdraw from Formula One and try his luck in the American IndyCar series. However, these stories were proved wrong with Williams' announcement before the Italian Grand Prix at Monza. Next year, Heinz Harald Frentzen will have a contract with Jordan.

CART star Alex Zanardi returns to Formula One after four years' absence.

Heinz Harald Frentzen was lucky to find a new berth at Jordan.

ITALIAN GRAND PRIX

No holding Ferrari

13 SEPTEMBER, MONZA. At the Italian Grand Prix, Michael Schumacher won the fourteenth race of the 1998 Formula One World Championship, with his team-mate Eddie Irvine in second place. This gave Schumacher his sixth win of the season and brought his World Championship points level with those of his chief rival Mika Hakkinen.

After the race, the jubilation of the Italian fans knew few limits. For the first time since 1988, they celebrated a double Ferrari victory on their home ground. After a fairly poor start to the season, luck seemed at last to be turning in Ferrari's direction.

Michael Schumacher passes Mika Hakkinen (above), and is acclaimed by the Ferrari pit crew as he crosses the finish line (left).

Yet a poor start to the race by Michael Schumacher made it seem unlikely that Ferrari would be in the running at all. As the lights went out at the start, Schumacher (who was in pole position for the first time since Hungary in 1997) could only look on helplessly as the two McLarens, followed by Jacques Villeneuve and Eddie Irvine, flew past him.

Schumacher overtook Villeneuve on the third lap, as well as passing Irvine without any struggle. But this did not alter the fact that the McLaren drivers had moved away from the rest of the field, with a lead of more than three seconds. However, predictions that McLaren-Mercedes were heading for an easy double victory proved to be premature.

Unexpectedly high brake wear on Hakkinen's car meant that he had to slow down and allow team-mate David Coulthard to pass him on the eighth lap. Schumacher naturally exploited Hakkinen's problem and rapidly closed up on the McLarens.

During lap 16, when Schumacher was already well up behind Hakkinen, McLaren's luck suddenly ran out. Coulthard's Silver Arrow, which then had a lead of more than nine seconds, was suddenly enveloped in a giant cloud of smoke. The car's Mercedes engine had thrown in the towel and Coulthard trundled off the track. Hakkinen and Schumacher had scarcely passed Coulthard when the Ferrari driver launched his attack. In the following bend, Schumacher succeeded in getting beside the Finn, who had been forced to slow because of the billowing cloud of smoke obscuring the track. The two drivers accelerated up the next straight side-by-side – but Schumacher had the better of it and took the lead.

Finnish fightback

The new leader now let loose and drove his car faultlessly to his first and only pitstop in lap 31. At this point, he was out of Hakkinen's field of view. Although the pitstop gave Hakkinen the lead once again, the position was reversed again during Hakkinen's pitstop in lap 34. New tyres with a lower air pressure were waiting for the McLaren – they were intended to compensate for the wear on the disc brakes. With Hakkinen six seconds

IN THE PRESS

Ferrari tornado over Monza

The Guardian "Ferrari make clean sweep after Coulthard's blow-up."

The Times "Schumacher proves first among equals."

Gazzetta dello Sport "Cry Ferrari! Schumi a world sovereign."

Il Matino "Ferrari master stroke. Ferrari legendary."

Corriere dello Sport "Everything for Ferrari. Schumi: triumph of giants. Irvine the perfect assistant. Hakkinen too tired to struggle."

Tuttosport "Red festival! Schumi first, World Championship title in his hand, Irvine second. Ferrari tornado over Monza. Delirium in the Ferrari pit."

Täglich Alles "Despite the Ferrari gala, Mika has match ball!"

L'Equipe "Red with happiness. Historic double for Ferrari."

ITALIAN GRAND PRIX

▲ *Eddie Irvine's second place made the Ferrari victory complete.*

David Coulthard returned to the pits accompanied by whistles and unambiguous gestures from the fans.

behind Schumacher and in second place, the plan initially seemed to work. Lap by lap, the McLaren slowly reeled in the Ferrari, and Hakkinen even drove the fastest lap of the entire race, with an impressive time of 1:25.139 mins.

During lap 46, however, when Hakkinen was only 2.6 seconds behind the leader, the brake system of the McLaren failed completely, and the car spun round when entering the second chicane. "While I was rotating, it passed through my head that there would be no points today," was Hakkinen's memory of the incident.

But Hakkinen escaped the spin with only a black eye. He was able to steer his car back on to the track and carry on – but minus any brakes. The following minutes looked like a mirror image of the Hungarian Grand Prix. Once again, a beaten McLaren limped towards the finishing line. Hakkinen refused to give in and carefully shepherded his crippled McLaren to the line, where he finished fourth, gaining three valuable World Championship points.

Eddie Irvine and Ralf Schumacher drew the main benefit from Hakkinen's misfortune. They easily passed the ailing McLaren, with Irvine following his team leader into second place, and Ralf becoming the second Schumacher on the winner's rostrum. Jean Alesi came in six seconds behind Hakkinen to gain a fifth place for Benetton, while the remaining point went to the other Jordan, driven by Damon Hill.

Red heaven

Arriving at the victor's podium of the Autodromo di Monza, anything up to 190,000 Ferrari supporters were in jubilant mood at the sight of the red-clad Schumacher and Irvine – plus a beaming Ralf Schumacher.

"I had a bad start, the wheels spun much too much," said a clearly delighted Michael Schumacher after the race. "In consequence, four other cars passed me. I looked as if I was having an outing instead of taking part in a race. But in the end, a double Ferrari victory in Monza with, as a bonus, brother Ralf on the podium. I can't imagine a better result."

Schumacher's victory at the Italian Grand Prix brought him level with Hakkinen, with 80 points each. Schumacher, who had been a full 24 points behind Hakkinen after the Monaco Grand Prix, did not miss the chance of firing a passing shot at his main rival: "Whoever has been so far in front and then sees the other draw level is, without doubt, psychologically damaged."

Following his team's success at Monza, Ferrari president Luca di Montezemolo also believed that Ferrari would have the advantage in the last two races of the season: "After this double victory, we must be in the running. Nevertheless, we said at the beginning of the season that our only objective was the World Championship title. The Monza victory was certainly no disadvantage for us from the psychological point of view. It was a message to our competitors."

At McLaren, no-one was taking the Ferrari "psychology games" very seriously. The McLaren team chiefs were more concerned with understanding how the brake defects on Hakkinen's car had occurred. They

Race Results

1	M. Schumacher	1:17:09.672
2	Irvine	1:17:47.649
3	R. Schumacher	1:17:50.824
4	Hakkinen	1:18:05.343
5	Alesi	1:18:11.544
6	Hill	1:18:16.360

Drivers' Championship

1	Hakkinen	80 points
2	M. Schumacher	80 points
3	Coulthard	48 points
4	Irvine	38 points
5	Villeneuve	20 points
6	Hill	17 points
	= Wurz	17 points
8	Fisichella	15 points
9	R. Schumacher	14 points
10	Frentzen	13 points

Constructors' Championship

1	McLaren-Mercedes	128 points
2	Ferrari	118 points
3	Williams-Mecachrome	33 points
4	Benetton-Mecachrome	32 points
5	Jordan-Mugen-Honda	31 points
6	Sauber-Petronas	10 points
7	Arrows-Hart	6 points
8	Stewart-Ford	5 points
9	Prost-Peugeot	1 point

vere faced with something of a iddle because this problem had not ppeared previously, neither during ests nor during the races. Despite the lisappointment felt in the McLaren amp, there was praise for Ferrari's erformance. "It's made the championship more exciting than we vould like," said McLaren MD Aartin Whitmarsh. "We've made too nany mistakes. You have to give 'errari credit. They've had uncharacteristically strong reliability nd have done a good job. If we'd one as good a job we wouldn't be aving this conversation. We are isappointed with that and it's omething we have to sort out."

'eace breaks out

'he expected reconciliation between Aichael Schumacher and David Coulthard also took place in Monza. Before the start of the race, the two rivers met to discuss matters in the ponsors' tent of the Williams team. fter a good hour, the doors opened again and Schumacher and Coulthard revealed the result of the "peace negotiations" to the assembled press. Coulthard emphasized once again that he had been hurt by Schumacher doubting his integrity; he was therefore happy that they had discussed the matter at length: "We explained to one another how we saw the situation in Belgium. In retrospect, we would both have reacted differently. I think the affair is now a thing of the past and I have no problem in meeting Michael again on the race track."

For his part, Schumacher apologized formally for his behaviour and explained that he was not proud of having lost his temper in Spa. "We must try to learn from this. David's rear light was not out as some people have suggested. I simply saw it too late because the spray behind his car was so thick. We must find a way of avoiding such accidents. Perhaps by means of even stronger rear lights or some other technical aid."

CIRCUIT

Autodromo Nazionale di Monza

Despite its many chicanes, Ferrari's home track is by far the fastest circuit in Formula One. In order to achieve speed on the straights, the drivers operate with very little wing but this means that the vehicles lose ground adhesion while driving through the slower sections of the circuit.

Curva Grande
Variante 1
Variante 2
Curve di Lesmo
Curva del Serraglio
Variante Ascari
Curva Parabolica

Track length 5.772 km (3.585 miles)
Race distance 305.908 km (191.005 miles) – 53 laps
1997 winner David Coulthard, McLaren-Mercedes
Lap record 1:24.808 min, Mika Hakkinen, McLaren-Mercedes, 1997

PRACTICE

Michael Schumacher is greeted with jubilation by the Ferrari crew.

With a lap time of 1:25.289 minutes, Michael Schumacher won the battle for pole position for the first time this season. Schumacher beamed with happiness at the result: "It was splendid here. However, it was about time. I was myself surprised and could not really believe it. It is now important that we use the correct strategy to dictate the race."

Schumacher chose the right moment for his "flying lap" during a qualifying session that, due to a short rain shower, started on a wet track. The track only began to dry out during the final minutes of the session. Seizing the moment, and with little traffic to get in his way, Schumacher produced his best time. Jacques Villeneuve in the Williams also reacted quickly, and posted a lap time of 1:25.561 minutes that put him just behind Schumacher on the first row of the grid.

The McLaren drivers, who had been dominant in qualifying during previous races, had to be satisfied with third and fourth places. Behind them was Eddie Irvine, always a danger for the McLarens.

Qualifying Results

1	M. Schumacher	Ferrari	1:25.289
2	Villeneuve	Williams-Mecachrome	1:25.561
3	Hakkinen	McLaren-Mercedes	1:25.679
4	Coulthard	McLaren-Mercedes	1:25.987
5	Irvine	Ferrari	1:26.159
6	R. Schumacher	Jordan-Mugen-Honda	1:26.309
7	Wurz	Benetton-Mecachrome	1:26.567
8	Alesi	Sauber-Petronas	1:26.637
9	Panis	Prost-Peugeot	1:26.681
10	Trulli	Prost-Peugeot	1:26.794
11	Fisichella	Benetton-Mecachrome	1:26.817
12	Frentzen	Williams-Mecachrome	1:26.836
13	Barrichello	Stewart-Ford	1:27.247
14	Hill	Jordan-Mugen-Honda	1:27.362
15	Herbert	Sauber-Petronas	1:27.510
16	Salo	Arrows-Hart	1:27.744
17	Verstappen	Stewart-Ford	1:28.212
18	Rosset	Tyrrell-Ford	1:28.286
19	Takagi	Tyrrell-Ford	1:28.346
20	Diniz	Arrows-Hart	1:28.387
21	Nakano	Minardi-Ford	1:29.101
22	Tuero	Minardi-Ford	1:29.417

Count Wolfgang Berghe von Trips (left) was killed in a tragic accident at Monza in1961, when his Ferrari, car no. 4, collided with Jim Clark's Lotus and left the track (above, above right, and above far right).

FLASHBACK

Count von Trips

"My worst fears have been realized. The race authorities have just officially confirmed that Count Wolfgang Berghe von Trips has had a fatal accident at the south bend."

Thousands of German motor-sport fans were devastated when they heard these words on the radio on 10 September 1961. Count von Trips was a much-loved figure in Germany for many reasons, including his personal magnetism, his dashing good looks, and his exuberant attitude to life. He once said: "I want to live to be 105 years old so I can have enough time to hear all the music I'd like to hear, read all the books that interest me, and have all the women I want."

But above all he seemed to promise Germany a level of success in motor racing it had never before achieved. On the day of his fatal crash, this gentleman among racing drivers was on the threshold of becoming the first German to win the Drivers' World Championship. However, it was not to be.

Count von Trips was born on 4 May 1928 into an aristocratic German family. Away from the race track, he went to agricultural college before working as an unsalaried clerk in a bank – both activities intended to equip him for a life as "lord of the manor". But his other plans were swept aside by his passionate enthusiasm for racing.

From bikes to cars

In 1950, von Trips sold a radio and a watch to raise the money to buy a BMW motorbike. After a few successes as a motorcycle racer, the Count changed over to racing cars. He turned up at the Mille Miglia with a Porsche 1300 and was immediately victorious in this class. Further successes followed, including second place in the Eifel race and third place at the final of the German sports car championship, a position that was enough to provide him with victory in the class.

These successes attracted the attention of Mercedes, who signed him up. Driving a 300 SLR, he gave impressive evidence of his ability in the Irish Tourist Trophy, taking third place behind his experienced colleagues Juan Manuel Fangio and Sterling Moss. The following year, he switched to Porsche where, with Hans Hermann, he won his class in the Sebering 12-hour race. A little later, together with Richard von Frankenberg, he also won the Le Mans 24-Hour race.

A disastrous debut

Count von Trips made his Formula One debut with Ferrari in 1956. The Italians took the Count on as substitute driver and allowed him to have a drive for the first time in the Italian Grand Prix at Monza. This first appearance did not last long, however, because the Count reduced his car to its component parts a few laps after the start when the drop arm failed. Despite this piece of bad luck, Ferrari continued to have confidence in him and gave him a second chance on 13 January 1957 in the Argentine Grand Prix.

Over the following years, Berghe von Trips established himself as a driver of the highest class, although not without having to overcome some bitter setbacks. During the 1000km race at the Nürburgring, he had a serious accident, fractured two vertebrae, and had to wear a plastic corset for two months. But the injured driver was aware of the risks of his profession and accepted them – he used to say: "A crash never finds us unprepared." He took his place in a car again shortly after this accident and won third place at the Italian Grand Prix in Monza in 1960.

And so to 1961, which should have been Count von Trips' year. On 22 May he won the Dutch Grand Prix, and he followed up this success with victory in the British Grand Prix. He went on to take second place in Belgium and Germany. The Count entered the last race of the season at Monza at the top of the World Championship table.

Death on the track

The practice results seemed to suggest that the trophy was his for the taking. For the first time in his career, von Trips put his Ferrari into pole position. After a bad start to the Grand Prix, however, things did not look so good. At the end of the first lap, his Ferrari was only in sixth place, with Jim Clark close behind him. In the following lap, von Trips pushed himself forward into fourth place. But the Scotsman's Lotus drew closer and closer to the German's Ferrari. Before the Curvetta, Clark tried to overtake. The cars touched and turned over. Whereas Clark's Lotus landed back on its wheels, the Ferrari shot straight up the embankment and through the fence into the crowd. Count Berghe von Trips was thrown from his car and died on the spot, as did 14 spectators. It was a tragic end for a full-blooded racing driver.

Von Trips was one of the "devil-may-care" drivers who have now disappeared from motor racing. They drove hard and they played hard – and they seldom lived long.

FLASHBACK

Monza: Tradition and tragedy

When the first Italian Grand Prix took place in 1921, the event almost folded through lack of interest. There were only six entries for the race on the triangular course at Montichiari, near Brescia. After this disappointing start, it was obvious to the Italian authorities that a new, more appropriate race track was needed if the leading drivers were to be induced to show more interest.

So, in February 1922, the Milan Automobile Club published its plan to build an *autodromo* in the Royal Park. Just three months later, on 15 May, Felice Nazzaro and Vincenzo Lancia dug the first spadeful of earth for the creation of what was to become the Autodromo di Monza.

There was enormous pressure to finish the building of the circuit on time, because the second Italian Grand Prix was scheduled to take place on the new track on 10 September of the same year. More than three thousand workers slaved around the clock to ensure that the circuit was completed in only 100 days. On 3 September, the track was inaugurated in pouring rain in front of 100,000 motorsport enthusiasts. The main attraction that day was the Grand Prix for Voiturettes which, to the delight of the *tifosi*, was won by Fiat.

At that time, the circuit consisted of a high-speed oval – modelled on the track at Indianapolis – and a 5.5 km (3.5 mile) road track. Now more than 70 years old, Monza is still in use, although substantially modified. Major changes were made to the circuit in the early 1970s, with the introduction of chicanes that cut down on the level of "slip-streaming" that had characterized Monza in the past. Since then there have been further modifications for safety reasons, but its fast corners and long straights ensure that its essential spirit remains unchanged.

Triumph and disaster

Including 1998, Monza has been the site of 69 Grands Prix, many of them spectacular races. But the traditional race track has also been the scene of some terrible tragedies. Many great racing drivers have died at Monza. Examples in Formula One are Alberto Ascari, killed in 1955, Count Wolfgang Berghe von Trips, who died at Monza in 1961, and Jochen Rindt in 1970. (Rindt was the only driver in the history of Formula One to be awarded the World Championship title posthumously.) The last fatal accident at Monza in Formula One occurred in 1978. During a mass pile-up, the Swedish Lotus driver Ronnie Petersen injured his legs so badly that he died a few hours later in a Milan clinic. Like Rindt and Count von Trips, Petersen was on the verge of winning the World Championship when his life was ended at Monza.

After the accident at the Parabolica, Jochen Rindt died on the spot in the wreckage of his Lotus.

LUXEMBOURG GRAND PRIX

Hakkinen and Schumacher raced neck-and-neck for much of the race, their content closely followed in the McLaren garage (inset).

LUXEMBOURG GRAND PRIX

Hakkinen is congratulated by team manager Ron Dennis after the race. Schumacher struggles to raise a smile.

Faultless Hakkinen drives into four-point lead

27 SEPTEMBER, NÜRBURGRING. The Ferrari team seemed to have the race sewn up – its cars were on the front row and this was a home Grand Prix for Michael Schumacher. But it was to be McLaren's day, as Mika Hakkinen crowned an error-free performance to extend his World Championship leadership by four points, with only one race left.

The seventh victory of the season by Mika Hakkinen was like a gift from heaven for the McLaren-Mercedes team. They subsequently celebrated in the British VIP tents, almost as if the result of the Luxembourg Grand Prix had given the team the World Championship they so desperately desired.

Team manager Ron Dennis, normally known in racing circles for his lack of emotion, responded emotionally to Hakkinen's success, hailing it as "probably the most important race in the history of the company". McLaren's joint owner and TAG chief, Mansour Ojjeh, also revelled in Hakkinen's victory: "It was Mika's day. Everyone thought that with the two Ferraris in front of us, it would be a boring race. Schumacher would drive ahead and Irvine would block us. He did it for a little while – but he was a gentleman."

And even Schumacher's manager, Willi Weber, recognized that his driver had been well and truly beaten: "It was a wonderful victory for motorsport, a splendid race by Mika Hakkinen. In my opinion, it was his best performance this year. He drove without error and withstood the pressure from Michael."

If there was happiness for some, then there was gloom for others. In the Ferrari camp, people were not so relaxed about the race. After both drivers had succeeded in out-qualifying both the McLarens, Ferrari expected victory. Using the blocking tactics that had been practised so successfully at the French Grand Prix, they were confident of success.

Ferrari tactics

Although Irvine got ahead of Schumacher at the start of the race, the German retook Irvine on the second lap. Irvine now acted in his traditional role of Schumacher's "body guard", holding off Hakkinen's McLaren and allowing Schumacher to build up a substantial lead. The spectators supporting Ferrari were also confident of a Schumacher victory. They were celebrating the assumed victor long before the finishing flag.

They did not, however, take into account Hakkinen's steely determination not to give up on the race. After a few laps, Hakkinen began to realize that Irvine was having problems with the Ferrari's handling. The problem, as ever, was in getting past him, which caused Hakkinen no

Mika Hakkinen's wife Erja celebrates her husband's triumph.

PRACTICE

Double pole for Ferrari

Michael Schumacher succeeded in driving to his second pole position in succession. He was using a vehicle with a wheel base 13 cm (5 in) shorter, in the hope of achieving better handling on the Eifel track. With a final time of 1:18.561 minutes, Schumacher confirmed the Ferrari plan. Eddie Irvine placed his car right behind Schumacher with a difference of only four-tenths of a second. This gave Ferrari their first one-two starting row of the season.

Mika Hakkinen only managed what was for him a lowly third place, and he was certainly not happy: "I was not satisfied with the car. I wanted to come out of the bends faster but it was not possible." For Hakkinen, the problem in the race lay in the two Ferraris ahead of him – and how he would get past them.

Qualifying times

1	M. Schumacher	Ferrari	1:18.561
2	Irvine	Ferrari	1:18.907
3	Hakkinen	McLaren-Mercedes	1:18.940
4	Fisichella	Benetton-Mecachrome	1:19.048
5	Coulthard	McLaren-Mercedes	1:19.169
6	R. Schumacher	Jordan-Mugen-Honda	1:19.455
7	Frentzen	Williams-Mecachrome	1:19.522
8	Wurz	Benetton-Mecachrome	1:19.569
9	Villeneuve	Williams-Mecachrome	1:19.631
10	Hill	Jordan-Mugen-Honda	1:19.807
11	Alesi	Sauber-Petronas	1:20.493
12	Barrichello	Stewart-Ford	1:20.530
13	Herbert	Sauber-Petronas	1:20.650
14	Trulli	Prost-Peugeot	1:20.709
15	Panis	Prost-Peugeot	1:21.048
16	Salo	Arrows-Hart	1:21.120
17	Diniz	Arrows-Hart	1:21.258
18	Verstappen	Stewart-Ford	1:21.501
19	Takagi	Tyrrell-Ford	1:21.525
20	Nakano	Minardi-Ford	1:22.078
21	Tuero	Minardi-Ford	1:22.146
22	Rosset	Tyrrell-Ford	1:22.822

CIRCUIT

Nürburgring

The critical point of the circuit is the Castrol S bend, just after the start-finish line – many drivers finish the race prematurely at this bend. Further tricky points are the bends at RTL, at the back of the track, and Coca Cola, just before the entry to the start-finish line. Overtaking manoeuvres are extremely difficult.

Drivers used to call the old Eifel circuit, with its extended northern loop, the "green hell", after the forests that surrounded the track and the sheer dangers that they all faced. After conversion work for safety reasons, the new, shorter track is now one of the most modern that Formula One has to offer.

Track length 4.568 km (2.831 miles)
Race distance 306.027 km (190.079 miles) – 67 laps.
1997 winner Jacques Villeneuve, Williams-Renault
Lap record 1:18.805 minutes, Heinz Harald Frentzen, Williams-Renault, 1997

little grief: "He lost the back-end in the corners a couple of times and was banging over the kerbs. He seemed to have some sort of brake or gear box problem and the fact that I couldn't overtake really annoyed me."

On lap 14, Hakkinen seized his chance and outbraked Irvine to grab second place. He was now just a little over eight seconds behind Schumacher. Hakkinen turned up the pressure and took a few tenths of a second from the leader on each lap. Schumacher's lead was slowly but remorselessly chipped away, before he took his first pitstop in lap 24. Hakkinen stayed out on the track for a further five laps, putting in a series of blisteringly fast laps. On lap 26 he drove the fastest time of the day at 1:20.45 minutes. A short while later Hakkinen roared into the pit lane.

Race Result

1	Hakkinen	1:32:14.789
2	M. Schumacher	1:32:17.000
3	Coulthard	1:32:48.952
4	Irvine	1:33:12.971
5	Frentzen	1:33:15.036
6	Fisichella	1:33:16.148

Drivers' Championship

1	Hakkinen	90 points
2	M. Schumacher	86 points
3	Coulthard	52 points
4	Irvine	41 points
5	Villeneuve	20 points
6	Hill	17 points
	= Wurz	17 points
8	Fisichella	16 points
9	Frentzen	15 points
10	R. Schumacher	14 points

Constructors' Championship

1	McLaren-Mercedes	142 points
2	Ferrari	127 points
3	Williams-Mecachrome	35 points
4	Benetton-Mecachrome	33 points
5	Jordan-Mugen-Honda	31 points
6	Sauber-Petronas	10 points
7	Arrows-Hart	6 points
8	Stewart-Ford	5 points
9	Prost-Peugeot	1 point

Any hopes Ferrari had of holding on to the lead disappeared when Hakkinen returned to the track after refuelling – he raced into the Castrol S bend just in front of a despairing Schumacher.

The epic struggle for the lead developed into a real showdown. Schumacher attempted to pressure Hakkinen into making a mistake, but the McLaren driver was having none of it and coolly reeled off the laps. On lap 47, after two-thirds of the race distance, Schumacher made his second stop. One lap later, Hakkinen too came into the pits – but nothing

An unhappy Schumacher broods over the result, while (insets) Fisichella, Frentzen, and Wurz battle for position – both on and off the track.

changed in the race order. On the contrary, when the McLaren driver returned to the track after his stop, the Ferrari was more than four seconds behind. Hakkinen then delivered a faultless performance for the remainder of the race – even if the lead at the end was down to two seconds.

In the Parc Fermé, an overjoyed Hakkinen climbed out of his McLaren and patted the Mercedes star painted on the front of the car. This was a symbolic thank you to his crew who had made the car so competitive.

After the race, Hakkinen was in the perfect position to answer those critics who had doubted his ability to handle the psychological pressures that all drivers face when up against Michael Schumacher. He had beaten the man who most people considered to be the best driver in the world on equal terms. Hakkinen explained his views on the situation: "I never doubted that McLaren and Mercedes could do the job and, personally, I didn't think about whether I can handle the pressure. But perhaps now I've shown the people who said 'Can Mika handle it?' that I can."

Psychological blow

Michael Schumacher was genuinely devastated by the result. In the sort of race that Schumacher had so often made his own, Hakkinen had "out-Schumachered" him. It was the sort of psychological blow that Schumacher had so regularly dished out to his opponents; now he was on the receiving end of this treatment. Schumacher, however, put a brave face on things when talking to the press: "Of course we are disappointed. But there's no reason for hanging our heads. We have a few weeks before the World Championship finale. This can be an advantage for us. It's up to us to have another pull on the oars."

Hakkinen pats his McLaren after another fine performance.

Ever the professional optimist, Schumacher insisted that he was ready for the final Grand Prix in Japan: "The layout of the track in Suzuka is the sort that suits Ferrari – as we saw in 1997. As far as the car is concerned, I am convinced that we are now on the same level as McLaren-Mercedes. There is practically no difference between the engines. It will be very close. There are days on which it is just impossible to win and today was one of them. But there is no question of giving up. We put McLaren Mercedes under pressure once again. And under pressure, they make mistakes – we have seen that."

Ferrari fears

But the Ferrari President, Luca di Montezemolo, probably displayed his team's real feelings regarding their setback at McLaren's hands on the Nürburgring. "That was the worst shock in my life," he said after the race. "I was turned to stone on Sunday and did not speak for an hour. The result changed me into a block of ice."

Norbert Haug, the thoughtful Mercedes motorsports boss, was keen to emphasize McLaren's new-found confidence: "It must be accepted that there have been difficulties, whether the rain in Spa-Francorchamps, the strategy in Hungary, or the motor in Hungary. But in general, it must be recognized that our concept leads in the right direction."

McLaren's influential technical director, Adrian Newey, amplified the comments made by Haug. But with the coming race in Japan very much in mind, he sounded a note of caution: "It was a most satisfying race. We started from behind and the whole team did a great job. But Michael has had the wind knocked out of his sails before and bounced back. You can never rule him out."

CALENDAR

2 October
Silverstone: More than 10,000 people take part in the 50th birthday celebrations of the circuit. The first motor races took place on the former military aerodrome in 1948. Great drivers and cars from the past were judged in a competition by the visitors to the Silverstone birthday celebration. The victors included Argentine driver Juan Manuel Fangio (best Formula One driver), Lotus 25 (best Formula One racing car), and Colin Chapman (best Formula One team manager).

15 October
Proposals from the individual commissions are put forward at the FIA World Congress in Paris concerning the rules and the list of next season's Grand Prix races,

1–31 October
Eddie Irvine does not participate in the Ferrari tests in Barcelona, which take place at the beginning of October, because of the need to cure his severe back trouble. He is replaced in the driving seat by the test driver Luca Badoer.

The Japan Tobacco Company has extended its contract with the Benetton team for a further two years. The cars will race in the colours of the Mild Seven brand until the end of the year 2000.

The distinctive light blue livery of the Benetton cars will continue into the new century, thanks to the sponsorship deal with Japan Tobacco.

The top racing teams plan to carry out testing with two separate test teams. There will be a conventional team, which will be responsible for the next race or two, and a development team, which will concern itself with improvements intended for inclusion within the Benetton car in the longer term.

Formula One boss Bernie Ecclestone is said to be involved in plans for the creation of a European football league consisting of high profile clubs such as Bayern Munich, Real Madrid, and Manchester United.

Tyre manufacturer Goodyear reacts strongly to the Nürburgring defeat. Thirty different tyre mixtures and designs are being tested in Barcelona in readiness for the forthcoming Suzuka Grand Prix, and the final battle with rival tyre manufacturer Bridgestone.

A comeback for Renault? The French engine manufacturer is considering returning to Formula One in the year 2001. First, however, a new 10-cylinder engine will be built for 1999 and this will be used under various designations by Williams (Mecachrome), BAR (Supertec), and Benetton (Playlife).

Peugeot will install a fourth development stage of the V10 engine in the Prost racing car for the season's finale in Suzuka. This engine already includes many components that will be incorporated in the 1999 design.

The departure of sponsorship-rich Pedro Diniz to Sauber is tearing a large hole in the development budget of the Arrows chief Tom Walkinshaw. In consequence, Arrows will probably continue to operate with the existing chassis for the 1999 season.

The new Formula One team BAR has been prevented from sending cars with different motifs (555 and Lucky Strike) on to the track for the next season. The British American Tobacco concern, which is part-owner of the team, is now considering making arrangements with another team – but only as sponsor.

The plans for the return of Honda to Formula One will probably be made known during the Suzuka racing weekend. A comprehensive test programme will be carried out next year before the Japanese company enters its own vehicle in the year 2000.

The course conversion work in Estoril in Portugal should be finished by the end of May 1999, even though no Grand Prix race is planned for it during the next season. However, there are plans to use the course as an official test track. The obviously disappointed operators of the race track are now hoping for a return of Formula One to the circuit in the year 2000 or 2001.

In order to ensure fairness, the Japanese tyre manufacturer Bridgestone is working with the teams currently using Goodyear tyres so that they have an opportunity to test-drive their product after the conclusion of the World Championship Grand Prix in Suzuka.

Quotes

"If Irvine again plays the rearguard game at Suzuka, that will not be in the spirit of the sport. We would like a fair decision, at best a Hakkinen-Schumacher duel."
Mercedes motorsport chief Norbert Haug in the German publication *Bild*

"So much happens in Formula One. It is often better to look away and think about real life."
McLaren driver Mika Hakkinen

"It would be very nice if Ferrari were rewarded for their years of hard work. They deserve it. Ferrari is Formula One."
FIA boss Bernie Ecclestone

TOBACCO BAN

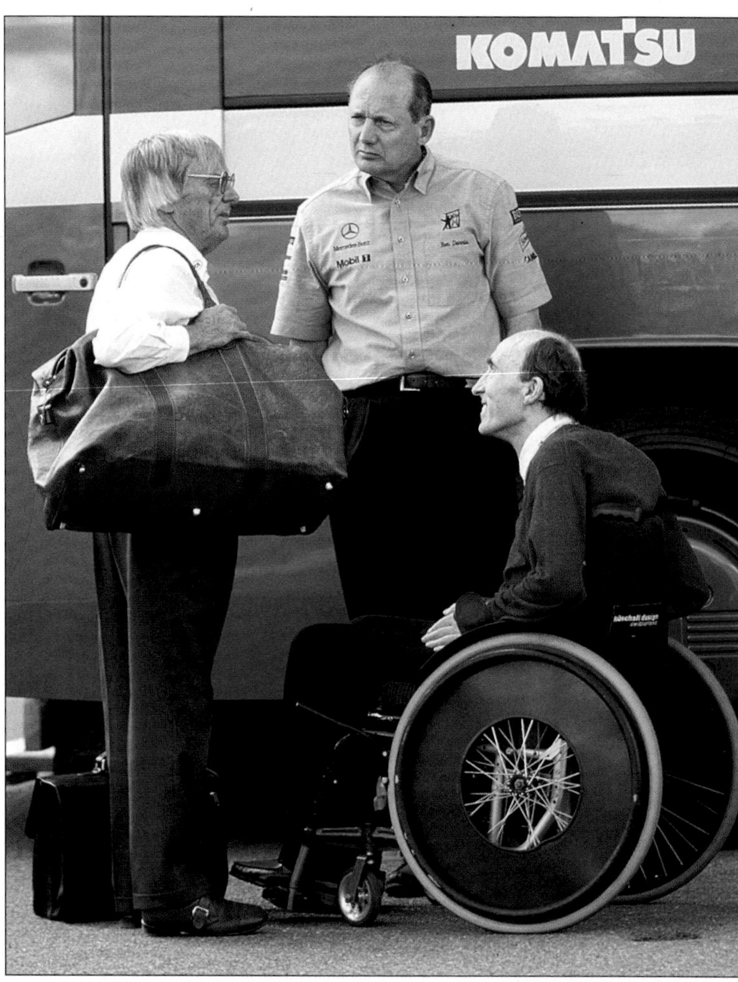

Bernie Ecclestone (left) confers with Ron Dennis and Frank Williams.

Far East Formula

15 October. The FIA and the influential Formula One figure Bernie Ecclestone announce their intention of pursuing new marketing directions for Formula One to escape advertising restrictions in Europe – two races will take place in the Far East.

The inclusion in next season's race calendar of a Grand Prix in the Malaysian capital of Kuala Lumpur had been expected by many people following speculation over the impending ban on tobacco advertising in most of Europe.

More surprising, however, was the announcement from the International Automobile Association (FIA) that a race was proposed for the Chinese city of Zhuhai. Because a total of 17 races (one more race than in 1998) has been planned for the 1999 season, the Argentine Grand Prix will now probably give way to the Zhuhai race – despite an existing contract with the Argentines. A final decision on the race calendar is to be made on 11 December 1998.

The Formula One year traditionally starts with the Australian Grand Prix, and concludes in Japan. Once again, Germany will have a second race with the Luxembourg Grand Prix being held at the Nürburgring.

THE FORMULA ONE 1999 GP CALENDAR

7 March	Australia/Melbourne
21 March	China/Zhuhai*
11 April	Brazil/São Paulo
2 May	San Marino/Imola*
16 May	Monaco/Monte Carlo
30 May	Spain/Barcelona
13 June	Canada/Montreal
27 June	France/Magny-Cours
11 July	Britain/Silverstone
25 July	Austria/Zeltweg
1 August	Germany/Hockenheim
15 August	Hungary/Budapest*
29 August	Belgium/Spa-Francorchamps
12 Sept	Italy/Monza
26 Sept	Luxembourg/Nürburgring
17 Oct	Malaysia/Sepang*
31 Oct	Japan/Suzuka

* Provisional
Substitute date: GP Argentina/Buenos Aires

RACING RETURN

BMW back in the fray

Having departed from Formula One in 1987, the Bayerische Motorenwerke (BMW) will return to Formula One for the new millennium. BMW will work with the Williams team to produce a car that will bring BMW the success it last gained in the 1980s.

In 1997, 10 years after its departure from Formula One, the Munich car manufacturer BMW announced a return to the top flight in motor racing. The Chairman of the Board, Bernd Pitschetsrieder, issued a statement at the International Automobile Exhibition (IAA) in Frankfurt that BMW would join with Williams to enter Formula One in the year 2000. A year later, the complex organizational arrangements are clearly already in place.

The parent company has created BMW Motorsport Limited as an independent company that will concentrate fully on Formula One matters. The managing director will be Karl-Heinz Kalbfell, who will also continue to lead the BMW AG Marketing Department.

He will be assisted by Paul Rosche as technical director, Thomas Giuliani as marketing director, Frederick Wilhelm Kreidt as financial director, and Gerhard Berger, who has been engaged as motorsport director.

The most important part within the team will be played by Paul Rosche, who has been working on engine development at BMW for 40 years. His record as an engineer includes some very successful engines, including the 1.5 litre turbo engine with which Nelson Piquet became World Champion in 1983. At 65, Rosche is yet again facing the challenge of Formula One. Rosche and his 80-strong team have already been working for almost two years on an engine that will be tested for the first time in a Williams vehicle in the spring of 1999.

A testing time

Rosche is keeping very quiet about the technical details of his new engine – which runs daily for three hours on the test stand. Detailed information would only be of limited value, however, as the decisive question is whether the Williams technical chief Patrick Head can combine the engine with the Williams chassis and aerodynamics to make a harmonious and effective whole. The engine is the single most important element in the equation, but it will take much time and hard work to make it the equal of the engines currently produced by Mercedes and Ferrari.

Rumours suggesting that BMW wished to purchase shares in Williams have been bluntly denied by Karl-Heinz Kalbfell: "There is no such intention. We need an independent partner." The new partnership will probably be called simply Williams-BMW, and the Bavarian company has declared that its famous blue-and-white quartered logo will be positioned on the nose of the car.

Gerhard Berger (left), suitably astride a BMW, and Nelson Piquet (above) driving a BMW-powered Brabham in 1981.

NEW HORIZONS

New job for Berger

Gerhard Berger announced his departure from Formula One last year. The question being asked was whether he would leave motorsport for good.

Berger's answer to the question of his future was made more rapidly than expected, when he was appointed as a director of BMW Motorsport for the next five years.

After almost 15 years in the sport, his move closed the circle of Berger's career. At the beginning, in 1985, Berger drove a BMW 635 in the touring class, and BMW eased Berger's entry into Formula One. Berger made his debut in 1984 at the steering wheel of an ATS-BMW, and was victorious two years later in a BMW-powered Benetton – the last Formula One victory that BMW would celebrate for quite a while.

Berger will represent his employers mainly on the race track and on important motor racing committees. These new duties will exclude any return to behind the wheel of a racing car. "My time as a racing driver is past," says Berger firmly. Despite this, Berger will continue to travel long distances. He will commute between Munich and the BMW Motorsport HQ at Grove in England, and Monaco, where he lives and has an office.

JAPANESE GRAND PRIX

Hakkinen powers to the title

1 NOVEMBER, SUZUKA. Finn Mika Hakkinen drove a faultless race to win the Japanese Grand Prix and the Formula One World Championship for McLaren, while Michael Schumacher's hopes of victory were confounded when he stalled on the starting grid.

A thousand days after his near fatal crash at Adelaide, Mika Hakkinen took the chequered flag at Suzuka to confirm his status as the world's top racing driver. During the season, he soaked up the pressure that any rival to Michael Schumacher customarily faces, and proved himself a worthy Champion by out-driving Schumacher on a number of occasions.

Although the eagerly anticipated duel between the two rivals never materialized, the race was not short on incident. Jarno Trulli stalled his Prost on the grid, forcing a second procession lap and a restart. Then, in front of 148,000 spectators, the unthinkable happened: Michael Schumacher stalled his Ferrari. An overheated clutch was said to be the fault, but whatever the reason, Schumacher's race was effectively over before it had started. The forlorn German driver had to join Trulli at the back of the grid as the race eventually got underway.

Hakkinen made an excellent start and roared away from the field to lead the race from start to finish. Eddie Irvine made a valiant effort to keep up with Hakkinen, but he was always slightly off the pace and eventually dropped back. David Coulthard was in third place, followed by the trio of Heinz Harald Frentzen, Damon Hill, and Jacques Villeneuve, engaged in a prolonged battle for fourth place.

Never say die

No one doubted that Schumacher would mount a determined fightback, but the speed with which he cut his way through the field presented an amazing spectacle. In the space of just 22 laps he had fought his way from the back of the grid to third place. Although it was extremely unlikely

Disaster for Ferrari: A race official flags Schumacher for stalling on the grid, effectively ending his title hopes.

JAPANESE GRAND PRIX

During his fight through the field, Schumacher (left) is held up by the battle between Hill's Jordan (centre) and Villeneuve's Williams.

CIRCUIT

Suzuka International Racing Course

Given Grand Prix status in 1987, Suzuka replaced the old Fuji speedway track that had formerly held the Japanese Grand Prix. Suzuka is a circuit that has become highly popular with the drivers. The circuit's figure-of-eight pattern is unique in Formula One. Combining a series of hilly lefts and rights, it also provides a fairly equal mix of clockwise and anti-clockwise driving. Vast, enthusiastic crowds make this concluding race of the season an atmospheric affair.

Triangle
'S' Curve
Hairpin
Degner Curve
Spoon Curve

Track length 5.86 km (3.64 miles)
Race distance 310.79 km (193.03 miles) – 53 laps
1997 winner Michael Schumacher, Ferrari
Lap record 1:38.942 min, Heinz Harald Frentzen, Williams-Renault, 1997

PRACTICE

Last battle for McLaren and Ferrari

For the last time this season, Michael Schumacher and Mika Hakkinen fought out their titanic struggle for grid position. Operating on a higher plane, way above the other drivers, the two Championship rivals gave everything to gain pole position. In the end it went to Schumacher who, on his second run, claimed the 20th pole of his career.

The two supporting drivers from Ferrari and McLaren lived up to their roles, with Coulthard achieving third position and Irvine fourth, the latter nearly two seconds slower than Schumacher. The stage was set for a perfect end to the season, with chances virtually even between Schumacher and Hakkinen.

Practice Results

1	M. Schumacher	Ferrari	1:36.29
2	Hakkinen	McLaren-Mercedes	1:36.47
3	Coulthard	McLaren-Mercedes	1:37.49
4	Irvine	Ferrari	1:38.19
5	Frentzen	Williams-Mecachrome	1:38.27
6	Villeneuve	Williams-Mecachrome	1:38.44
7	R. Schumacher	Jordan-Mugen-Honda	1:38.46
8	Hill	Jordan-Mugen-Honda	1:38.60
9	Wurz	Benetton-Mecachrome	1:38.95
10	Fisichella	Benetton-Mecachrome	1:39.08
11	Herbert	Sauber-Petronas	1:39.23
12	Alesi	Sauber-Petronas	1:39.44
13	Panis	Prost-Peugeot	1:40.03
14	Trulli	Prost-Peugeot	1:40.11
15	Salo	Arrows-Hart	1:40.38
16	Barrichello	Stewart-Ford	1:40.50
17	Takagi	Tyrrell-Ford	1:40.61
18	Diniz	Arrows-Hart	1:40.68
19	Verstappen	Stewart-Ford	1:40.94
20	Nakano	Minardi-Ford	1:41.31
21	Tuero	Minardi-Ford	1:42.35
NON-QUALIFIER			
22	Rosset	Tyrrell-Ford	

The end for Schumacher, as he coasts to a halt after his high-speed blow-out on 'ap 32. On points, Mika Hakkinen was now the new World Champion.

Under the scrutiny of waiting cameramen, Michael Schumacher returns to the Ferrari pits after his disastrous tyre explosion.

hat Schumacher would be able to :lose with Hakkinen, it was a fine)erformance. But in chasing the eaders, Schumacher paid a price in yre wear. His front tyres were badly potted, but it was his right rear that xploded on lap 32 (although his unning over debris left by two other ars crashing earlier may have been a actor in the blow-out).

At the moment the tyre failed, ;chumacher was travelling at 266 :m/h (165 mph), but he managed to ring the now three-wheeled Ferrari under control and park it on the grass

Race Result

	Hakkinen	1:27:22.535
:	Irvine	1:27:29.026
	Coulthard	1:27:50.197
	Hill	1:28:36.026
	Frentzen	1:28:36.392
	Villeneuve	1:28:38.402

Drivers' Championship

1	Hakkinen	100 points
2	M. Schumacher	86 points
3	Coulthard	56 points
4	Irvine	47 points
5	Villeneuve	21 points
6	Hill	20 points
7	Frentzen	17 points
	= Wurz	17 points
9	Fisichella	16 points
0	R. Schumacher	14 points

Constructors' Championship

1	McLaren-Mercedes	156 points
2	Ferrari	133 points
3	Williams-Mecachrome	38 points
4	Jordan-Mugen-Honda	34 points
5	Benetton-Mecachrome	33 points
6	Sauber-Petronas	10 points
7	Arrows-Hart	6 points
8	Stewart-Ford	5 points
9	Prost-Peugeot	1 points

erge. Thus, for the second year in uccession, Schumacher stood watching the new World Champion race ound the circuit in front of him. chumacher's blow-out excited joy nd despondency in the McLaren and 'errari camps respectively.

Hakkinen's elation on receiving the news that he was the new Champion was tempered by the need for him to maintain his concentration: "It was disturbing my performance a little bit, which I would say is quite normal, but then I seemed to calm down quite a lot and it was quite easy to control the situation. But there is always one problem when you are leading like that – and it happened to me with about 10 laps to go – which is the tendency for your mind to start thinking about other things. I almost started whistling in the car."

During the final laps of the race, Hakkinen slowed down to preserve tyres and minimize the possibility of mechanical error, crossing the line six seconds ahead of Eddie Irvine and nearly half a minute in front of his team-mate David Coulthard.

Jordan resurgent

At the final chicane, Damon Hill outbraked the Williams of Heinz Harald Frentzen and took fourth place for Jordan. Hill had driven solidly throughout the race, and his final overtaking manoeuvre was arguably a less than subtle way of telling Frentzen – his new team-mate for 1999 – who was the number one Jordan driver. After a terrible start to the season, the Jordan team had fought back and were delighted to gain fourth place in the Constructors' Championship, just behind Williams.

If 1998 had been a poor year for Williams, it was nothing to the disappointment felt by Ferrari in so narrowly missing their first World Championship since 1983. Schumacher graciously described Hakkinen as a worthy winner, and did much to restore his public reputation by coming up to Hakkinen at the end of the race to shake his hand. But there was no hiding the feeling that Schumacher thought the season could have been his. Team manager Jean Todt summed up the dilemma faced by Ferrari: "We have shown we are capable of winning Grands Prix, but we must show that one day we will be able to win a World Championship." Ferrari president Luca di Montezemolo was more upbeat, however, and promised victory in 1999.

A chivalrous moment: Michael Schumacher (with Eddie Irvine) shakes hands with Mika Hakkinen to congratulate him on his victory.

JAPANESE GRAND PRIX

orld Champion Mika Hakkinen locks up his brakes in recognition of the tribute from the McLaren team, while (inset) he is surrounded by well-wishers.

Mika Hakkinen emphatically answered his critics by winning the Formula One World Championship in commanding style.

NEW WORLD CHAMPION

From under-achiever to World Champion

The reputation of being a solid if not extraordinary driver has been pinned to Mika Hakkinen for much of his Formula One career. He took the first hurdles very rapidly on the way into Formula One: CART championship, Formula Ford, and Formula Three. In 1991, his debut in the world of Formula One took place in a Lotus-Judd at the Phoenix Grand Prix in Arizona. Despite a respectable seventh place on the starting grid, his debut ended in failure when he failed to finish. Nevertheless, he reached the victor's podium (third place) by his third race, although those were the only points he gained that year.

In his second season at Lotus, Hakkinen achieved an eighth place in the overall driver listings – something of a miracle in view of the poor resources available to him.

After two years with Lotus, Hakkinen's career line seemed to flatten out when he signed a contract as a test driver with McLaren. Without complaint, he carried on with his duties until he was given a chance to prove himself towards the end of 1993, when he replaced Michael Andretti. The main driver at McLaren was Ayrton Senna, and in one race he managed to outqualify the brilliant Brazilian. Hakkinen also achieved third place at the Japanese Grand Prix. In 1994 Hakkinen was taken on by McLaren as the permanent second driver to Senna, and he achieved a creditable fourth place in the drivers' World Championship.

Thereafter, Hakkinen's career seemed to be on hold. In 1995 he finished in seventh place, and he gained overall fifth places in both the 1996 and 1997 Championships. However, critics claimed that Hakkinen lacked aggression. These critics, however, overlooked the fact that the McLaren cars he was driving were far from up to the standards set by Williams and Benetton. Too often, technical defects – rather than any lack of driving skill on Hakkinen's part – were the factors that produced the poor results. The Finnish ex-World Champion Keke Rosberg (now Hakkinen's manager) made the point: "I think he is much more competent behind the steering wheel than many will admit." By winning the title against Michael Schumacher, who was driving a very competitive Ferrari, the "quiet man" of Formula One has made the critics think again.

HAKKINEN'S ROAD TO THE WORLD CHAMPIONSHIP

Australian Grand Prix: Mika Hakkinen wins the curtain-raiser in Melbourne. The Grand Prix ended for Michael Schumacher in the fifth lap because of engine trouble. The Finn led by 10 points to 0.
Brazilian Grand Prix: A third place for Schumacher. Hakkinen was again first over the finishing line and therefore led Schumacher by 20 points to 4 in the Championship table.
Argentine Grand Prix: Ferrari driver Michael Schumacher celebrates his first victory. Mika Hakkinen was in second place. Points position: 26 to 14 in favour of Hakkinen.
San Marino Grand Prix: Schumacher is second behind David Coulthard. Hakkinen had to park his car during lap 17 because of gear box damage. Nevertheless, Hakkinen retained his leadership in the drivers' table with 26 points to 20.
Spanish Grand Prix: An effortless victory by Hakkinen in Barcelona. Schumacher takes third place. Points: 30 to 24 for Hakkinen.
Monaco Grand Prix: An on-form Mika Hakkinen deals effortlessly with the narrow street-circuit in Monte Carlo and comes first. After an unplanned pit-stop due to a collision, Michael Schumacher only managed tenth place. This victory allowed the McLaren driver to extend his lead to 22 points overall (46 to 24).
Canadian Grand Prix: First place goes to Schumacher. Hakkinen had to give up in the first lap as a result of a defect in the accelerator mechanism of his car. The current points position: Hakkinen on 46 to Schumacher's 34.
French Grand Prix: Schumacher wins again and Hakkinen has to be content with third place. Hakkinen's lead has been cut to 6 points – 50 to 44.
British Grand Prix: Michael Schumacher's fine run continues with a third win in a row. Mika Hakkinen was second and just holds his overall lead with 2 points (56 to 54) in the World Championship table.
Austrian Grand Prix: The tide turns against Ferrari, with a first place for Hakkinen. Third place goes to Schumacher. The score has moved to 66 to 58 points in favour of the McLaren driver.
German Grand Prix: For the sixth time this season, Hakkinen crosses the line in first place. Schumacher was fifth. A comfortable points lead for Mika Hakkinen begins to build – 76 to 60.
Hungarian Grand Prix: First place goes to Michael Schumacher, with only a single point assigned to sixth-placed Mika Hakkinen. The McLaren driver holds his lead, nevertheless, with 77 points to 70.
Belgian Grand Prix: Both the World Championship hopefuls drop out after collisions with other vehicles, the victory going to Jordan driver Damon Hill. Unaltered points position: 77 to 70.
Italian Grand Prix: Schumacher wins in Monza. Hakkinen is fourth. 80 points to 80 – for the very first time this season both the leading drivers have equal World Championship points.
Luxembourg Grand Prix: Victory for Hakkinen over Schumacher, who has to be satisfied with second place. As a consequence, Hakkinen goes to the spectacular showdown in Japan with a marginal lead of 4 points (90 to 86).
Japanese Grand Prix: Victory in the race and in the World Championship goes to Mika Hakkinen. After a bad start, Ferrari's Michael Schumacher has to retire with a blown tyre. The final score: 100 points to Hakkinen, 86 to Schumacher.

Mika Hakkinen, shown here celebrating his victory on the Nürburgring, and now a worthy World Champion.

23·6

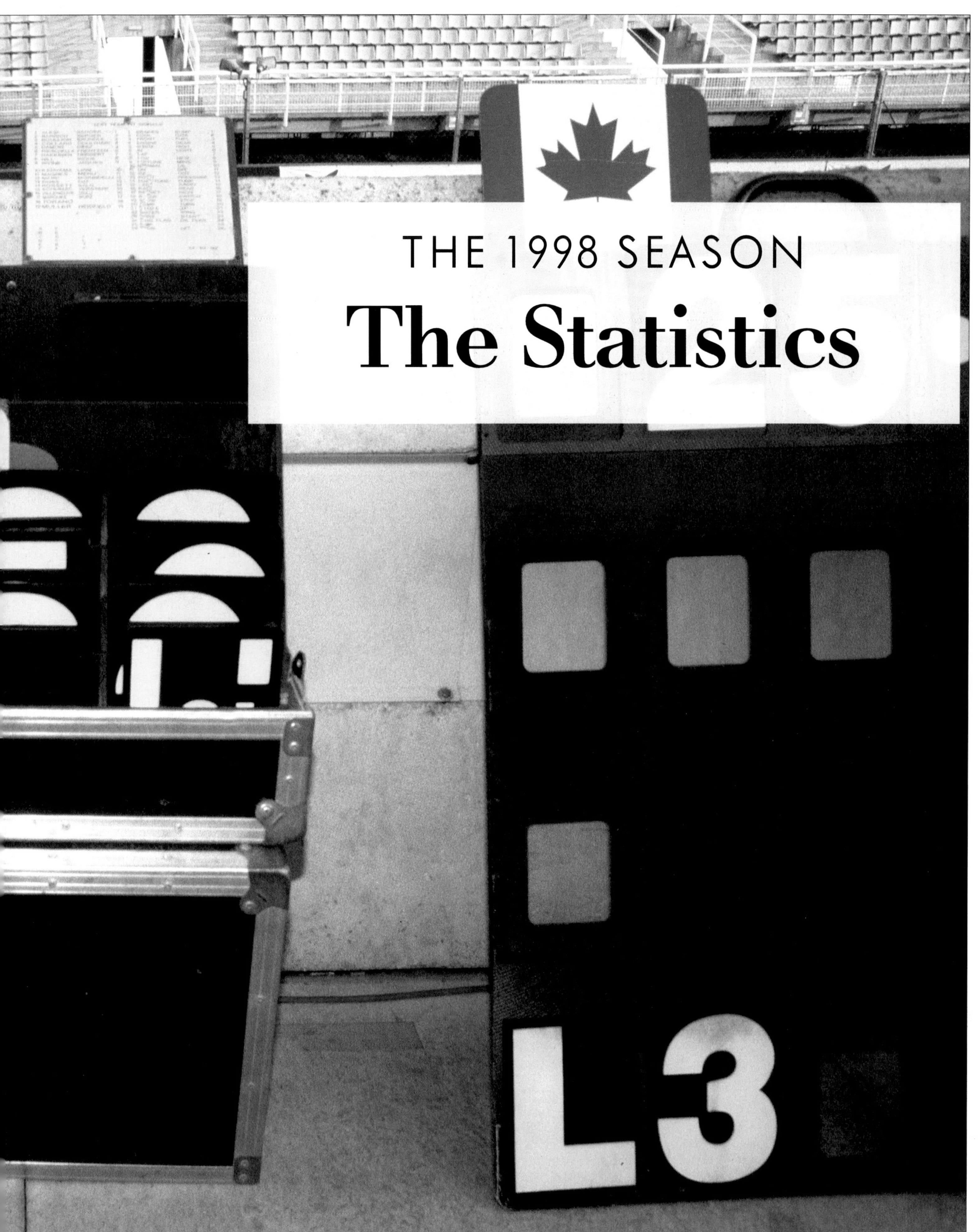

THE 1998 SEASON

The Statistics

Australian Grand Prix

8 March, Melbourne

First World Championship race; track length: 5.302 km; race distance: 58 laps (307.516 km); lap record: 1:30.585 min (210.710 kmh/130.929 mph), Heinz-Harald Frentzen, Williams-Renault (1997); fastest lap: Mika Hakkinen: 1:37.7min; weather: fine and mild; spectators: 103,000

RACE RESULT

Driver	Team	Laps	Time (hours)	Ave. (mph)	Difference
1 Hakkinen	McLaren-Mercedes	58	1:31:45.996	124.958	
2 Coulthard	McLaren-Mercedes	58	1:31:46.698	124.943	0.702 sec
3 Frentzen	Williams-Mecachrome	57	1:31:54.664	122.611	1 lap
4 Irvine	Ferrari	57	1:31:55.743	122.564	1 lap
5 Villeneuve	Williams-Mecachrome	57	1:32:30.546	121.819	1 lap
6 Herbert	Sauber-Petronas	57	1:32:30.970	121.809	1 lap
7 Wurz	Benetton-Mecachrome	57	1:32:33.611	121.751	1 lap
8 Hill	Jordan-Mugen-Honda	57	1:32:34.894	121.723	1 lap
9 Panis	Prost-Peugeot	57	1:32:52.446	121.339	1 lap

RETIREMENTS

Driver	Team	Lap	Reason	Position before retirement
Fisichella	Benetton-Mecachrome	43	Bodywork damage	7
Alesi	Sauber-Petronas	41	Engine failure	8
Trulli	Prost-Peugeot	26	Gear box failure	7
Rosset	Tyrrell-Ford	25	Gear problems	13
Salo	Arrows-Hart	23	Power failure	11
Tuero	Minardi-Ford	22	Engine failure	14
Nakano	Minardi-Ford	8	Back axle broken	16
M. Schumacher	Ferrari	5	Engine failure	3
Diniz	Arrows-Hart	2	Hydraulic failure	18
R. Schumacher	Jordan-Mugen-Honda	1	Collision with Magnussen	14
Magnussen	Stewart-Ford	1	Collision with R. Schumacher	15
Takagi	Tyrrell-Ford	1	Spun off	13
Barrichello	Stewart-Ford	0	Gear box failure	14

PITSTOPS

Lap		Duration* (sec)	Lap		Duration* (sec)
8	Nakano	1:07.593	28	Villeneuve	26.102
12	Tuero	26.182	28	Panis	27.245
18	Rosset	26.533	29	Alesi	27.278
18	Tuero	31.836	33	Frentzen	24.314
19	Hill	26.976	33	Irvine	29.968
19	Salo	25.448	36	Hakkinen***	11.242
20	Wurz	22.398	36	Wurz	25.529
22	Fisichella	22.885	39	Hill	24.907
24	Hakkinen	23.546	40	Hakkinen	26.981
25	Coulthard	23.319	42	Coulthard**	21.931
27	Herbert	27.977	41	Fisichella	23.775

* including driving to and from pit
** fastest pitstop
*** Hakkinen drove through the pit lane without stopping

Brazilian Grand Prix

29 March, São Paulo

Second World Championship race; track length: 4.292 km; race distance: 72 laps (309.024 km); lap record: 1:18.397 min (197.089 kmh/122.465 mph), Jacques Villeneuve, Williams Renault (1997); fastest lap: 1:19.337 min (194.754 kmh/121.014 mph), Mika Hakkinen, McLaren-Mercedes; weather: cloudy, drizzle at end; spectators: 52,611

RACE RESULT

Driver	Team	Laps	Time (hours)	Ave. (mph)	Difference
1 Hakkinen	McLaren-Mercedes	72	1:37:11.747	118.535	
2 Coulthard	McLaren-Mercedes	72	1:37:12.849	118.512	1.102 sec
3 M. Schumacher	Ferrari	72	1:38:12.297	117.317	1:00.550 min
4 Wurz	Benetton-Mecachrome	72	1:38:19.200	117.179	1:07.453 min
5 Frentzen	Williams-Mecachrome	71	1:37:14.445	116.835	1 lap
6 Fisichella	Benetton-Mecachrome	71	1:37:19.574	116.732	1 lap
7 Villeneuve	Williams-Mecachrome	71	1:37:23.653	116.651	1 lap
8 Irvine	Ferrari	71	1:37:28.184	116.560	1 lap
9 Alesi	Sauber-Petronas	71	1:37:42.228	116.281	1 lap
10 Magnussen	Stewart-Ford	70	1:37:41.719	114.653	1 lap
11 Herbert*	Sauber-Petronas	67	1:33:34.057	114.543	Retired

** Retired but still assessed because of the distance travelled*

Damon Hill finished the race as tenth but was later disqualified because his Jordan was underweight

RETIREMENTS

Driver	Team	Lap	Reason	Position before retirement
Herbert	Sauber-Petronas	67	Engine failure	12
Panis	Prost-Peugeot	63	Gear box failure	10
Barrichello	Stewart-Ford	56	Gear box failure	12
Rosset	Tyrrell-Ford	52	Gear box failure	16
Tuero	Minardi-Ford	44	Spun off	15
Diniz	Arrows-Hart	26	Gear box failure	15
Takagi	Tyrrell-Ford	19	Engine failure	15
Salo	Arrows-Hart	18	Engine failure	17
Trulli	Prost-Peugeot	17	Fuel pressure	20
Nakano	Minardi-Ford	3	Spun off	16
R. Schumacher	Jordan-Mugen-Honda	0	Spun off	8

PITSTOPS

Lap		Duration* (sec)	Lap		Duration* (sec)
22	Rosset	37.063	41	Herbert	36.519
24	Magnussen	41.362	42	Alesi	35.265
26	M. Schumacher	33.656	43	Panis	39.871
27	Frentzen	33.455	45	Frentzen	33.532
27	Irvine	33.938	46	Wurz	34.914
29	Villeneuve	34.602	47	Fisichella	33.805
36	Coulthard	35.893	48	Villeneuve**	33.185
36	Barrichello	41.078	49	Rosset	39.146
36	Hill	36.749	49	Magnussen	39.580
39	Hakkinen	37.402	53	M. Schumacher	38.450
40	Tuero	41.452	55	Irvine	33.307

* including driving to and from pit
** fastest pitstop

Argentine Grand Prix

12 April, Buenos Aires

Third World Championship race; track length: 4.259 km; race distance: 72 laps (306.648 km); lap record: 1:27.981 min (174.269 kmh/108.286 mph), Gerhard Berger, Benetton-Renault (1997); fastest lap: 1:28.179 min (173.878 kmh/108.043 mph), Alexander Wurz, Benetton-Mecachrome; weather: cloudy, windy, cool;

RACE RESULTS

	Driver	Stable	Laps	Time (hrs)	Ave (mph)	Difference
1	M. Schumacher	Ferrari	72	1:48:36.175	105.201	
2	Hakkinen	McLaren-Mercedes	72	1:48:59.073	104.832	22.899 sec
3	Irvine	Ferrari	72	1:49:33.920	104.277	57.745sec
4	Wurz	Benetton-Mecachrome	72	1:49:44.309	104.112	1:08.134min
5	Alesi	Sauber-Petronas	72	1:49:54.461	103.952	1:18.286min
6	Coulthard	McLaren-Mercedes	72	1:49:54.926	103.929	1:19.751min
7	Fisichella	Benetton-Mecachrome	72	1:50:04.612	103.792	1:28.438min
8	Hill	Jordan-Mugen-Honda	71	1:49:17.761	103.080	1 lap
9	Frentzen	Williams-Mecachrome	71	1:49:43.772	102.673	1 lap
10	Barrichello	Stewart-Ford	70	1:49:03.354	101.851	2 laps
11	Trulli	Prost-Peugeot	70	1:49:18.377	101.618	2 laps
12	Takagi	Tyrrell-Ford	70	1:50:15.941	100.734	2 laps
13	Nakano	Minardi-Ford	69	1:49:18.217	100.168	3 laps
14	Rosset	Tyrrell-Ford	68	1:48:49.538	99.149	4 laps
15	Panis*	Prost-Peugeot		1:39:39.861	103.483	Retired

** Retired but still assessed because of the distance travelled*

RETIREMENTS

Driver	Stable	Lap	Reason	Position before retirement
Panis	Prost-Peugeot	65	Engine failure	8
Tuero	Minardi-Ford	63	Accident	15
Villeneuve	Williams-Mecachrome	52	Collision with Coulthard	6
Herbert	Sauber-Petronas	46	Collision with Hill	9
R. Schumacher	Jordan-Mugen-Honda	22	Spun off	18
Salo	Arrows-Hart	18	Gear box failure	16
Magnussen	Stewart-Ford	17	Transmission failure	20
Diniz	Arrows-Hart	13	Gear box failure	19

PITSTOPS

Lap	Driver	Duration* (sec)	Lap	Driver	Duration* (sec)
18	R. Schumacher	28.306	**39**	Herbert	27.296
27	Alesi	26.044	**39**	Trulli	27.731
28	M. Schumacher	25.999	**40**	Wurz	27.696
28	Hill	26.698	**40**	Barrichello	34.156
29	Irvine	25.762	**42**	Hakkinen	26.241
32	Coulthard	27.649	**42**	Panis	27.686
34	Rosset	30.424	**43**	Frentzen	28.139
35	Tuero	1:01.645	**45**	Barrichello	31.805
37	Villeneuve	29.088	**46**	Hill	35.037
37	Fisichella	27.448	**50**	Alesi	25.127
38	Frentzen	55.876	**53**	M. Schumacher**	24.472
38	Takagi	30.051	**55**	Irvine	24.760
38	Nakano	36.775			

* including driving to and from pit
** fastest pitstop

San Marino Grand Prix

26 April, Imola

Fourth World Championship race; track length: 4.93km; race distance: 62 laps (305.66 km); lap record: 1:25.531 min (207.503 kmh/128.936 mph), Heinz Harald Frentzen, Williams-Renault (1997); fastest lap: 1:19.337 min (194.754 kmh/121.014 mph), Mika Hakkinen, McLaren-Mercedes; weather: cloudy, drizzle at end; spectators: 52,611

RACE RESULTS

	Driver	Team	Laps	Time (hrs)	Ave. (mph)	Difference
1	Coulthard	McLaren-Mercedes	62	1:34:24.593	120.619	
2	M. Schumacher	Ferrari	62	1:34:29.147	120.522	4.554 sec
3	Irvine	Ferrari	62	1:35:16.368	119.526	51.776 sec
4	Villeneuve	Williams-Mecachrome	62	1:35:19.183	119.467	54.590 sec
5	Frentzen	Williams-Mecachrome	62	1:35:42.069	118.991	1:17.477 min
6	Alesi	Sauber-Petronas	61	1:34:30.693	118.544	1 lap
7	R. Schumacher	Jordan-Mugen-Honda	60	1:34:34.790	116.515	2 laps
8	Tuero	Minardi-Ford	60	1:35:48.285	115.025	2 laps
9	Salo	Arrows-Hart	60	1:35:55.865	114.874	2 laps
10	Hill*	Jordan-Mugen-Honda	57	1:29:29.923	116.969	Retired
11	Panis*	Prost-Peugeot	56	1:27:03.370	118.139	Retired

** Retired but still assessed because of the distance travelled*

RETIREMENTS

Driver	Team	Lap	Reason	Position before retirement
Hill*	Jordan-Mugen-Honda	57	Engine failure	7
Panis*	Prost-Peugeot	56	Engine failure	7
Rosset	Tyrrell-Ford	48	Engine failure	12
Takagi	Tyrrell-Ford	40	Engine failure	10
Trulli	Prost-Peugeot	34	Throttle failure	10
Nakano	Minardi-Ford	27	Engine failure	15
Diniz	Arrows-Hart	18	Engine failure	14
Hakkinen	McLaren-Mercedes	17	Gear box failure	5
Fisichella	Benetton-Mecachrome	17	Accident	7
Wurz	Benetton-Mecachrome	17	Engine failure	19
Herbert	Sauber-Petronas	12	Suspension failure	13
Magnussen	Stewart-Ford	8	Gear box failure	20
Barrichello	Stewart-Ford	0	Spun off	17

PITSTOPS

Lap	Driver	Duration* (sec)	Lap	Driver	Duration* (sec)
1	Hill	32,328	**27**	Irvine	24.531
1	Magnussen	31,748	**27**	Frentzen	25.030
1	Wurz	59,839	**27**	Salo	54.989
18	Salo	29,915	**29**	Salo	30.015
18	Rosset	27,848	**36**	R. Schumacher	31.920
20	Takagi	25,473	**36**	Rosset	26.520
20	Nakano	33,423	**40**	Alesi	26.860
21	R. Schumacher	29,236	**41**	Frentzen	26.769
22	Alesi	24,763	**41**	Panis	25.229
22	Trulli	25,479	**41**	Hill	29.324
22	Tuero	28,265	**44**	Coulthard	24.302
23	Panis	24,639	**42**	Tuero	28.677
24	Hill	27,892	**44**	Irvine	23.769
26	Coulthard	24,585	**44**	Villeneuve	28.918
26	M. Schumacher	25,022	**46**	M. Schumacher **	23.299
26	Villeneuve	28,113			

* including driving to and from pit
** fastest pitstop

Spanish Grand Prix

10 May, Barcelona

Fifth World Championship race; track length: 4.728 km; race distance: 65 laps (307.32 km); lap record: 1:22.242 min (206.960 kmh/128.599 mph), Giancarlo Fisichella, Jordan-Peugeot (1997); fastest lap: 1:24.275 min (201.967 kmh/125.496 mph), Mika Hakkinen, McLaren-Mercedes; weather: slightly cloudy, warm, windy; spectators: 65,000

RACE RESULTS

Driver	Team	Laps	Time (hrs)	Ave. (mph)	Difference
1 Hakkinen	McLaren-Mercedes	65	1:33:37.621	122.325	
2 Coulthard	McLaren-Mercedes	65	1:33:47.060	122.120	9.439 sec
3 M. Schumacher	Ferrari	65	1:34:24.716	121.308	47.094 sec
4 Wurz	Benetton-Mecachrome	65	1:34:40.159	120.978	1:02.538 min
5 Barrichello	Stewart-Ford	64	1:33:54.435	120.083	1 lap
6 Villeneuve	Williams-Mecachrome	64	1:33:55.147	120.068	1 lap
7 Herbert	Sauber-Petronas	64	1:33:58.147	120.004	1 lap
8 Frentzen	Williams-Mecachrome	63	1:33:42.553	118.456	2 laps
9 Trulli	Prost-Peugeot	63	1:33:46.888	118.364	2 laps
10 Alesi	Sauber-Petronas	63	1:33:47.986	118.341	2 laps
11 R. Schumacher	Jordan-Mugen-Honda	63	1:33:49.657	118.306	2 laps
12 Magnussen	Stewart-Ford	63	1:34.01.002	118.069	2 laps
13 Takagi	Tyrrell-Ford	63	1:34:37.620	117.307	2 laps
14 Nakano	Minardi-Ford	63	1:34:41.328	117.230	2 laps
15 Tuero	Minardi-Ford	63	1:34:42.163	117.213	2 laps
16 Panis*	Prost-Peugeot	60	1:28:29.202	119.471	Retired

* Retired but still assessed because of the distance travelled

RETIREMENTS

Driver	Team	Lap	Reason	Position before retirement
Panis*	Prost-Peugeot	60	Hydraulic failure	8
Hill	Jordan-Mugen-Honda	46	Engine failure	9
Fisichella	Benetton-Mecachrome	28	Collision with Irvine	5
Irvine	Ferrari	28	Collision with Fisichella	4
Salo	Arrows-Hart	21	Engine failure	12
Diniz	Arrows-Hart	20	Engine failure	21

PITSTOPS

Lap	Duration* (sec)	Lap	Duration* (sec)
2 Frentzen	35.395	**33** Trulli	31.385
18 Panis	27.989	**34** Alesi	27.670
19 Magnussen	29.445	**38** Tuero	29.976
19 R. Schumacher	28.489	**40** M. Schumacher	28.983
21 Takagi	28.000	**40** Frentzen	29.628
21 Tuero	30.033	**40** Takagi	28.614
21 Frentzen	29.818	**40** Nakano	31.159
22 Barrichello	27.409	**42** Panis	27.456
22 Herbert	26.694	**42** R. Schumacher	27.647
22 Hill	27.241	**42** Magnussen	29.417
23 Wurz	28.239	**42** Tuero	28.682
23 Nakano	29.053	**44** Barrichello	28.329
24 Trulli	26.009	**44** Herbert	26.194
24 Alesi	25.243	**45** Hakkinen	30.994
25 Irvine	26.982	**45** Hill	27.212
25 Fisichella	27.380	**45** Villeneuve	28.248
26 Hakkinen	27.261	**46** Coulthard**	25.156
27 Coulthard	25.920	**46** Wurz	26.669
27 M. Schumacher	26.056	**48** M. Schumacher	25.794

* including driving to and from pit
** fastest pitstop

Monaco Grand Prix

24 May, Monte Carlo

Sixth World Championship race; track length: 3.367 km; race distance: 78 laps (307.32 km); old lap record: 1:53.315 min (106.937 kmh/66.448 mph), Michael Schumacher, Ferrari (1997); new lap record: 1:22.948 min (146.13 kmh/90.801 mph), Mika Hakkinen, McLaren-Mercedes; weather: slightly cloudy, mild;

RACE RESULTS

Driver	Team	Laps	Time (hrs)	Ave. (mph)	Difference
1 Hakkinen	McLaren-Mercedes	78	1:51:23.595	87.898	
2 Fisichella	Benetton-Mecachrome	78	1:51:35.070	87.748	11.475 sec
3 Irvine	Ferrari	78	1:52:04.973	87.357	41.378 sec
4 Salo	Arrows-Hart	78	1:52:23.958	87.111	1:00.363 min
5 Villeneuve	Williams-Mecachrome	77	1:51:58.811	86.317	1 lap
6 Diniz	Arrows-Hart	77	1:52:06.752	86.215	1 lap
7 Herbert	Sauber-Petronas	77	1:52:35.186	85.839	1 lap
8 Hill	Jordan-Mugen-Honda	76	1:51:47.513	85.339	2 laps
9 Nakano	Minardi-Ford	76	1:51:48.485	85.327	2 laps
10 M. Schumacher	Ferrari	76	1:52:16.789	84.968	2 laps
11 Takagi	Tyrrell-Ford	76	1:52:31.704	84.780	2 laps
12 Alesi*	Sauber-Petronas	72	1:44:13.825	86.712	Retired

* Retired but still assessed because of the distance travelled

RETIREMENTS

Driver	Team	Lap	Reason	Position before retirement
Alesi	Sauber-Petronas	72	Gear box failure	5
Trulli	Prost-Peugeot	56	Gear box failure	10
Panis	Prost-Peugeot	49	Lost a wheel	13
R. Schumacher	Jordan-Mugen-Honda	44	Suspension	11
Wurz	Benetton-Mecachrome	42	Accident	4
Magnussen	Stewart-Ford	30	Suspension	12
Coulthard	McLaren-Mercedes	17	Engine failure	2
Barrichello	Stewart-Ford	11	Suspension failure	12
Frentzen	Williams-Mecachrome	9	Collision with Irvine	6
Tuero	Minardi-Ford	0	Accident	21

PITSTOPS

Lap	Duration*(sec)	Lap	Duration*(sec)
16 Panis	26.111	**41** Nakano	29.992
20 Takagi	26.702	**42** Wurz	27.200
30 M. Schumacher**	24.328	**42** Takagi	29.909
30 Alesi	24.876	**43** Diniz	28.466
31 Fisichella	27.644	**43** Hill	26.200
37 Hakkinen	28.603	**45** Irvine	25.317
37 Trulli	30.548	**45** R. Schumacher	35.483
38 M. Schumacher	4:05.291	**54** Villeneuve	24.449
38 Herbert	26.312	**55** Alesi	24.352
41 Salo	27.368		

* including driving to and from pit
** fastest pitstop

Canadian Grand Prix

7 June, Montreal

Seventh World Championship race; track length: 4.421 km; race distance: 69 laps (305.049 km); old lap record: 1:19.635 min (199.856 kmh/124.185 mph), David Coulthard, McLaren-Mercedes (1997); new lap record: 1:19.379 min (200.501 kmh/124.586 mph), Michael Schumacher, Ferrari; weather: cloudy and cool; spectators: 100,912

RACE RESULTS

Driver	Team	Laps	Time (hrs)	Ave. (mph)	Difference
1 M. Schumacher	Ferrari	69	1:40:57.355	112.652	
2 Fisichella	Benetton-Mecachrome	69	1:41:14.017	112.343	16.662 sec
3 Irvine	Ferrari	69	1:41:57.414	111.546	1:00.059 min
4 Wurz	Benetton-Mecachrome	69	1:42:00.587	111.488	1:03.232 min
5 Barrichello	Stewart-Ford	69	1:42:18.868	111.156	1:21.513 min
6 Magnussen	Stewart-Ford	68	1:41:26.707	110.484	1 lap
7 Nakano	Minardi-Ford	68	1:41:27.937	110.462	1 lap
8 Rosset	Tyrrell-Ford	68	1:42:17.371	109.572	1 lap
9 Diniz	Arrows-Hart	68	1:42:19.361	109.537	1 lap
10 Villeneuve	Williams-Mecachrome	63	1:41:14.604	102.902	6 laps

RETIREMENTS

Driver	Team	Lap	Reason	Position before retirement
Tuero	Minardi-Ford	53	Collision with Villeneuve	9
Hill	Jordan-Mugen-Honda	42	Electric failure	11
Panis	Prost-Peugeot	39	Engine failure	3
Frentzen	Williams-Mecachrome	20	Spun off	4
Coulthard	McLaren-Mercedes	18	Gear box failure	1
Herbert	Sauber-Petronas	18	Spun off	9
Salo	Arrows-Hart	18	Accident	12
Hakkinen	McLaren-Mercedes	0	Gear box failure	2
R. Schumacher	Jordan-Mugen-Honda	0	Transmission failure	5
Alesi	Sauber-Petronas	0	Collision with Trulli	9
Trulli	Prost-Peugeot	0	Collision with Alesi	10
Takagi	Tyrrell-Ford	0	Clutch defect	16

PITSTOPS

Lap		Duration* (sec)	Lap		Duration* (sec)
1	Irvine	53.521	**38**	Irvine	25.540
14	Diniz	29.034	**39**	Hill	28.182
15	Rosset	30.607	**39**	Nakano	29.094
20	M. Schumacher	25.532	**40**	Wurz	27.997
21	Barrichello	29.162	**41**	Hill	36.699
21	Rosset	30.341	**42**	Hill	2:52.748
23	Villeneuve	7:40.133	**44**	Fisichella	27.419
23	Tuero	35.029	**48**	Barrichello	26.631
35	M. Schumacher	27.034	**50**	M. Schumacher	24.092
35	Magnussen	27.799	**55**	Irvine**	23.516
37	Diniz	31.445	**62**	Rosset	25.249

* including driving to and from pit
** fastest pitstop

French Grand Prix

28 June, Magny-Cours

Eighth World Championship race; track length: 4.25 km; race distance: 71 laps (301.75 km); lap record: 1:17.070 min (198.521 kmh/123.355 mph), Nigel Mansell, Williams-Renault (1992); fastest lap: 1:17.523 min (197.36 kmh/122.634 mph), David Coulthard, McLaren-Mercedes; weather: cloudy, windy, warm; spectators: 75,000

RACE RESULTS

Driver	Team	Laps	Time (hrs)	Ave. (mph)	Difference
1 M. Schumacher	Ferrari	71	1:34:45.026	118.659	
2 Irvine	Ferrari	71	1.35:04.601	118.251	19.575 sec
3 Hakkinen	McLaren-Mercedes	71	1:35:04.773	118.248	19.747 sec
4 Villeneuve	Williams-Mecachrome	71	1:35:51.991	117.277	1:06.965 min
5 Wurz	Benetton-Mecachrome	70	1:34:47.515	116.935	1 lap
6 Coulthard	McLaren-Mercedes	70	1:34:52.416	116.835	1 lap
7 Alesi	Sauber-Petronas	70	1:34:54.330	116.795	1 lap
8 Herbert	Sauber-Petronas	70	1:35:37.415	115.918	1 lap
9 Fisichella	Benetton-Mecachrome	70	1:35:53.089	115.602	1 lap
10 Barrichello	Stewart-Ford	69	1:34:46.884	115.276	2 laps
11 Panis	Prost-Peugeot	69	1:35:02.913	114.952	2 laps
12 Verstappen	Stewart-Ford	69	1:35:21.800	114.573	2 laps
13 Salo	Arrows-Hart	69	1:35:43.315	114.144	2 laps
14 Diniz	Arrows-Hart	69	1:36:03.194	113.750	2 laps
15 Frentzen*	Williams-Mecachrome	68	1:32:26.742	116.475	Retired
16 R. Schumacher	Jordan-Mugen-Honda	68	1:35:42.686	112.500	3 laps
17 Nakano*	Minardi-Ford	65	1:30:51.169	113.285	Retired

* Retired but still assessed because of the distance travelled

RETIREMENTS

Driver	Yeam	Lap	Reason	Position before retirement
Frenzten	Williams-Mecachrome	68	Mechanical failure	8
Nakano	Minardi-Ford	65	Engine failure	16
Takagi	Tyrrell-Ford	60	Engine failure	15
Trulli	Prost-Peugeot	55	Spun off	17
Tuero	Monardi-Ford	41	Gear box failure	19
Hill	Jordan-Mugen-Honda	19	Hydraulic leakage	14
Rosset	Tyrrell-Ford	16	Engine failure	17

PITSTOPS

Lap		Duration* (sec)	Lap		Duration* (sec)
2	Trulli	1:21.652	**35**	Takagi	26.723
15	Takagi	26.413	**35**	Tuero	30.959
16	R. Schumacher	27.167	**39**	Diniz	28.578
17	Wurz	25.111	**43**	Irvine	26.628
17	Hill	26.616	**45**	M. Schumacher	26.537
18	Fisichella	24.600	**45**	Nakano	28.192
18	R. Schumacher	2:22.308	**45**	Panis	26.239
20	Frentzen	26.576	**45**	Verstappen	25.816
21	Hakkinen	25.830	**46**	Alesi	25.378
21	Verstappen	28.725	**46**	Trulli	26.539
22	M. Schumacher	25.905	**47**	Herbert	25.848
22	Nakano	27.796	**47**	Barrichello	25.654
22	Coulthard	34.293	**48**	Villeneuve	26.031
23	Irvine	25.451	**50**	Wurz	25.114
23	Alesi	25.883	**51**	Frentzen	24.759
23	Barrichello	26.668	**51**	Takagi	26.467
24	Villeneuve	25.997	**52**	Fisichella	26.386
24	Herbert	45.659	**54**	Hakkinen	25.698
25	Trulli	25:814	**55**	Coulthard	53.598
29	Panis	25.631	**53**	R. Schumacher	25.176
31	Salo	28.109	**56**	Coulthard	31.297
33	Wurz**	24.101	**63**	Coulthard	27.156
34	Fisichella	31.547			

* including driving to and from pit
** fastest pitstop

British Grand Prix

12 July, Silverstone

Ninth World Championship race; track length: 5.14 km; race distance: 60 laps (308.4 km); lap record: 1:24.475 min (219.047 kmh/136.109 mph), Michael Schumacher, Ferrari (1997); fastest lap: 1:35.704 min (193.346 kmh/120.140 mph), Michael Schumacher, Ferrari; weather: variously heavy rain, cool, windy; spectators: 110,000

RACE RESULTS

Driver	Team	Laps	Time (hrs)	Ave. (mph)	Difference
1 M. Schumacher	Ferrari	60	1:47:02.450	107.379	
2 Hakkinen	McLaren-Mercedes	60	1:47:24.915	107.004	22.465 sec
3 Irvine	Ferrari	60	1:47:31.649	106.893	29.199 sec
4 Wurz	Benetton-Mecachrome	59	1:47:29.402	105.148	1 lap
5 Fisichella	Benetton-Mecachrome	59	1:47:30.546	105.129	1 lap
6 R. Schumacher	Jordan-Mugen-Honda	59	1:47:54.075	104.747	1 lap
7 Villeneuve	Williams-Mecachrome	59	1:48:20.879	104.315	1 lap
8 Nakano	Minardi-Ford	58	1:48:26.357	102.460	2 laps
9 Takagi	Tyrrell-Ford	56	1:47:37.746	99.670	4 laps

RETIREMENTS

Driver	Team	Lap	Reason	Position before retirement
Alesi	Sauber-Petronas	53	Electric failure	4
Diniz	Arrows-Hart	45	Spun off	11
Panis	Prost-Peugeot	40	Spun off	9
Barrichello	Stewart-Ford	39	Spun off	11
Verstappen	Stewart-Ford	38	Engine failure	11
Coulthard	McLaren-Mercedes	37	Spun off	2
Trulli	Prost-Peugeot	37	Spun off	15
Rosset	Tyrrell-Ford	29	Spun off	16
Tuero	Minardi-Ford	29	Spun off	17
Herbert	Sauber-Petronas	27	Spun off	10
Salo	Arrows-Hart	27	Spun off	11
Frentzen	Williams-Mecachrome	15	Spun off	6
Hill	Jordan-Mugen-Honda	13	Spun off	8

PITSTOPS

Lap		Duration* (sec)	Lap		Duration* (sec)
13	R. Schumacher	30.004	23	Trulli	55.064
16	Verstappen	32.413	26	Panis	32.593
18	Fisichella	30.627	29	Nakano	32.996
18	Barrichello	32.816	35	R. Schumacher	32.978
18	Diniz	31.499	35	Irvine	30.382
19	M. Schumacher	28.883	39	Villeneuve	32.583
19	Rosset	32.243	39	Diniz	4:19.224
19	Villeneuve	31.458	40	Hakkinen	27.851
19	Wurz	32.998	40	M. Schumacher	30.509
20	Salo	29.099	40	Alesi	33.843
21	Coulthard	28.352	40	Wurz	36.840
21	Takagi	33.961	40	R. Schumacher	32.886
22	Alesi	29.144	41	Villeneuve	33.080
22	Irvine**	26.509	43	Fisichella	30.760
23	Hakkinen	27.978	43	Takagi	31.860

* including driving to and from pit
** fastest pitstop

Austrian Grand Prix

26 July, Zeltweg

Tenth World Championship race; track length: 4.319 km; race distance: 71 laps (306.649 km); lap record: 1:11.814 min (216.709 kmh/134.657 mph), Jacques Villeneuve, Williams-Renault (1997); fastest lap: 1:12.878 min (213.348 kmh/132.568 mph), David Coulthard, McLaren-Mercedes; weather: slightly cloudy, warm; spectators: 55,000

RACE RESULTS

Driver	Team	Laps	Time (hrs)	Ave. (mph)	Difference
1 Hakkinen	McLaren-Mercedes	71	1:30:44.086	126.000	
2 Coulthard	McLaren-Mercedes	71	1:30:49.375	125.877	5.289 sec
3 M. Schumacher	Ferrari	71	1:31:23.176	125.101	39.093 sec
4 Irvine	Ferrari	71	1:31:28.062	124.990	43.977 sec
5 R. Schumacher	Jordan-Mugen-Honda	71	1:31:34.740	124.838	50.655 sec
6 Villeneuve	Williams-Mecachrome	71	1:31:37.288	124.780	53.202 sec
7 Hill	Jordan-Mugen-Honda	71	1:31:57.710	124.318	1:13.624 min
8 Herbert	Sauber-Petronas	70	1:30:56.888	123.934	1 lap
9 Wurz	Benetton-Mecachrome	70	1:30:58.611	123.882	1 lap
10 Trulli	Prost-Peugeot	70	1:31:33.536	123.107	1 lap
11 Nakano	Minardi-Ford	70	1:31:44.313	122.866	1 lap
12 Rosset	Tyrrell-Ford	69	1:33:28.193	118.867	2 laps

RETIREMENTS

Driver	Team	Lap	Reason	Position before retirement
Verstappen	Stewart-Ford	51	Engine failure	12
Tuero	Minardi-Ford	30	Spun off	14
Fisichella	Benetton-Mecachrome	21	Collision with Alesi	2
Alesi	Sauber-Petronas	21	Collision with Fisichella	5
Frentzen	Williams-Mecachrome	16	Engine failure	6
Barrichello	Stewart-Ford	8	Brake failure	9
Diniz	Arrows-Hart	3	Collision with Salo	18
Salo	Arrows-Hart	1	Collision with Diniz	20
Panis	Prost-Peugeot	0	Clutch defect	10
Takagi	Tyrrell-Ford	0	Spun off	20

PITSTOPS

Lap		Duration* (sec)	Lap		Duration* (sec)
1	Coulthard	38.584	36	Coulthard	28.421
2	Tuero	47.733	37	Herbert	26.912
3	Tuero**	15.286	38	Trulli	28.768
18	M. Schumacher	39.545	38	Nakano	30.150
19	Hill	26.884	42	M. Schumacher	27.450
21	Fisichella	28.395	43	R. Schumacher	26.404
21	Rosset	28.330	43	Villeneuve	28.563
22	Wurz	27.546	45	Hill	26.546
25	Verstappen	27.181	46	Verstappen	25.995
26	R. Schumacher	27.079	48	Wurz	26.617
26	Tuero	27.862	48	Rosset	29.429
28	Irvine	26.375	52	Irvine	25.472
34	Hakkinen	29.464			

* including driving to and from pit
** fastest pitstop

German Grand Prix

2 August, Hockenheim

Eleventh World Championship race; track length: 6.823 km; race distance: 45 laps (307.035 km); lap record: 1:41.590min (241.524 kmh/150.076 mph), Riccardo Patrese, Williams-Renault; fastest lap: 1:46.471 min (193.346 kmh/120.140 mph), David Coulthard, McLaren-Mercedes; weather: cloudy, cool; spectators: 140,000

RACE RESULTS

Driver	Team	Laps	Time (hrs)	Ave. (mph)	Difference
1 Hakkinen	McLaren-Mercedes	45	1:20:47.984	141.671	
2 Coulthard	McLaren-Mercedes	45	1:20:48.410	141.658	0.427 sec
3 Villeneuve	Williams-Mecachrome	45	1:20:50.561	141.595	2.578 sec
4 Hill	Jordan-Mugen-Honda	45	1:20:55.169	141.461	7.185 sec
5 M. Schumacher	Ferrari	45	1:21:00.597	141.303	12.613 sec
6 R. Schumacher	Jordan-Mugen-Honda	45	1:21:17.722	140.807	29.739 sec
7 Fisichella	Benetton-Mecachrome	45	1:21:19.010	140.770	31.027 sec
8 Irvine	Ferrari	45	1:21:19.633	140.752	31.650 sec
9 Frentzen	Williams-Mecachrome	45	1:21:20.768	140.719	32.785 sec
10 Alesi	Sauber-Petronas	45	1:21:36.355	140.271	48.37 2 sec
11 Wurz	Benetton-Mecachrome	45	1:21:45.978	139.996	57.99 5 sec
12 Trulli	Prost-Peugeot	44	1:20:53.714	138.359	1 lap
13 Takagi	Tyrrell-Ford	44	1:21:07.369	137.970	1 lap
14 Salo	Arrows-Hart	44	1:21:13.440	137.798	1 lap
15 Panis	Prost-Peugeot	44	1:21:52.283	136.709	1 lap
16 Tuero	Minardi-Ford	43	1:22:35.459	132.438	2 laps

RETIREMENTS

Driver	Team	Lap	Reason	Position before retirement
Herbert	Sauber-Petronas	37	Gear box	11
Nakano	Minardi-Ford	36	Gear box	16
Barrichello	Stewart-Ford	27	Gear box	13
Verstappen	Stewart-Ford	24	Transmission failure	17
Diniz	Arrows-Hart	2	Throttle	19

PITSTOPS

Lap		Duration* (sec)	Lap		Duration* (sec)
7	Panis	31.305	**23**	Wurz	31.460
14	R. Schumacher	28.636	**23**	Verstappen	30.009
15	Barrichello	28.455	**24**	M. Schumacher	30.165
19	Tuero	2:46.346	**24**	Trulli	30.313
20	Takagi	32.658	**24**	Salo	32.115
21	Alesi	30.262	**24**	Nakano	31.506
22	Fisichella	30.103	**25**	Irvine	31.440
22	Frentzen	30.127	**26**	Hakkinen	29.764
22	Herbert	29.912	**27**	Coulthard	29.019
22	Panis	33.076	**29**	R. Schumacher**	27.554
23	Villeneuve	30.939	**36**	Panis	34.525
23	Hill	30.446			

* including driving to and from pit
** fastest pitstop

Hungarian Grand Prix

16 August, Budapest

Twelfth World Championship race; track length: 3.972 km; race distance: 77 laps (305.844 km); lap record: 1:18.308 min (182.418 kmh/113.349 mph), Nigel Mansell, Williams-Renault (1992); fastest lap: 1:19.349 min (193.346 kmh/120.140 mph), Michael Schumacher, Ferrari; weather: cloudy, warm; spectators: 115,000

RACE RESULTS

Driver	Team	Laps	Time (hrs)	Ave. (mph)	Difference
1 M. Schumacher	Ferrari	77	1:45:25.550	108.157	
2 Coulthard	McLaren-Mercedes	77	1:45:34.983	107.996	9.433 sec
3 Villeneuve	Williams-Mecachrome	77	1:46:09.994	107.402	44.444 sec
4 Hill	Jordan-Mugen-Honda	77	1:46:20.626	107.223	55.075 sec
5 Frentzen	Williams-Mecachrome	77	1:46:22.060	107.199	56.520 sec
6 Hakkinen	McLaren-Mercedes	76	1:45:29.932	106.678	1 lap
7 Alesi	Sauber-Petronas	76	1:45:41.361	106.476	1 lap
8 Fisichella	Benetton-Mecachrome	76	1:45:56.357	106.235	1 lap
9 R. Schumacher	Jordan-Mugen-Honda	76	1:46:15.311	105.919	1 lap
10 Herbert	Sauber-Petronas	76	1:46:20.059	105.840	1 lap
11 Diniz	Arrows-Hart	74	1:45:27.272	103.914	3 laps
12 Panis	Prost-Peugeot	74	1:45:29.999	103.870	3 laps
13 Verstappen	Stewart-Ford	74	1:45:53.909	103.480	3 laps
14 Takagi	Tyrrell-Ford	74	1:46:08.141	103.248	3 laps
15 Nakano	Minardi-Ford	74	1:47:45.727	101.689	3 laps
16 Wurz*	Benetton-Mecachrome	69	1:36:02.908	106.382	Retired

* Retired but still assessed because of the distance travelled

RETIREMENTS

Driver	Team	Lap	Reason	Position before retirement
Wurz	Benetton-Mecachrome	69	Transmission failure	7
Barrichello	Stewart-Ford	54	Gear box	15
Trulli	Prost-Peugeot	28	Engine failure	12
Salo	Arrows-Hart	18	Gear box	11
Irvine	Ferrari	13	Gear box	4
Tuero	Minardi-Ford	13	Engine failure	20

PITSTOPS

Lap		Duration* (sec)	Lap		Duration* (sec)
18	Takagi	30.773	**44**	Coulthard	30.058
22	Nakano	32.454	**44**	Hakkinen	30.648
23	Trulli	34.207	**44**	Takagi	31.245
24	Hill	29.660	**46**	Diniz	30.433
25	M. Schumacher	30.356	**48**	Herbert	29.908
24	Barrichello	30.929	**48**	Barrichello	32.393
26	Coulthard	29.984	**48**	Nakano	1:01.896
26	R. Schumacher	21.421	**49**	Wurz	31.361
26	Diniz	30.373	**50**	Fisichella	31.508
26	Verstappen	31.433	**50**	Verstappen	30.803
26	Panis	30.200	**51**	Hill	29.576
28	Hakkinnen	30.610	**51**	Alesi	29.985
28	Wurz	30.262	**51**	Panis	31.037
29	Frentzen	38.066	**52**	R. Schumacher	30.588
29	Fisichella	31.088	**54**	Frentzen	30.371
30	Alesi	28.933	**55**	Villeneuve	29.588
31	Villeneuve	34.231	**62**	M. Schumacher	30.046
32	Herbert	29.607			
43	M. Schumacher**	28.938			

* including driving to and from pit
** fastest pitstop

Belgian Grand Prix

30 August, Spa-Francorchamps

Thirteenth World Championship race; track length: 6.968 km; race distance: 44 laps (306.592 km); lap record: 1:51.095 min (225.99 kmh/140.424 mph), Alain Prost, Williams-Renault (1993); fastest lap: 2:03.766 min (202.679 kmh/125.939 mph), Michael Schumacher, Ferrari; weather: misty, rain, cool; spectators: 100,000

RACE RESULTS

	Driver	Team	Laps	Time (hrs)	Ave. (mph)	Difference
1	Hill	Jordan-Mugen-Honda	44	1:43:47.407	110.125	
2	R. Schumacher	Jordan-Mugen-Honda	44	1:43:48.339	110.108	0.932 sec
3	Alesi	Sauber-Petronas	44	1:43:54.647	109.997	7.240 sec
4	Frentzen	Williams-Mecachrome	44	1:44:19.650	109.558	32.242 sec
5	Diniz	Arrows-Hart	44	1:44:39.089	109.218	51.682 sec
6	Trulli	Prost-Peugeot	42	1:44:42.230	104.201	2 laps
7	Coulthard	McLaren-Mercedes	39	1:43:51.212	97.550	5 laps
8	Nakano	Minardi-Ford	39	1:46:01.069	95.559	5 laps

RETIREMENTS

Driver	Team	Lap	Reason	Position before retirement
Fisichella	Benetton-Mecachrome	26	Collision with Nakano	5
M. Schumacher	Ferrari	25	Collision with Coulthard	1
Irvine	Ferrari	25	Spun-off	7
Tuero	Minardi-Ford	17	Electric failure	12
Villeneuve	Williams-Mecachrome	16	Accident	4
Takagi	Tyrrell-Ford	10	Spun-off	10
Verstappen	Stewart-Ford	8	Engine failure	10
Wurz	Benetton-Mecachrome	0	Steering defect	7
Hakkinen	McLaren-Mercedes	0	Collision with Herbert	3
Herbert	Sauber-Petronas	0	Collision with Hakkinen	
Panis	Prost-Peugeot	0	Mass collision at start	
Barrichello	Stewart-Ford	0	Mass collision at start	
Salo	Arrows-Hart	0	Mass collision at start	
Rosset	Tyrrell-Ford	0	Mass collision at start	

PITSTOPS

Lap	Driver	Duration* (sec)	Lap	Driver	Duration* (sec)
9	Coulthard	30.867	21	Trulli	32.831
9	Tuero	31.603	24	Irvine	31.793
10	Irvine	40.142	24	Coulthard	13:17.692
10	R. Schumacher	31.506	24	Nakano	33.211
16	M. Schumacher	31.147	26	Nakano	13:45.304
16	Hill	34.088	27	R. Schumacher	33.342
16	Alesi	31.000	28	Hill**	30.663
16	Frentzen	31.822	28	Alesi	33.789
16	Fisichella	38.510	28	Frentzen	32.134
21	Diniz	33.346			

* including driving to and from pit
** fastest pitstop

Italian Grand Prix

13 September, Monza

Fourteenth World Championship race; track length: 5.77 km; race distance: 53 laps (305.81 km); lap record: 1:24.808 min (244.929 kmh/152.192 mph), Mika Hakkinen, McLaren-Mercedes (1997); fastest lap: 1:25.139 min (243.977 kmh/151.600 mph), Mika Hakkinen, McLaren-Mercedes; weather: slightly cloudy, warm; spectators: 190,000

RACE RESULTS

	Driver	Team	Laps	Time (hrs)	Ave. (mph)	Difference
1	M. Schumacher	Ferrari	53	1:17:09.672	147.632	
2	Irvine	Ferrari	53	1:17:47.649	146.431	37.977 sec
3	R. Schumacher	Jordan-Mugen-Honda	53	1:17:50.824	146.332	41.152 sec
4	Hakkinen	McLaren-Mercedes	53	1:18:05.343	145.878	55.671 sec
5	Alesi	Sauber-Petronas	53	1:18:11.544	145.685	1:01.892 min
6	Hill	Jordan-Mugen-Honda	53	1:18:16.360	145.536	1:06.688 min
7	Frentzen	Williams-Mecachrome	52	1:17:11.164	144.798	1 lap
8	Fisichella	Benetton-Mecachrome	52	1:17:11.752	144.779	1 lap
9	Takagi	Tyrrell-Ford	52	1:18:15.640	142.810	1 lap
10	Barrichello	Stewart-Ford	52	1:18:22.050	142.615	1 lap
11	Tuero	Minardi-Ford	51	1:17:59.838	140.534	2 laps
12	Rosset	Tyrrell-Ford	51	1:18:12.566	140.153	2 laps
13	Trulli	Prost-Peugeot	50	1:17:27.397	138.737	3 laps

RETIREMENTS

Driver	Team	Lap	Reason	Position before retirement
Verstappen	Stewart-Ford	39	Gear box failure	9
Villeneuve	William-Mecachrome	37	Spun off	4
Salo	Arrows-Hart	32	Throttle	10
Wurz	Benetton-Mecachrome	24	Gear box failure	7
Coulthard	McLaren-Mercedes	16	Engine failure	1
Panis	Prost-Peugeot	15	Problems with vibration	19
Nakano	Minardi-Ford	13	Engine failure	18
Herbert	Sauber-Petronas	12	Spun off	14
Diniz	Arrows-Hart	10	Gear box failure	18

PITSTOPS

Lap	Driver	Duration* (sec)	Lap	Driver	Duration* (sec)
8	Panis	29.589	32	Irvine	19.919
13	Takagi	20.308	32	Alesi	19.872
13	Panis	6:36.370	33	Villeneuve	20.743
14	Hill	20.577	34	Hakkinen	20.643
17	Barrichello	37.675	34	Takagi	20.321
18	Verstappen	20.588	34	Barrichello	26.101
22	Salo	26.134	35	Fisichella	41.408
24	Trulli	1:44.959	35	Frentzen	31.175
25	Rosset	23.207	35	Verstappen	19.808
30	R. Schumacher	21.496	36	Hill**	19.154
31	M. Schumacher	21.015			
31	Tuero	21.545			

* including driving to and from pit
** fastest pitstop

Luxembourg Grand Prix

27 September, Nürburgring

Fifteenth World Championship race; track length: 4.556 km; race distance: 67 laps (305.252 km); lap record: 1:18.805 min (208.128 kmh/129.325 mph), Heinz Harald Frentzen, Williams Renault (1997); fastest lap: 1:20.450 min (203.873 kmh/126.681 mph), Mika Hakkinen, McLaren-Mercedes; weather: variable cloud, cool; spectators: 140,000

RACE RESULT

Driver	Team	Laps	Time (hours)	Ave. (mph)	Difference
1 Hakkinen	McLaren-Mercedes	67	1:32:14.789	123.363	
2 M. Schumacher	Ferrari	67	1:32:17.000	123.314	2.212 sec
3 Coulthard	McLaren-Mercedes	67	1:32:48.952	122.606	34.164 sec
4 Irvine	Ferrari	67	1:33:12.971	122.080	58.183 sec
5 Frentzen	Williams-Mecachrome	67	1:33:15.036	121.973	1:00.248 min
6 Fisichella	Benetton-Mecachrome	67	1:33:16.148	122.011	1:01.360 min
7 Wurz	Benetton-Mecachrome	67	1:33:19.578	121.936	1:04.790 min
8 Villeneuve	Williams-Mecachrome	66	1:32:20.752	121.391	1 lap
9 Hill	Jordan-Mugen-Honda	66	1:32:22.990	121.342	1 lap
10 Alesi	Sauber-Petronas	66	1:32:29.424	121.202	1 lap
11 Barrichello	Stewart-Ford	65	1:32:28.610	119.382	2 lap
12 Panis	Prost-Peugeot	65	1:32:29.872	119.355	2 lap
13 Verstappen	Stewart-Ford	65	1:32:52.806	118.864	2 lap
14 Salo	Arrows-Hart	65	1:32:53.413	118.851	2 lap
15 Nakano	Minardi-Ford	65	1:32:56.589	118.783	2 lap
16 Takagi	Tyrrell-Ford	65	1:32:57.269	118.769	2 lap
Tuero*	Minard-Ford	56	1:32:50.967	102.439	11 lap

* Tuero finished but was not included in the assessment because of the distance travelled.

RETIREMENTS

Driver	Team	Lap	Reason for retirement	Position before retirement
R. Schumacher	Jordan-Mugen-Honda	53	Brake disc failure	14
Herbert	Sauber-Petronas	37	Engine failure	12
Rosset	Tyrrell-Ford	36	Engine failure	19
Trulli	Prost-Peugeot	6	Gear box failure	14
Diniz	Arrows-Hart	6	Hydraulic failure	16

PITSTOPS

Lap	Duration* (sec)	Lap	Duration* (sec)
1 Tuero	11:53.081	34 Barrichello	30.501
20 Rosset	28.776	39 Nakano	29.979
22 R. Schumacher	28.591	42 Fisichella	28.172
22 Verstappen	30.382	42 Salo	28.320
22 Takagi	29.309	43 Frentzen	27.307
23 Fisichella	29.567	43 Wurz	28.714
24 M. Schumacher	26.933	43 Panis	28.193
24 Wurz	30.821	43 Verstappen	29.434
25 Irvine	28.417	45 Tuero	29.624
25 Panis	28.749	45 Villeneuve	27.569
25 Salo	30.376	45 Takagi	27.535
26 Frentzen	27.546	47 M. Schumacher	25.895
26 Hill	27.476	48 Hakkinen**	24.858
26 Herbert	26.052	48 R. Schumacher	26.710
27 Alesi	26.865	48 Alesi	26.470
28 Hakkinen	27.178	49 Irvine	25.509
29 Coulthard	27.359	51 Hill	26.544
31 Villeneuve	30.683	52 Coulthard	25.669

* including driving to and from pit
** fastest pitstop

Japanese Grand Prix

1 November, Suzuka

Sixteenth World Championship race; track length: 5.864 km; race distance: 53 laps (310.596 km); lap record: 1:38.942 min (213.361 kmh/132.576 mph), Heinz Harald Frentzen, Williams-Renault (1997); fastest lap: 1:40.190 min (210.703 kmh/130.925 mph), Michael Schumacher, Ferrari; weather: cloudy, warm; spectators 148,000

RACE RESULT

Driver	Team	Laps	Time (hours)	Ave. (mph)	Difference
1 Hakkinen	McLaren-Mercedes	51	1:27:22.535	127.523	
2 Irvine	Ferrari	51	1:27:29.026	127.366	6.491 sec
3 Coulthard	McLaren-Mercedes	51	1:27:50.197	126.854	27.662 sec
4 Hill	Jordan-Mugen-Honda	51	1:28:36.026	125.761	1:13.491 min
5 Frentzen	Williams-Mecachrome	51	1:28:36.392	125.752	1:13.857 min
6 Villeneuve	Williams-Mecachrome	51	1:28:38.402	125.705	1:15.867 min
7 Alesi	Sauber-Petronas	51	1:28:58.588	125.229	1:36.053 min
8 Fisichella	Benetton-Mecachrome	51	1:29:03.837	125.106	1:41.301 min
9 Wurz	Benetton-Mecachrome	50	1:27:37.673	124.661	1 lap behind
10 Herbert	Sauber-Petronas	50	1:27:43.035	124.535	1 lap behind
11 Panis	Prost-Peugeot	50	1:28:20.327	123.658	1 lap behind
12 Trulli*	Prost-Peugeot	48	1:25:12.668	123.066	3 laps behind

* Retired but still assessed because of the distance travelled.

RETIREMENTS

Driver	Team	Lap	Reason for retirement	Position before retirement
Trulli	Prost-Peugeot	48	Breakdown	12
Nakano	Minardi-Ford	40	Electric failure	13
M. Schumacher	Ferrari	31	Tyre blow-out	3
Takagi	Tyrrell-Ford	28	Collision with Tuero	15
Tuero	Minardi-Ford	28	Collision with Takagi	16
Barrichello	Stewart-Ford	25	Hydraulic leakage	16
Verstappen	Stewart-Ford	21	Gear box failure	17
Salo	Arrows-Hart	14	Hydraulic failure	12
R. Schumacher	Jordan-Mugen-Honda	13	Engine failure	8
Diniz	Arrows-Hart	2	Spun off	15

PITSTOPS

Lap	Duration* (sec)	Lap	Duration* (sec)
9 Barrichello	31.668	22 Barrichello	33.212
14 Hill	33.020	28 Irvine	29.670
14 Wurz	31.474	28 Takagi	32.241
15 Irvine	30.693	29 Fisichella	33.233
15 Fisichella	30.415	30 Wurz	33.985
16 M. Schumacher*	29.395	30 Panis	32.638
16 Verstappen	33.099	31 Nakano	32.775
16 Nakano	32.735	32 Hakkinen	31.513
16 Panis	33.974	33 Hill	31.593
16 Takagi	32.637	33 Villeneuve	31.223
18 Hakkinen	30.832	34 Frentzen	29.683
18 Villeneuve	31.711	35 Alesi	30.239
18 Trulli	33.021	35 Trulli	31.481
18 Tuero	33.134	36 Herbert	30.859
19 Frentzen	32.292	38 Coulthard	31.562
19 Alesi	31.451	39 Irvine	29.520
20 Herbert	31.123		
21 Coulthard	30.963		

* including driving to and from pit

DRIVERS' WORLD CHAMPIONSHIP

	Australia, Melbourne	Brazil, São Paulo	Argentina, Buenos Aires	San Marino, Imola	Spain, Barcelona	Monaco, Monte Carlo	Canada, Montreal	France, Magny-Cours	Britain, Silverstone	Austria, Zeltweg	Germany, Hockenheim	Hungary, Budapest	Belgium, Spa-Francorchamps	Italy, Monza	Luxembourg, Nürburgring	Japan, Suzuka	TOTAL
1 Hakkinen	10	10	6	–	10	10	–	4	6	10	10	1	–	3	10	10	100
2 M. Schumacher	–	4	10	6	4	–	10	10	10	4	2	10	–	10	6	–	86
3 Coulthard	6	6	1	10	6	–	–	1	0	6	6	6	0	–	4	4	56
4 Irvine	3	0	4	4	–	4	4	6	4	3	0	0	–	6	3	6	47
5 Villeneuve	2	0	–	3	1	2	0	3	0	1	4	4	–	–	0	1	21
6 Hill	0	–	0	–	–	0	–	–	–	0	3	3	10	1	0	3	20
7 Wurz	0	3	3	–	3	–	3	2	3	0	0	–	–	–	0	0	17
8 = Frentzen	4	2	0	2	0	–	–	0	–	–	0	2	3	0	2	2	17
9 Fisichella	–	1	0	–	–	6	6	0	2	–	0	0	–	0	1	0	16
10 R. Schumacher	–	–	–	0	0	–	–	0	1	2	1	0	6	4	–	–	14
11 Alesi	–	0	2	1	0	0	–	0	–	–	0	0	4	2	0	0	9
12 Barrichello	–	–	0	–	2	–	2	0	–	–	–	0	–	0	0	–	4
13 Salo	–	–	–	0	–	3	–	0	–	–	0	0	–	–	0	–	3
= Diniz	–	–	–	–	–	1	0	0	–	–	–	0	2	–	–	–	3
15 Herbert	1	0	–	–	0	0	–	0	–	0	–	0	–	–	–	0	1
= Magnussen	–	0	–	–	0	–	1	–	–	–	–	0	–	–	–	–	1
= Trulli	–	–	0	–	0	–	–	–	–	0	0	–	1	0	–	0	1

CONSTRUCTORS' WORLD CHAMPIONSHIP

	Australia, Melbourne	Brazil, São Paulo	Argentina, Buenos Aires	San Marino, Imola	Spain, Barcelona	Monaco, Monte Carlo	Canada, Montreal	France, Magny-Cours	Britain, Silverstone	Austria, Zeltweg	Germany, Hockenheim	Hungary, Budapest	Belgium, Spa-Francorchamps	Italy, Monza	Luxembourg, Nürburgring	Japan, Suzuka	TOTAL
1 McLaren	16	16	7	10	16	10	–	5	6	16	16	7	0	3	14	14	156
2 Ferrari	3	4	14	10	4	4	14	16	14	7	2	10	–	16	9	6	133
3 Williams	6	2	0	5	1	2	0	3	0	1	4	6	3	0	2	3	38
4 Jordan	0	–	0	0	0	0	–	0	1	2	4	3	16	5	0	3	34
5 Benetton	0	4	3	–	3	6	9	2	5	0	0	0	–	0	1	0	33
6 Sauber	1	0	2	1	0	0	–	0	–	0	0	0	4	2	0	0	10
7 Arrows	–	–	–	0	–	4	0	0	–	–	0	0	2	–	0	–	6
8 Stewart	–	0	–	–	2	–	3	0	–	–	–	0	–	0	0	–	5
9 Prost	0	–	0	0	0	–	–	0	–	0	0	0	1	0	0	0	1

0 = race completed but no World Championship points gained – = retired or did not start

Points for drivers and teams – first place: 10 points; second place: 6 points; third place: 4 points; fourth place: 3 points; fifth place: 2 points; sixth place: 1 point.

FLAGS OF FORMULA ONE

Black and white check
This finishing flag is waved when a car crosses the finishing line.

Blue held still
Another car wishes to overtake – let it pass.
Blue waved
Let other car pass immediately – otherwise a penalty is threatened.

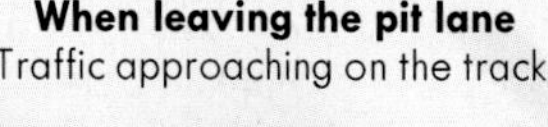

When leaving the pit lane
Traffic approaching on the track.

Yellow and red stripes
Caution, slippery section. Indicates that water or oil is on the track.

Red
Race is interrupted or cut short.

Yellow held still
Danger, do not overtake.
Yellow waved
Immediate danger, slow down, no overtaking.
Yellow waved twice
Track completely or partially blocked.

Green
Cancels the yellow flag and indicates that there is no longer a danger on the track.

Black and white diagonal
Warning for non-sporting behaviour.

Black
Together with a white starting number, the black flag indicates that the driver must go to the pit within the next lap and then immediately to the race management.

Black with orange spot
Driver whose starting number is indicated within the flag has technical problems and must return to the pit.

White held still
Caution – service or other slow vehicle on the track.
White waved
Driver of a fast vehicle may be hindered by a slower vehicle.

FORMULA ONE – WORLD CHAMPIONS SINCE 1950

Year	Winner	Team
1950	Giuseppe Farina	Alfa Romeo
1951	Juan Manuel Fangio	Alfa Romeo
1952	Alberto Ascari	Ferrari
1953	Alberto Ascari	Ferrari
1954	Juan Manuel Fangio	Maserati/Mercedes
1955	Juan Manuel Fangio	Mercedes
1956	Juan Manuel Fangio	Ferrari
1957	Juan Manuel Fangio	Maserati
1958	Mike Hawthorne	Ferrari
1959	Jack Brabham	Cooper-Climax
1960	Jack Brabham	Cooper-Climax
1961	Phil Hill	Ferrari
1962	Graham Hill	BRM
1963	Jim Clark	Lotus-Climax
1964	John Surtees	Ferrari
1965	Jim Clark	Lotus-Climax
1966	Jack Brabham	Brabham-Repco
1967	Denis Hulme	Brabham-Repco
1968	Graham Hill	Lotus-Ford
1969	Jackie Stewart	Matra-Ford
1970	Jochen Rindt	Lotus-Ford
1971	Jackie Stewart	Tyrell-Ford
1972	Emerson Fittipaldi	Lotus-Ford
1973	Jackie Stewart	Tyrell-Ford
1974	Emerson Fittipaldi	McLaren-Ford
1975	Niki Lauda	Ferrari
1976	James Hunt	McLaren-Ford
1977	Niki Lauda	Ferrari
1978	Mario Andretti	Lotus-Ford
1979	Jody Scheckter	Ferrari
1980	Alan Jones	Williams-Ford
1981	Nelson Piquet	Brabham-Ford
1982	Keke Rosberg	Williams-Ford
1983	Nelson Piquet	Brabham-BMW
1984	Niki Lauda	McLaren-Porsche
1985	Alain Prost	McLaren-Porsche
1986	Alain Prost	McLaren-Porsche
1987	Nelson Piquet	Williams-Honda
1988	Ayrton Senna	McLaren-Honda
1989	Alain Prost	McLaren-Honda
1990	Ayrton Senna	McLaren-Honda
1991	Ayrton Senna	McLaren-Honda
1992	Nigel Mansell	Williams-Renault
1993	Alain Prost	Williams-Renault
1994	Michael Schumacher	Benetton-Ford
1995	Michael Schumacher	Benetton-Renault
1996	Damon Hill	Williams-Renault
1997	Jacques Villeneuve	Williams-Reanult
1998	Mika Hakkinen	McLaren-Mercedes

CONSTRUCTORS' WORLD CHAMPIONSHIP*

Year	Team	Year	Team
1958	Vanwall	1979	Ferrari
1959	Cooper-Climax	1980	Williams-Ford
1960	Cooper-Climax	1981	Williams-Ford
1961	Ferrari	1982	Ferrari
1962	BRM	1983	Ferrari
1963	Lotus-Climax	1984	McLaren-TAG-Porsche
1964	Ferrari	1985	McLaren-TAG-Porsche
1965	Lotus-Climax	1986	Williams-Honda
1966	Brabham-Repco	1987	Williams-Honda
1967	Brabham-Repco	1988	McLaren-Honda
1968	Lotus-Ford	1989	McLaren-Honda
1969	Matra-Ford	1990	McLaren-Honda
1970	Lotus-Ford	1991	McLaren-Honda
1971	Tyrell-Ford	1992	Williams-Renault
1972	Lotus-Ford	1993	Williams-Renault
1973	Lotus-Ford	1994	Williams-Renault
1974	McLaren-Ford	1995	Benetton-Renault
1975	Ferrari	1996	Williams-Renault
1976	Ferrari	1997	Williams-Renault
1977	Ferrari	1998	McLaren-Mercedes
1978	Lotus-Ford		

* The constructors' title has only been awarded since 1958

RECORDS*

Drivers

World Championship titles: Fangio 5
Number of Grand Prix races: Patrese 256
Victories: Prost 51
Second places: Prost 35
Third places: Berger 21
Victories in one season: Mansell (1992) & Schumacher (1995) both 9
Successive victories in one season: Brabham (1960), Clark (1965), Mansell (1992) 5
Victories in the same Grand Prix: Prost (France, Brazil), Senna (Monaco) 6
Successive victories in the same Grand Prix: Senna 5 (Monaco 1989-1993)
Podium places: Prost 106
Greatest number of kilometres driven in the lead: Senna 13,706
World Championship points: Prost 798.5
World Championship points in one season: Mansell 108 (1992)
Fastest laps: Prost 41
Fastest laps in one season: Mansell 8 (1992)
Pole positions: Senna 65
Pole positions in one season: Mansell 14 (1992)
Successive pole positions: Prost 7 (1993)
Start/finish victories: Senna 19
Youngest Grand Prix winner: Bruce McLaren 1959, USA, 22 years, 104 days
Oldest Grand Prix winner: Luigi Fagioli (1951, France) 53 years
Youngest World Champion: Emerson Fittipaldi (1972) 25 years
Oldest World Champion: Juan Manuel Fangio (1957) 46 years
Youngest driver at the start: Mike Thackwell (1980, Monaco), 19 years
Oldest driver at the start: Louis Chiron (1955, Monaco), 55 years

Teams

Constructors' title: Williams 9
Grand Prix victories: Ferrari 113
Victories in one season: McLaren 15 (1988)
Successive victories in one season: McLaren 11 (1988)
World Championship points: Ferrari 2997
World Championship points in one season: McLaren 199 (1988)
Double victories in one season: McLaren 10 (Senna, Prost 1988)
Pole positions: Ferrari 121
Successive pole positions: Williams 24 (1992, 1993)
Pole positions in one season: Williams 15 (1992, 1993), McLaren 15 (1988, 1989)
Victories on the same race track: Ferrari 11 (Monza)

Races

Smallest number of cars at the finish: 4 (Monaco, 1966)
Shortest Grand Prix: 24 min 24.899sec, Australian Grand Prix, 1991 (cut short after 14 laps because of rain)

* To January 1998

Photography Credits

Bertelsmann Lexikon Verlag, Gütersloh; Bongarts, Hamburg; Daimler-Benz Classic, Stuttgart; dpa, Frankfurt; Horstmüller, Düsseldorf; Keystone Pressedienst GmbH, Hamburg; Pressebild-Agentur Schirner, Meerbusch; Sven Simon, Essen; Sipa Press, Paris; Sportimage, Hamburg.

Front cover DPPI/Action-Plus Photographic (main picture); LAT (Hakkinen, Schumacher, Coulthard); Allsport/photo Mark Thompson (Hill).
Back cover Allsport/photo Clive Mason (top left); LAT (top right, middle left, middle right); Allsport/photo David Taylor (bottom).